Service-Learning

Engineering In Your Community

Marybeth Lima, PhD
Louisiana State University

William C. Oakes, PhD, PE
Purdue University

A percentage of the sales from this book
will support service-learning projects for
those areas affected by Hurricane Katrina.

Editor
John L. Gruender
Managing Editor
Great Lakes Press, Inc.

Great Lakes Press, Inc.
Okemos, MI   St. Louis, MO
PO Box 550 / Wildwood, MO 63040
(636) 273-6016
custserv@glpbooks.com
www.glpbooks.com

International Standard Book Number: 1-881018-94-6 (softcover)

All comments and inquiries should be addressed to:

Great Lakes Press, Inc.
c/o John Gruender, Editor
PO Box 550
Wildwood, MO 63040-0550

jg@glpbooks.com
phone (636) 273-6016
fax (636) 273-6086

www.glpbooks.com

Library of Congress Control Number: 2004103270 (softcover)

Printed in the USA by Sheridan Books, Inc., Ann Arbor and Chelsea, Michigan.

10 9 8 7 6 5 4 3 2 1

Important Information

This book belongs to: _____

_____

_____

_____

phone: _____

Contents

Preface

TO THE STUDENT

This book was developed for students in all disciplines of engineering and engineering technology enrolled in courses that incorporate community-based projects to teach engineering principles. We have tried to provide a wide range of information that is useful for students beginning their study of engineering (first- and second-year students) as well as more experienced students, including seniors in capstone courses. Even high school students with an interest in engineering and technology will be able to make good use of much of the material contained in this textbook.

You are probably holding this book in your hands because you are taking a course that incorporates service-learning. Service-learning is an approach to teaching and learning in which you master your learning objectives by working with a community partner to address an important community need. The primary purpose of this book is to help expose you to the fundamentals of engineering and the skill sets that you will need (including problem-solving, analysis, teamwork, communication, and project management skills) to be a successful engineer or technologist. What makes this book different from other introductory engineering resources is that the engineering fundamentals and skill sets are presented in the context of solving community problems and achieving community goals. Because of this, you will see information presented in this textbook that may be new to you—for example, social context in engineering, communicating and interacting with community entities, and liability issues in community design.

We wrote this book because there is a significant need for future engineers like you to fully understand how to practice engineering in a community context. It is our hope that this book will help you to develop your personal and professional life as both an engineer and as a citizen. We believe that an engineer with strong technical skills can contribute significantly to society, but an engineer with strong technical skills coupled with an understanding of how to apply engineering in the service of the community will provide an even greater benefit to society.

A description of the chapters contained in this book is as follows. Chapters one and two introduce service-learning and engineering, and provide a context for effectively using these principles to address societal and ethical issues. Chapters three and four deal with the "nuts & bolts" of the engineering profession, including the way in which engineers approach problem-solving, and methods for creating, analyzing, and evaluating technical concepts. Chapters five, six, and seven describe effective techniques for communicating, working in teams, and managing engineering projects. Chapter eight provides information on the use of engineering standards in design, and safety and ethical issues unique to engineering and service-learning. Chapter nine summarizes successful service-learning projects from different engineering disciplines and provides advice for completing a service-learning project successfully. Chapter 10 highlights resources and information that you may find necessary to complete engineering projects. Reflecting on what you have learned through service-learning is a critically important part of an engineering education; chapter 11 provides guidance on this technique.

If you have any comments or suggestions for us, please contact our editor, John Gruender, at jg@glpbooks.com or (800) 837-0201. We are interested in your feedback and welcome any suggestions for improving this book in coming editions! We wish you the best in all your engineering endeavors.

Marybeth Lima   William Oakes
Louisiana State University   *Purdue University*

Acknowledgments

FROM MARYBETH LIMA

My contribution to this project is dedicated to my partner, Lynn Hathaway, whose unwavering support and wisdom has made my life and my work a joy.

My family and friends have provided caring hearts, sympathetic ears, and when necessary, a well-placed kick to get me going. For this, I thank my mother, Kathleen Rogers, my father, John Lima, my brother John Lima, Jr., and my cousin, Chris Rogers. My friends Ann Christy, Diana Glawe, Connie Kuns, Carol Lee Moore, and Sue Nokes have carried me through this project as they have helped to carry me through my life.

I've learned more about service-learning from Jan Shoemaker than from anyone else; thanks for teaching me, sharing books, anecdotes, knowledge, and wisdom, and especially for providing inspiration when I was tired. I learned more about writing from Richard Delong than from anyone else. Thank you, Dick, for taking the time to work with me in a capacity well outside your job description.

Though I have worked on service-learning projects with many people, several stand out in terms of their work ethic, vision, and spirit. All have inspired me, including Judy Bethly, Becky Ropers-Huilman, Kenny Kohler, Georgia Jenkins, Belinda Martinez, Robert Martinez, Deborah Normand, and Carol O'Neil. My success in service-learning is also linked to those people whose leadership and mentoring allowed my program to thrive, including Richard Bengtson, Kenneth Koonce, Saundra McGuire, Pauline Rankin, and Greg Vincent. I would also like to acknowledge those who taught me to successfully navigate the university system, especially Emily Toth, Dominique Homberger, J. Marcos Fernandez, and Michelle Masse. Nina Asher, Leslie Morreale, Bill Pinar, and Brian Ropers-Huilman were continually supportive of this effort. Tom Bride kept me going with his bottomless stash of peanut butter crackers and fun-size candy bars. Carmen Board and Robin Myers kept me centered with yoga and massage, respectively. Danielle Bayham, Rhonda Shepard, and Angie Singleton have helped me to keep my professional life as efficient, organized and officially authorized as possible.

Students are an integral part of any service-learning program, and while many have contributed their time and immense talents, Tessa Byrne, Lakiesha Claude,

ix

Stuart Feilden, Julianne Forman, Bilal Ghosn, and Brandon Kilbourne stand out in particular. Alicia Abadie and John Michael Assad critically reviewed five chapters of this book for the much needed student perspective.

In closing, I would like to thank my co-author, Bill Oakes, and the editor of this project, John Gruender, for their support and industriousness in making this project a reality.

Dr. Marybeth Lima

Marybeth received a B.S. in Agricultural Engineering ('88) and a PhD in Food, Agricultural and Biological Engineering ('96) from the Ohio State University. She is an Associate Professor in the Biological and Agricultural Engineering Department at Louisiana State University. Her current responsibilities include teaching undergraduate and graduate courses in biological engineering and advising senior engineering students on capstone design projects. Her research contributions have included the broad areas of biological engineering and engineering education. Specific research projects include the use of ohmic heating to improve drying and extraction processes, and determining optimal milling parameters for new rice varieties.

Marybeth has performed extensive work in engineering education and has pioneered the use of educational techniques such as service-learning in engineering and the integration of communication and teaming skills across the Biological Engineering curriculum. She has worked with the local community, engineering students, and public schools to design and build public works accessible to everyone. She is passionately committed to improving the community through engineering-community partnerships that bring the principles of engineering alive for children, and tangibly use engineering to enhance democratic society.

Marybeth has been nationally recognized for her service-learning work by the American Society for Engineering Education and The Society for Engineering in Biological, Food, and Agricultural Systems. She has received numerous teaching and service awards including the Brij Mohan Distinguished Professor Award and the LSU Service-Learning Faculty Fellowship. In 2004, she received the Gulf South Summit Award for Service-Learning in Higher Education and was a finalist for the Thomas Ehrlich Faculty Award for Service-Learning. She was the recipient of the 2005 Ernest A. Lynton Award for Faculty Professional Service and Academic Outreach.

FROM WILLIAM (BILL) OAKES

My contribution to this project is dedicated to my wife Kristin and daughters Jessica, Carolyn, Elizabeth, and Katherine. They are the loves of my life.

My wife and best friend Kristin deserves extra thanks for the love, support, and guidance she has provided. God has truly blessed me to give me such a wonderful life partner and friend. She has been a mentor in education as I transitioned from my role as a design engineer to that of a professor. She added her suggestions and editing to this text. Her own impact in our local community is enormous, and an inspiration. She is also an awesome mother for our daughters.

Thanks also goes to my parents for being such great role models for engaging personally and professionally in the community. They have given me a strong conviction for engagement. They have been awesome parents and provided loving support for all we have done.

I am extremely grateful to Professors Leah Jamieson and Edward Coyle for inviting me to become a Co-Director of the Engineering Projects in Community Service (EPICS) Program. This program provided my introduction to service-learning and has been the most exciting thing I have worked on during my career. They both have been very generous, providing a tremendous amount of mentoring, opportunities, and encouragement. Pam Brown was also a great supporter, colleague, and friend as we worked together on the EPICS program over several years. Edward Zlotkowski helped to broaden and deepen my understanding of service-learning and also has been a great mentor, supporter, and friend. John Spencer has been incredible as a corporate supporter of service-learning and a wonderful friend. There are also many other EPICS faculty, staff, and students who have helped shape my experience and views on service-learning.

Finally, I have to thank our editor John Gruender for his perseverance and leadership on this project, and my co-author Marybeth Lima for her dedication, inspiration, and insightful contributions.

Dr. William C. Oakes

Bill received his B.S.M.E. ('85) and M.S.M.E. ('87) from Michigan State University. After receiving his masters, he accepted a position with GE Aircraft Engines where he worked primarily as a mechanical design engineer. He also became involved in campus recruiting and interviewing for GE. He returned to school at Purdue in Mechanical Engineering to earn his Ph.D. (received in '97). After receiving his Ph.D., he remained at Purdue University and is currently an associate professor in Engineering Education where he teaches first-year engineering courses using service-learning. He also teaches Mechanical Engineering courses and is a co-director of the Engineering Projects in Community Service (EPICS) Program.

He is the director of the first-year engineering learning communities where he integrates service-learning throughout the learning community cohorts for over 200 students each year. He also serves as an academic adviser for first-year engineering students. Bill has received numerous teaching awards at Purdue and is a member of Purdue's Teaching Academy. He is an Indiana Campus Compact Fellow and a Purdue Service-Learning Fellow. He has received the NSPE Education Excellence Award (2004) and was a co-recipient of the 2005 National Academy of Engineering's Bernard M. Gordon Prize for innovation in engineering and technology education. He has given service-learning workshops on more than twenty campuses across the country. He's married and has four terrific daughters. In his spare time, he has served as the youth coordinator, Sunday school teacher, and elder at Sunrise Christian Reformed Church in Lafayette, IN.

Chapter 1

Introduction

Engineers create products, systems, and processes to better people's lives. Today's engineers, in fact, can bring their expertise to bear on a broader range of issues than was traditionally considered, e.g., community, health, social and environmental issues. Engineers have a great deal to contribute, and they can and should become engaged in solutions to problems in their local communities as citizens and professionals. In particular, opportunities abound for engineering students to offer their expertise to organizations and agencies that lack the resources to have paid technical staffs. Engaging in service as a student is an excellent opportunity to experience engineering in practice and to see the connection between your future and the solution to society's pressing issues.

—Dr. William Wulf, President of the
National Academy of Engineering

Today is one of the most exciting times to be entering engineering. Modern technology has brought tremendous advances that have improved the quality and longevity of people's lives beyond anything imagined centuries ago, and engineers have played a pivotal role in these advances. Many people associate engineering with high-tech innovation like the newest computers, the tallest skyscrapers or the fastest aircraft. While engineers designed all these, engineering is much more. As Dr. Wulf, President of the National Academy of Engineering, points out, engineers have a great deal to contribute to issues in our local and global communities. Engineering that applies directly to human and social issues is less visible and often overlooked. Today's technological advances have opened doors and opportunities to address many of the human and societal needs of our day:

- Environmental Engineering—Environmental engineers work to clean up existing environmental dangers and to prevent future risks to people's health. New technologies are improving our air and water quality. Environmental

1

engineers work with other engineers to improve processes and to reduce
and eliminate harmful emissions.

- Medical Engineering—Engineers work to introduce diagnostic equipment to
  identify diseases earlier than ever before, and treatments can prolong people's lives and improve the quality of life.
- Assistive Technologies—Engineers can design and produce devices and
  systems or adapt existing ones to enable children and adults to overcome
  barriers that disabilities present and to open options to them not available
  before.
- Education—Engineers work with educators to design, develop, and produce learning environments and educational materials to enhance the educational experience of child and adult learners and to provide access to a
  broader range of learners. New technologies allow learning environments to
  adapt to an individual learner's pace and his or her learning styles.
- Human Services—Information technology can improve the efficiency and
  capabilities of human service organizations and agencies to provide more
  services with the same resources. Technology can coordinate and target resources at specific community needs and assess the programs' impact on
  the communities.
- Biology—Biological engineering has introduced ways to treat diseases, improve nutrition and safety of food, and mitigate and prevent environmental
  problems

The potential impact on our communities and their people is enormous, yet
many communities go lacking in services. Many community agencies and organizations and the communities that they serve lack the budgetary resources to
implement these advances. Products that do exist are often too expensive or require customization by people with technical training. Few community agencies or
organizations have financial resources to employ technical staffs to take advantage of these technologies. In many parts of our country and around the globe,
the communities and people with greatest needs are those with the fewest resources to address these needs.

These challenges provide opportunities for the engineering community from a
commercial and service perspective. Products and services can be brought to
market that are affordable and usable by people without technical backgrounds.
While market forces can address some of a community's needs and opportunities, many needs do not hold the promise of large profits to drive attention and
resources from the private sector and must be addressed through community
and volunteer programs. The engineering community is a major player in these
activities.

What many organizations and agencies need is part-time help from volunteers
or service-learning students and not a full-time technical staff. Many companies
have programs to provide volunteers and services for local organizations. Professional engineers and engineering faculty donate their time to serve the community. Another resource exists within the universities, however, and that is the stu-

dents. Campus organizations organize groups to serve in the local communities; special events like spring break trips enable students to serve in other parts of the country and world. Many students entering college have participated in some form of community service before they came to college so most students are comfortable with the idea of serving the community.

A tremendous resource of engineering expertise resides in our nation's universities and colleges. Engineering students, even in their first years of study, possess skills and abilities that can have an enormous impact in our local communities. While students can and should volunteer their time in communities, models for integrating community service with academic coursework can provide services to the underserved and enhance the learning of the course content. This integration is called service-learning.

Real Engineering Context

As Dr. Wulf has pointed out, service-learning provides needed resources to our community and world and can be a fantastic opportunity to learn about the practice of engineering because the issues and situations are real. That means the solutions are not always straightforward and the work constraints can change, just like engineering in practice. Engineers work to apply mathematic and scientific principles to better society and this application involves people. In a classroom, simulating the twists and turns a real design may take is difficult without a real customer who acts as a real customer. For many years, engineering professors have simulated these experiences by bringing in industrial projects to class. This is a great thing to do and can benefit student learning, but it often lacks the real customer interaction. The customers in these cases are company representatives interested in helping the college and recruiting their students so they want to make a good impression. Few companies will bring their most pressing technical issues to a college. If they are critical to a business, the company will hire people to work on that problem themselves. Community agencies that have no technical staffs will present their most compelling technical issues to a class and will engage them with emotion since they need results. The ability to do their job may rely on the result. The same principles and processes that are applied to more traditional engineering applications are applied to engineering solutions in local and global communities, which is one aspect that makes engineering service-learning so powerful an educational experience.

Alumni of service-learning attest that their service-learning experience prepared them for their work as practicing engineers

> The Project I work on today at Intel Corp. spans several years with hundreds of engineers working together. [Service-learning] gave me a forum to develop the skills to succeed in a project-based environment.
> —Moyolosla Ajaja, Software Engineer, Intel Corp.

Service-learning programs provide means for active learning and discovery through engagement in the community. The community engagement provided me with an opportunity to apply the knowledge and skills learned in the classroom to address community needs. Service-learning programs also provide a valuable opportunity to develop and work as a team. As a team, you work together towards a common goal by combining experiences with critical thought to reach the solution. Most importantly, service-learning programs instill pride in community citizenship. My experience in Service-learning inspired myself and fellow team members to establish a scholarship in honor of a former professor. The scholarship will be awarded to a student at our alma mater who is enrolled in a service-learning program and who displays commitment to learning, team, and community.

—Chad Shockley, BSCE 1999, MSCE 2001,
Environmental Advisor, ExxonMobil

Over three semesters, I worked within a service-learning class that was partnered with the local Habitat for Humanity chapter. The service learning class was able to assist Habitat for Humanity to reduce costs and overall build times. However, the reward to the students was even more valuable. The skills that are learned while enrolled in such a class are truly applicable in the workforce. I recommend that any student, regardless of major, participate in a similar class to develop the skills that will assist them in finding a job and advancing in their professional career.

—Brent Phillips, BSME, Consultant, Accenture, Chicago, IL.

Employers that work with service-learning programs can attest to the preparation that service-learning provides.

As an industry-based practitioner, I can attest to the similarities between [service-learning] and private-sector projects in the business world. Students gain experience in teamwork, leadership, and communication. They see the benefits of good engineering practices including designing for ease of use, testability, and maintenance while delivering real value to the community.

—Jon Reid, Chief Technology Officer for Savitar, Inc. and
adjunct advisor for the EPICS (Engineering Project in
Community Service) program at Purdue University

Service-learning provides opportunities for students to see community and societal applications for their future profession. This concept is so important to engineering that the Accreditation Board for Engineering and Technology (ABET) lists developing an understanding the impact of engineering solutions in a global and societal context and a knowledge of contemporary issues in its eleven outcomes that all engineering programs in the United States are held accountable for to be considered accredited. Understanding how engineering and technological decisions can have an impact on social issues is an important part of engineering. Service-learning can benefit all eleven outcomes for ABET as we will show later in this chapter.

Integrating Service, the University, and Engineering

The idea of integrating service and learning at the university dates to the 1860s in the United States with the Morrill Act that created the land grant universities. Each state has a land grant university that has service to the state and its citizens as a key part of its mission. The author and philosopher John Dewey furthered these ideas with his writings on integrating experience and education in the early decades of the 20th century. The 1960s saw numerous campus-based and community-based initiatives arise in connection with public issues. Earnest Boyer enhanced these connections as President of The Carnegie Foundation for the Advancement of Teaching in the 1990s with his redefinition of scholarship within the university that integrates service to the local communities. He wrote that university scholarship should include engagement in the community.

> *You cannot hope to build a better world without improving the individuals. To that end each of us must work for . . . [self] improvement, and at the same time share a general responsibility for all humanity, our particular duty being to aid those to whom we think we can be most useful.*
> —Marie Curie

Engineers at the university have a long history of engagement and activity with communities. Extension offices at the land grant universities and technical assistance programs provide a means for local organizations and companies to tap into the expertise at the university. Many corporations have service expectations of their employees, especially their executives. General Electric, for example, has an organization comprised of managers and employees dedicated to helping in their communities called the ELFUN organization, which serves in the local communities near GE facilities. As part of their mission and values, many engineering professional societies provide services to the community and their student chapters work with local organizations near campus. The National Society of Black Engineers (NSBE) hosts a local service project at the site of its national conference each year. Most of the engineering honoraries have service as part of their mission and activities. For example, Tau Beta Pi, the engineering-wide honorary, requires service of all its initiates. Many individual professors serve as free consultants to local community organizations.

So What Is New in Service-Learning?

If service to the community is old, then what makes service-learning new? Service-learning is a pedagogy or educational methodology that directly and intentionally integrates classroom learning with service to the community. Research has found that this combination can improve the academic learning of course material, give participants a deeper understanding of the social issues they address, and provide valuable community services.

Most of the efforts for engagement in the community (extension services, technical assistance programs, economic development initiatives, student organizations, and the work of individual faculty serving as pro-bono consultants to local community organizations) have no direct link with classroom learning. Similarly, most class content in engineering programs has no link with the community or service. Service-learning intentionally and systematically links the service and experiences in the community with classroom content, and vice versa, for the enhancement of each. People involved in these activities have found that these learning benefits are real and that the applications of engineering into community issues provides a realistic context for their later work as engineering professionals.

Definitions of Service-Learning

Many other disciplines have imbedded service-learning into their college curricula as well as many K-12 schools. You or your classmates may have participated in service-learning activities before. With all of the possible ways to implement service-learning, developing a concise definition can be difficult and many formal definition variations exist. Most definitions share a great deal of commonality, and Hatcher and Bringle (1997) developed one of the more concise and complete definitions:

> *We view service-learning as a credit-bearing educational experience in which students participate in an organized service activity that meets identified community needs and reflect on the service activity in such a way as to gain further understanding of the course content, a broader appreciation of the discipline, and an enhanced sense of civic responsibility.*

Service-learning has developed so much visibility and interest that the US Congress addressed the issue and integrated a legal definition into the National and Community Act of 1990:

(23) Service-Learning—*The term "service-learning" means a method:*
    (A)   *under which students or participants learn and develop through active participation in thoughtfully organized service that—*
        (i)   *is conducted in and meets the needs of a community;*
        (ii)   *is coordinated with an elementary school, secondary school, institution of higher education, or community service program, and with the community; and*
        (iii)   *helps foster civic responsibility; and*
    (B)   *that—*
        (i)   *is integrated into and enhances the academic curriculum of the students, or the educational components of the community service program in which the participants are enrolled; and*
        (ii)   *provides structured time for the students or participants to reflect on the service experience.*

Congressional Definition: *THE NATIONAL AND COMMUNITY SERVICE ACT OF 1990* [As amended through December 17, 1999, P.L. 106–170]

Components of Service-Learning

Service-learning has distinct and important components. As a participant, you must understand their importance and how they fit together. These components are not necessarily unique to service-learning, but taken as a whole, they are what makes service-learning distinct.

1. *Service*—A key component of service-learning is service to an under-serviced area or people. In engineering, service can take many forms. It may involve direct contact with people through educational programs for children or the elderly. It may involve projects delivered to underserved populations to address a need, such as a solar power system for a remote village in the Andeas mountains. It can take the form of research, data analysis, and results interpretation and presentation. This service might be a shortterm need filled during the course or could be part of a larger, ongoing project.

2. *Academic Content*—Service-learning is not a substitute for learning engineering principles and content but rather a means to learn engineering principles and content more effectively. The decisions made by practicing engineers can have significant impact on people's lives, and an engineer must be well grounded in science, math, and the engineering sciences. In service-learning, the service is directly linked to course studies to help students learn that material more effectively. If it is a design course, with engineering design principles being taught, the service provides an environment in which to learn. In an engineering science course, the service reinforces course concepts.

   As in a traditional course, students should expect to be graded and evaluated based on their demonstration of academic learning. Just as you are not given credit for your study hours, you will not be given credit simply for your service hours. You will be graded on how you take the lessons from the service and the other parts of the course and integrate them into demonstration of academic achievement through exams, reports, or presentations.

3. *Partnerships and Reciprocity*—Service-learning involves partnerships with students, faculty, the community, and in some cases companies. Students performing service-learning are not doing something *for* the community, but rather *with* the community. Each partnership member contributes to the project's goals and each benefits from it. When service-learning is done well, the partnerships become reciprocal. In reciprocal partnerships, all partners contribute to the work, receive benefits from the work, and learn from the work and the other partners. Community members commonly approach these partnerships with skepticism based on previous experiences with student groups. As student participants, you may need to take initiative to move past such skepticism and look for ways to gain the respect and confidence of those in your partnerships. Doing so will give you access to the community's expertise and allow you to understand how to integrate and uti-

lize the available resources to implement and sustain your work after your course ends. Partners do not leave partners hanging after the work is over. Good engineering utilizes available resources and creates sustainable systems, and your work will need to be sustained after you leave using the community's resources.

4. *Mutual Learning*—Many practicing engineers will tell you that after they graduate, they learn much from technicians and hourly workers with years of experience but without engineering degrees. Good engineers learn how to gain these individuals' respect, so they can tap this experience and knowledge to better their own work. Part of this respect is to acknowledge contributions and to treat them as sources of expertise. For service-learning to work, this principle must be practiced with community members, service-providers, and service recipients. Respect defines reciprocal partnerships, but it goes much deeper than that for the student participants. The community will be learning about the technology and expertise you bring. Learning opportunities abound in the service-learning experience if you are open to them. Looking for these opportunities will help you project the kind of respect to those you work with that will open them up to sharing and will allow you to be more effective in your work. Opportunities to learn an engineering application in a real setting is an important part of service-learning as is the learning that occurs in the community you are serving, the issues you are addressing, and the people on whom you will have an impact.

5. *Analysis and Reflection*—The idea of recording your experiences so that you can analyze, reflect, or revisit them later is common practice in engineering. Thomas Edison filled hundreds of notebooks with data, notes, and observations. Engineers have found analyzing their work useful so that they can improve on later designs and projects.

In service-learning, the practice of recording, analyzing and reflecting is important for several reasons. One of the most important is connecting the service to the academic content. This can be difficult since service-learning presents technical challenges in untraditional ways. To make these connections, instructors may guide students through activities to analyze and reflect upon their work, how they are accomplishing the work, the implications of their work, and its connections with the academic course content and larger social issues. These kinds of activities are called metacognitive activities and have improved learning (Bransford, 2000) in many contexts, not just service-learning. Metacognition or reflection can help students understand the following:

- The academic material covered by the course;
- How the course material relates to the service;
- The implications of the social context and issues associated with the need being met;
- The role of engineering in the context of large social issues.

Activities promoting analysis and reflection can take several forms and can include open-ended questions, written or oral guided discussion topics, periodic written summaries of the work being undertaken and its implications, and assigned readings.

Reflection activities are designed to help participants process their experience. It is human nature to see things through a filter based on your own experiences and understanding. Service-learning provides many opportunities to be placed into unique environments and to have experiences that are different from those that you're used to. Your instructor may design activities to help you process these experiences so that you see other views and possibilities. Service-learning experiences can bring us into situations where our preconceptions come into play. We all have filters through which we view the world and service-learning is an excellent environment to explore these filters and to examine how they affect the way we learn and work.

Balance Between Service and Learning

Service-learning creates a balance between service-based learning and academic learning. Each complements the other. Eyler and Giles (1999) have illustrated variations within this balance with the following table. Service-learning integrates academic and community needs to the benefit of both. Service is not just performed as an add-on side project nor is the service the primary focus of the experience. Both are balanced and each enhances the other.

service-LEARNING	Learning goals are primary; service outcomes are secondary
SERVICE-learning	Service outcomes are primary; learning goals are secondary
service learning	Service and learning goals are separate
SERVICE-LEARNING	Service and learning goals have equal weight; each enhances the other for all participants

One of the byproducts of this balance is tension, in which service and learning goals are in conflict. Since you are providing a service, part of the service-learning experience designed to enhance the learning may be slowing your progress on the project. You could provide more service if you did not spend so much time participating in reflection activities, for example. Similarly, you may need to do other activities on the service component for the people you are serving that might seem tangential to learning the course material and are taking time away that could be used for studying. Even with the best design programs, these tensions are often felt because both parts are necessary and build upon each other. Remember that with service-learning, you are in a balanced system, and that by balancing the two dimensions, each part will be better.

How Is Service-Learning Different from Other Courses and Experiences?

Understanding how service-learning is different from other learning experiences is useful. Service-learning has many of the same components as other learning opportunities available to engineering students but the collection of these components is unique to service-learning and it is the collection that provides service-learning with its distinctive benefits. Engineering students need many experiences to prepare them for practice and for life as a professional and citizen in the world. Service-learning is one piece that complements the other learning environments in which engineering students are engaged. Here are the distinctive aspects you will encounter.

- *Traditional Classrooms*—Traditional courses are often taught in lecture style with a professor in the front of the room presenting material using a black or white board, an overhead projector, or PowerPoint. Service-learning is experiential learning, with students learning through participation in an experience which is imbedded in a social context. Some students do not feel taught in experiential learning; they feel that they have to learn things themselves, which is true. Your instructor will be more of a coach, who facilitates your learning than a presenter of knowledge.
- *Laboratory and Design Courses*—Non-service-learning courses, such as design and laboratory courses, are experiential learning environments. While these share the experiential aspects, they typically lack a connection with social contexts, which the service experience provides with activities such as reflection to allow participants to understand the connections between the learning and the service.
- *Internships and cooperative education*—The authors recommend internships (typically summer engineering jobs) and cooperative educational assignments (co-op) (program that alternate work assignments and semesters or quarters on campus) to all engineering students. They are important to gain experience with the private sector and to experience an engineering career. These experiences are independent from academic components and focus almost exclusively on experience and practice. They are also separate from social contexts.
- *Extracurricular Activities and Opportunities*—Many student organizations engage in volunteer and community service activities, which are terrific experiences and provide valuable services to the campus and local community. These activities are typically isolated from academic coursework and usually conceived purely as a service activity. These activities rarely include guided reflection activities that enhance learning and reinforce academic content.

Learning Benefits

One of service-learning's central benefits is that it provides an effective means to learn the kind of material taught in college disciplines. The connection with service to the community provides learners with a concrete connection to what would otherwise be abstract concepts. Eyler and Giles summarized this finding:

". . . students are [sometimes] able to marshal a body of knowledge to solve problems presented in class but fail to see a problem, much less the relevance of what has been learned, in a different setting. The new

situation does not provide the cues associated with what has been learned; the key words from the classroom are not present in the wider environment. A service-learning student will have more ways to access this understanding." Eyler and Giles, 1999

The connection to the community can provide motivation and a context that has been cited by cognitive scientists who study how people learn.

Learners of all ages are more motivated when they can see the usefulness of what they are learning and when they can use that information to do something that has an impact on others especially in their local community   (John Bransford et al., *How People Learn*)

The reflection that is used in service-learning follows a learning cycle model where reflection or metacognitive activities are used to help students process the material that has been covered or experienced and has been proven effective to enhance learning, not just in service-learning. Metacognitive, or reflection activities, serve to reinforce learning concepts on technical aspects of course material as well as to help process the social and human experiences that are a part of service-learning.

In engineering, developing a deep understanding of the fundamental aspects of mathematics and science as well as engineering practice including design is vital to your education. Service-learning provides an excellent environment to see relevant community connections. Since your work's results will likely be used by the community, the results must be safe, reliable, and meet the intended technical specifications. Use of sound engineering principles is vital to the work's success, and people will be depending on your ability to deliver a technically sound product. Service-learning's pedagogy is an effective way to learn engineering principles and is one of the main reasons that instructors use service-learning.

Many students wonder how an experience or class might benefit them as they prepare for an engineering career: "How will this help me get a job or internship or co-op position?" Service-learning can provide an excellent environment to prepare students for engineering practice and give them an experience that will help them succeed as a practicing engineer. A service-learning experience deals with real people and constraints, which create many of the messy issues of real problem solving. Many service-learning experiences require real problem solving to deal with unexpected issues, and the ability to handle these messy issues is important. Many students will put their service-learning experience on their résumés since it is not a typical classroom experience. They can use that experience to demonstrate how they can handle issues they will encounter in practice.

Your engineering classes will prepare you for the application of technical engineering principles to future problems, but engineers need other characteristics to be effective in practice that are more difficult to simulate in a traditional classroom. Major engineering corporations have found that experience with the complex issues of real people and situations is valuable for their engineers. Boeing Company has been one of the most active corporations in engineering education and has published a list of desired attributes of an engineer and posted it on its company website. The list includes technical fundamentals in math and science along with understanding the engineering context in terms of societal needs, ethical standards, ability to think creatively and critically, and the ability to adapt to change. Service-learning can provide an environment that can challenge and draw upon the entire range of attributes listed by Boeing and held as important to many engineers.

Desired Attributes of an Engineer

An understanding of the social context and issues related to the problem you are addressing is necessary to be able to deliver an effective solution. If you do not understand the issues and implications of those issues, you may deliver something that does not address the true needs of the people you are serving. The social context and issues around the needs you are addressing are important aspects of the service-learning experience and should be taken as an important part of the learning process even if they are not traditional engineering topics. As we have mentioned earlier, corporations such as Boeing and GE value societal awareness and engagement so that they can design better products and provide quality communities for their employees and neighbors.

Desired Attributes of an Engineer

- **A good understanding of engineering science fundamentals**
  - Mathematics (including statistics)
  - Physical and life sciences
  - Information technology (far more than computer literacy)
- **A good understanding of design and manufacturing processes**
  - Understands engineering, for example
- **A multidisciplinary systems perspective**
- **A basic understanding of the context in which engineering is practiced**
  - Economics (including business practices)
  - History
  - The environment
  - Customer and societal needs
- **Good communication skills**
  - Written, oral, graphic, and listening
- **High ethical standards**
- **An ability to think critically, creatively, independently, and cooperatively**
- **Flexibility or the ability and self-confidence to adapt to rapid or major change**
- **Curiosity and a desire to learn for life**
- **A profound understanding of the importance of teamwork**

---

http://www.boeing.com/companyoffices/pwu/attributes/attributes.html

The social context has value for the engineer and provides a motivated customer. Your community partners will serve several roles but one of them is a customer for your work. Whether you are doing an analysis, report, presentation, or design, your community partner will serve as the customer for your work. Making sure that you and your classmates meet the needs of the community will require good communication skills. A strong benefit for service-learning students is that most of the people you interact with in the communities will not have a technical background, which means that you will not be able to use technical jargon and will have to explain things in a way that makes sense. Being able to communicate effectively with diverse audiences is crucial to your success as an engineer.

> *The ideal engineer is a composite . . . not a scientist . . . not a mathematician . . . not a sociologist or a writer; but . . . may use the knowledge and techniques of any or all of these disciplines in solving engineering problems.*   —N.W. Dougherty.

The context for service-learning is almost always new to students and not what they envisioned applying engineering toward, which means they have to be creative. With real customers and people, your assignments and specifications may change as you progress through your assignment. This does not happen in a traditional classroom; once you are given an assignment, the description does not usually change. However, in these settings, just as in the real world, things will change (see the Boeing list). Your experiences will prepare you for these and other situations you will encounter later as an engineer.

Students should be prepared for the unexpected in their service. Providing services and products in underserved areas may place you into situations that you would not otherwise encounter and almost certainly would not experience in a traditional class. You will encounter situations and people different from ones you would have normally come in contact with. Your instructor may prepare you for situations and help process your experiences. Keep an open mind to new situations and look for places where your preconceptions may act as a filter; keeping these things in mind will help you to clearly frame your issue. A computer cannot think and adapt to a new situation but we can. We do this by making assumptions and analogies to what we know and how it relates to now and what is normal. Learning what these preconceptions are and how they affect your views and actions is a learning experience that will benefit you personally and professionally throughout your career.

Processing these aspects of your experience is important and is one of the reasons that reflection is a key component to the service-learning experience. Some of your experiences and lessons will not align with the academic course learning objectives but will service you well professionally and personally.

You will need to learn about the social issues and needs that require solutions, and some issues will not have easy solutions. Many we address in service-learning will remain with our society for most or all of our lifetime, and the experiences we have can help us be informed citizens to work toward solutions. Take advantage of these learning opportunities to ask questions and explore issues.

A byproduct for many participants is that they leave with a broader under-standing of what engineering is and what engineers can do. What Dr. Wolf men-tioned at the start of this text is that engineering can and should be about making our local and global communities a better place for all. It will take creative, entre-preneurial, and technically sound individuals with a deep understanding of rele-vant social issues to bring technology's benefits to the underserved people throughout the world. Your service-learning experience may be the first step in this process.

One of the great lessons for students is how to capitalize on and learn from the community's expertise. Students in service-learning typically join a community, lo-cally or abroad, that has many needs. The students commonly feel they are doing something for the community. One of the components of service-learning is part-nerships. You and your classmates must address problems with the community. The community you are working with existed before you arrived and will remain after you leave. You can do many things to help make the community better, but you need to understand that you are not essential to the solutions; the community residents are. The most effective way to address needs is to capitalize on local community resources and expertise. Doing so will provide a more effective solu-tion and will continue the benefits of your work after you leave.

A typical mistake for a young engineer to make is to approach hourly workers who do not have college degrees as people less knowledgeable. Trades people will tell stories about countless arrogant college grads who thought they had all the answers. These people often know a great deal about the products and processes and can make a great contribution.

The author had an experience in a summer job in a manufacturing facility that summed up the experience. One machinists pulled me aside and showed me how an engineer had increased the cost of a part he was machining. The machinist knew they could reduce the cost and when I asked why he did not let the engineer know, his response hit a chord and taught me a lesson to this day. He said that the engineer would not listen, but if he had, he would have taken the credit for himself. No relationship or trust existed between them. In service-learning, many people will be able to help you do your work better and will teach you many les-sons, but you need to be able to identify them. They may not come forward right away. I was in that machine shop for several weeks before they felt respected. Learning to treat those you are working with in a respectful way and to listen and learn from them is a lesson and discipline that will allow you to do better work in your service-learning and will help you in your professional and personal life.

One of the universal goals of service-learning, whether in elementary school, high school, or college, is to instill an enhanced sense of citizenship in the par-ticipants. In the last presidential election, only half the eligible voters cast ballots and only one third of college age students cast ballots. In non-presidential election years, the voting rate has been lower. Through your experiences, you will become engaged in your local community. This does not imply service-learning has a polit-ical agenda, but an engaged citizenry is a requirement for a flourishing democracy.

Despite the strong history of service and direct applications, the engineering profession has not embraced service to the community as a practice expectation.

Figure 1.1 Students tour Habitat for Humanity's Global Village.

Law, for example, has imbedded the expectation of pro bono work into its professional responsibilities. Lawyers embrace this ethic as they understand that access to legal counsel is critical for our free society and all citizens do not have the means to pay for these services. We, as an engineering community, have not formalized this concept. In your service-learning experience, you will see how much of an impact you can have in your career through professional volunteering. With technology's advantages, access to this technology is important and all citizens do not have the resources to pay for these benefits.

What Fields Can Do Service-Learning?

Engineering students have implemented service-learning in various ways in almost all disciplines. More detailed case studies are provided in chapter 9 of this text. Below are some examples of how this has been applied.

Aerospace Engineers—Work with a local children's museum to design and build an interactive wind tunnel to bring the fundamental concept of flight to children or design economical means for satellite communications systems for missionaries in developing areas of the world.

Agricultural Engineers—Work with local farmers with disabilities to design and build equipment to allow the farmers to continue to farm.

Architectural Engineers—Work with a local children's clinic for children with emotional challenges to design and build a play environment that accommodates their special needs.

Biological Engineers—Work with local elementary schools to design and build playgrounds that are safe and fun for the children.

Biomedical Engineers—Work with therapists to adapt mobility devices such as wheelchairs for children's customized needs.

Chemical Engineers—Work with local environmental organizations to gather and analyze local environmental data to address local community problems.

Civil Engineers—Work with a local Habitat for Humanity affiliate to improve the design and construction efficiency of their homes. Environmentally friendly building materials are introduced and will reduce the homes' operating costs.

Computer Engineers—Work with the local agencies for homelessness prevention to design and deploy a secure, distributed database system allowing agencies to track clients and maintain confidentiality.

Electrical Engineers—Work with therapists of a local children's clinic to design and build customized electromechanical devices for children with disabilities.

First-Year Engineering Students—Teach middle school children about what it takes to go to college and present their choice of engineering in a fun and engaging way.

Industrial Engineers—Work with a local organization that employs adults with mental and physical disabilities and impairments to develop customized fixtures to allow the employees to complete the tasks contracted to the organization.

Materials Engineers—Work with a local community recycling organization to improve a recycling program.

Mechanical Engineers—Work with the university's Dean of Students to develop classroom furniture that is accessible to students with disabilities.

Software Engineers—Work with local educators to develop interactive software to teach Spanish to school children.

The Changing Face of Engineering Education

A final introductory endorsement of service-learning comes from the examination of the criteria that all engineering programs must follow for accreditation through the Accreditation Board of Engineering and Technology or ABET (ABET 2000, 2002). ABET established a list of outcomes that all programs must meet that reflect the understanding that today's engineers are being asked to do much more than just make calculations. They are expected to work on multidisciplinary teams in a multicultural environment, manage multiple projects, and compete in a diverse global marketplace. The technology explosion has created a situation in which much of the knowledge students gain in college may be considered obsolete within a few years. The Internet and the advancement of computer tools have changed the way engineers work and the businesses in which they work.

Service-learning is well positioned to help engineering programs meet educational challenges difficult to accomplish in traditional courses. It is an important way to help students master traditional elements of the engineering curriculum as we have noted earlier. ABET's criteria are mapped against service-learning in the appendix to this chapter.

How to Use This Text

Service-learning provides a compelling context in which students can apply the knowledge acquired in their engineering courses to real problems with real constraints. Students apply knowledge in a context different from their normal classroom environment. Thus, students are challenged to evaluate and to synthesize classroom knowledge and tools to ask how these can best be utilized to solve the problems.

This text has been designed as a resource for engineering students engaged in service-learning activities. Readers will find that most of the material is not merely of interest in a service-learning context, but is relevant to any engineering project and to good engineering practice in general. Topics in subsequent chapters include the engineering design process, teamwork, project planning, communications, and problem solving. These are included in many engineering texts and should serve as a resource for non-service-learning projects. We have, however, included aspects that are specifically applicable for service-learning applications and provided examples in these other chapters that relate to community-based work.

The reader will find a few atypical chapters, such as the chapter on reflection and analysis or the chapter on engineering and society.

While no text can provide a complete and comprehensive reference for all that students will encounter in a service-learning experience, we have included materials that are the most likely to be beneficial for engineering project work. As students prepares for their engineering career, they will accumulate resources and this text will be one of those. We have included examples of other service-learning projects we hope will stimulate your thinking to come up with innovative ways to bring you engineering expertise to bear on issues in your local communities as well as those far away.

Summary

Engineering is a lifelong pursuit. One of the goals of any engineering program is to make its graduates lifelong learners. We want to start students on their journey as engineering professionals and lifelong learners. By framing engineering into a community context, we start students on the way to being engaged professionals and citizens. The education you are receiving and the skills you are developing can have a profound impact on your local, state, national, and global community. Your professional engagement in the issues of today is what will solve many of the problems facing you and your fellow citizens. Your civic engagement is what will keep our democracy alive and flourishing. We hoped in writing this text to contribute in some small way to all of the above.

Appendix: ABET Criteria and Service-Learning

ABET's Engineering Criteria 2000 (EC 2000) states that engineering programs must demonstrate that their graduates have the following:

a. an ability to apply knowledge of mathematics, science, and engineering
b. an ability to design and conduct experiments, as well as to analyze and interpret data
c. an ability to design a system, component, or process to meet desired needs   d.   an ability to function on multidisciplinary teams
e. an ability to identify, formulate, and solve engineering problems
f. an understanding of professional and ethical responsibility
g. an ability to communicate effectively
h. the broad education necessary to understand the impact of engineering solutions in a global and societal context
i. a recognition of the need for, and an ability to engage in, lifelong learning
j. a knowledge of contemporary issues
k. an ability to use the techniques, skills, and modern engineering tools necessary for engineering practice

Service-learning can be mapped into ABET's criteria to enhance a student's ability to meet these outcomes.

1. An ability to apply knowledge of mathematics, science, and engineering

    Service-learning provides an opportunity for students to apply concepts and theory learned in the traditional classroom to problems situated in contexts different from those to which they are accustomed. Success here requires that students be able to synthesize the knowledge they have acquired in their courses and apply that knowledge to community-based issues.

2. An ability to design and conduct experiments, as well as to analyze and interpret data

    Service-learning requires students to design, produce, and deliver real products used by real people. This real world context provides a compelling need to analyze and predict issues. Furthermore, students see first hand the faces of those who will use their products, and this adds a compelling reason for them to understand the project's issues.

3. An ability to design a system, component, or process to meet desired needs

    Since service-learning requires the delivery of real products and real services to solve real problems, students are able to experience

(box continues)

(*continued*)

the entire design process from initial problem definition and specification development to design to manufacture and delivery of a completed product or service.

4. An ability to function on multidisciplinary teams

   Because service-learning problems are real and complex, they invariably require a multidisciplinary solution. They require engineering
   students to work with students from other disciplines or, at a minimum, to consult with experts in other fields to find solutions to community needs. Service-learning creates a compelling environment in
   which to engage in multidisciplinary work. Rare is the problem in the
   real world that can be solved within the confines of a single academic
   discipline.

5. An ability to identify, formulate, and solve engineering problems

   Service-learning provides a compelling context in which students
   can experience the process of identifying and formulating problems
   that require technical solutions. Service-learning requires students to
   work with their community partners to identify engineering issues in
   a community context and to decide how their expertise and resources
   can best be utilized to address those issues.

6. An understanding of professional and ethical responsibility

   The context in which service-learning projects are situated provides a natural opportunity for students to examine their profession's professional and ethical responsibilities. The multidimensional
   reflection and analysis imbedded in the service-learning process ensures that students will explore these issues in a guided manner to
   deepen their overall understanding of their roles as engineering
   professionals.

7. An ability to communicate effectively

   Service-learning necessitates extensive communication with community partners, i.e., individuals who most often do not possess a
   technical background. For this reason, students learn how vital clear
   communication is between team members and their clientele. Analytic and reflective activities provide opportunities for students to improve their communication skills. Furthermore, because the students
   are producing real products used in a context outside of class, they
   will become aware of the need to provide sufficient documentation to
   continue and/or service the project.

8. The broad education necessary to understand the impact of engineering solutions in a global and societal context

   Service-learning provides a context in which students can directly
   explore the impact of engineering solutions on society. The utilization
   of engineering skills in social settings provides an opportunity for
   students to receive a broader education than would otherwise be the

(*box continues*)

(*continued*)

> case. Reflection and analysis help ensure that social contexts and is-
> sues will be explored in a guided and intentional manner.
> 9. A recognition of the need for, and an ability to engage in, lifelong
>   learning
>   Service-learning applications often require knowledge and/or
>   skills new to students and beyond their class learning. Thus, they gain
>   a firsthand appreciation of the ability to acquire skills and that they
>   need to do this to solve real problems. They can use reflection exer-
>   cises to reinforce this awareness.
> 10. A knowledge of contemporary issues
>   The community context of service-learning projects guarantees
>   that students will become directly involved in contemporary social is-
>   sues. Such direct involvement helps students appreciate society's
>   complex issues.
> 11. An ability to use the techniques, skills, and modern engineering tools
>   necessary for engineering practice.
>   Service-learning provides a compelling context in which students
>   can apply the knowledge acquired in their engineering courses to real
>   problems with real constraints. Students are asked to apply knowl-
>   edge in a context different from that of their normal classroom envi-
>   ronment. Thus, they are constantly challenged both to evaluate and
>   to synthesize the knowledge and tools they have acquired in the
>   classroom and to ask how these can best be utilized to solve the
>   problems at hand.

REFERENCES

ABET (2000). *Criteria for Accrediting Engineering Programs.* The Engineering Accreditation Commission of The Accreditation Board for Engineering and Technology. http://www.abet.org/eac/eac.htm.

ABET (2002). *Engineering Criteria 2002-2003,* Accreditation Board for Engineering and Technology, http://www.abet.org/criteria.html, May 2002.

Boeing Company (1996), http://www.boeing.com/companyoffices/pwu/attributes/
attributes.html

Boyer, E. L. *Scholarship Reconsidered: Priorities of the Professoriate.* Princeton,
NJ: Carnegie Foundation for the Advancement of Teaching, 1990.

Bransford, JD, Brown, AL and Cocking, RR. Eds. *How People Learn.* National
Academic Press: Washington DC., 2000.

Dewey, J. *Experience and Education,* New York: Macmillan, 1951 (originally published in 1938).

Eyler, J. and Giles, DE, Jr. *Where's The Learning in Service-Learning?* San Francisco, CA: Jossey-Bass Publishers, 1999.

Hatcher, J.A. and Bringle, R.G. Reflection: Bridging the Gap Between Service and Learning, *College Teaching*, 45 (4), 153–158, 1997.

Jamieson, LH, Oakes, WC & Coyle, EJ. EPICS: Serving the community through engineering design projects. In *Learning to Serve: Promoting Civil Society Through Service-learning.* Norwell, MA: Kluwer Academic Publishers, 2002.

Michaud, F, Clavet, A, Lachiver, G, Lucas, M. *Designing Toy Robots to Help Autistic Children—An Open Design Project for Electrical and Computer Engineering Education.* Proceedings from the 2000 Annual Conference of the ASEE, Charlotte, NC.

Oakes, WC & Rud, AG, Jr. The EPICS model in engineering education: Perspective on problem solving abilities needed for success beyond school. In *Beyond Constructivism: A Models & Modeling Perspective*, H. Doerr & R. Lesh, Eds. Hillsdale, NJ: Lawrence Erlbaum Associates, Inc., 2001.

Oakes, William; Duffy, John; Jacobius, Thomas; Linos, Panos; Lord, Susa; Schultz, William, W; and Smith, A. Service-Learning In Engineering, *Proceedings of the 2002 Frontiers in Education Conference*, Boston, MA, Nov. 2002.

Stanton, TK; Giles, DE; and Nadinne, IC *Service-Learning: A Movement's Pioneers Reflect on Its Origins, Practice, and Future.* San Francisco, CA: Jossey-Bass Publishers, 1999.

Simon, LAK; Kenny, M; Brabeck, K; & Lerner, RM, Eds. *Learning to Serve: Promoting Civil Society Through Service-learning.* Norwell, MA: Kluwer Academic Publishers, 2002.

Stott, Nathaniel W.; Schultz, William W. Brei, Diann, Winton; Hoffman, Deanna M; and Markus, Greg. *ProCEED: A Program for Civic Engagement in Engineering Design,* Proceedings from the 2000 Annual Conference of the ASEE, Charlotte, NC, 2000.

Tsang, E, Ed. *Projects that Matter: Concepts and Models for Service-Learning in Engineering.* AAHE, Washington DC, 2000.

Tinto, V. *Leaving College: Rethinking the Causes and Cures of Student Attrition*, Chicago: University of Chicago Press, 1993

Waterman, AS, Ed. *Service-Learning: Applications from the Research,* Mahwah, NJ: Lawrence Erlbaum Associates, Publishers, 1997.

Zlotkowski, E, Ed. *Successful Service-Learning Programs: New Models of Excellence in Higher Education.* Bolton, MA: Anker Publishing Company, Inc., 1998.

Zlotkowski, E, Ed. *Service-Learning and the First-Year Experience.* University of South Carolina: National Resource Center for the First-Year Experience & Students in Transition, 2002.

EXERCISES

1. Write a one-page essay on how technology can be used to address (at least in part) one socially-related need in your local community.

2. Prepare a short oral presentation on how technology can be used to address (at least in part) one socially-related need in your local community.

3. Write a one page essay on how technology can be used to address (at least in part) one socially-related need in the developing world.

4. Prepare a short oral presentation on how technology can be used to address (at least in part) one socially-related need in the developing world.

5. Select three social-related issues and write a paragraph on how technology can be used to address these issues.

6. Prepare a one-page essay on how community-based work will help prepare you for a future career as an engineer.

7. Prepare a short oral presentation on how community-based work will help prepare you for a future career as an engineer.

8. Write a two-page proposal to a company asking them to support your class' efforts in service-learning. Outline why they would want to sponsor your class, including direct and indirect benefits for themselves and the community. Suggest ways they could help your class in addition to financial support. See section 7.3.2 for information on writing a successful proposal.

9. Write a letter that could be emailed to a friend on why she or he should enroll in a service-learning class.

10. Prepare an "elevator speech", a one-minute presentation, on why a student should enroll in a service-learning course.

11. Write a one-page paper on the challenges and opportunities for personal and professional growth doing service-learning.

12. Write a one-page essay on what you expect the service-learning experience to be like. What do you think you will be doing? How do you think you will feel in the service experience?

13. Take the list of desired attributes of an engineer developed by the Boeing Company and map service-learning into each attribute in a similar manner to what was done with the ABET outcomes in this chapter's appendix.

14. Write a one-page essay on how service-learning could be implemented in other courses in your major.

15. Prepare a short oral presentation on how service-learning could be implemented in other courses in your major.

16. Write a one-page essay about the expertise and resources in the community that could help you and your classmates accomplish your project's goals.

17. Write a one-page essay about the expertise and resources in the community to help you and your classmates learn the course material.

Chapter 2

Engineering in a Societal Context

When you help, you see life as weak. When you fix, you see life as broken. When you serve, you see life as whole. Fixing and helping may be the work of the ego, and service the work of the soul.

—Rachel Naomi Remen

2.1 INTRODUCTION

One of the main goals of engineering is to serve society. Most definitions of engineering include this concept. The Accreditation Board of Engineering and Technology (ABET) is a national organization in charge of ensuring that the information engineering colleges teach is technically sound and professionally valid. ABET's definition of engineering is as follows:

> "Engineering is the profession in which a knowledge of the mathematical and natural sciences gained by study, experience, and practice is applied with judgment to develop ways to utilize, economically, the materials and forces of nature for the benefit of humankind."

Engineers have played a vital role in the development of our society, from the design and construction of public works such as buildings, parks, and sewage treatment plants to technology development for transportation, communication, health, and environmental quality issues. Although the engineering profession has made important societal contributions, the relationship between engineering and society is not always explicit. In order to be a successful engineer, understanding society and societal context is as important as understanding engineering and technological contexts. Engineering decisions may be value decisions and social policy decisions. Societal context drives engineering, but sometimes engineering drives societal context. The purpose of this chapter is to introduce the profession of engineering in a societal context and to offer recommendations for how engineers can best serve democratic society.

We will start by examining the individual engineering disciplines, including the problems with which they tend to work, and their employment descriptions.

2.2 THE ENGINEERING PROFESSIONS

The following descriptions of the types of engineering were taken from the U.S. Department of Labor, Bureau of Labor Statistics, Occupational Outlook Handbook (www.bls.gov) unless otherwise noted. Job information includes the year 2000.

Aerospace

 Aerospace engineers are responsible for developing extraordinary machines from airplanes that weigh over a half a million pounds to spacecraft that travel over 17,000 miles an hour. They design, develop, and test aircraft, spacecraft, and missiles and supervise the manufacturing of these products. Aerospace engineers who work with aircraft are aeronautical engineers, and those working specifically with spacecraft are astronautical engineers.

Aerospace engineers develop new technologies for use in aviation, defense systems, and space exploration often specializing in areas such as structural design, guidance, navigation and control, instrumentation and communication, or production methods. They often use Computer-Aided Design (CAD), robotics, lasers and advanced electronic optics to assist them. They may specialize in a particular aerospace product, such as commercial transports, military fighter jets, helicopters, spacecraft, or missiles and rockets. Aerospace engineers may be experts in aerodynamics, thermodynamics, celestial mechanics, propulsion, acoustics, and guidance and control systems.

Aerospace engineers typically are employed within the aerospace industry although their skills are becoming increasingly valuable elsewhere. For example, aerospace engineers in the motor vehicles manufacturing industry design vehicles that have lower air resistance, which increases the vehicles' fuel efficiency.

Agricultural

 Agricultural engineers apply knowledge of engineering technology and biological science to agriculture. They design agricultural machinery and equipment and agricultural structures. They develop ways to conserve soil and water and improve the agricultural product processing. Agricultural engineers work in research and development, production, sales, and management.

More than one third of the 2,400 agricultural engineers employed in 2000 worked for engineering and management services, and they supplied consultant services to farmers and farm-related industries. Others worked in various industries, including crops and livestock as well as manufacturing and government.

Biological[1]

 Biological engineers integrate applied biology into fundamental engineering principles to design processes and systems that influence, control, or use biological materials and organisms for society's benefit. The discipline applies the principles of analysis, synthesis, and design to physical problems and processing systems associated with plants, animals, humans, and their environments.

Biological engineers work various industries, including environmental consulting, biotechnology, the bioprocess and food sector, government, and manufacturing. Many pursue advanced degrees in medical, veterinary, or dental school, or in engineering (usually biological or biomedical).

Biomedical

 By combining biology and medicine with engineering, biomedical engineers develop devices and procedures that solve medical and health related problems. Many do research, along with life scientists, chemists, and medical scientists, on the engineering aspects of the biological systems of humans and animals. Biomedical engineers design devices used in medical procedures, such as the computers used to analyze blood or the laser systems used in corrective eye surgery. They develop artificial organs, imaging systems such as ultrasound, and devices for automating insulin injections or controlling body functions. Most engineers in this specialty require a sound background in one of the more basic engineering specialties, such as mechanical or electronics engineering, in addition to specialized biomedical training. Some specialties within biomedical engineering include biomaterials, biomechanics, medical imaging, rehabilitation, and orthopedic engineering.

Biomedical engineers held about 7,200 jobs in 2000. Manufacturing industries employed 30 percent of all biomedical engineers, primarily in the medical instruments and supplies industries. Many others worked for health services. Some worked on a contract basis for government agencies or as independent consultants.

Chemical

 Chemical engineers apply the principles of chemistry and engineering to solve problems involving the production or use of chemicals, building a bridge between science and manufacturing. They design equipment and develop processes for large-scale chemical manufacturing, plan and test methods of manufacturing the products and treating the byproducts, and supervise production. Chemical engineers work in manufacturing industries other than chemical manufacturing, such as

---

[1] Biological Engineering is a new discipline and is not yet included in the Occupational Outlook Handbook.

those producing electronics, photographic equipment, clothing, pulp, and paper. They work in the healthcare, biotechnology, and business services industries.

The knowledge and duties of chemical engineers overlap many fields. Chemical engineers apply principles of chemistry, physics, mathematics, and mechanical and electrical engineering. They can specialize in oxidation or polymerization and pollution control or the production of fertilizers, pesticides, automotive plastics, and chlorine bleach. They must be aware of all aspects of chemicals manufacturing and how it affects the environment, the safety of workers, and customers. Because chemical engineers use computer technology to optimize all phases of research and production, they need to understand how to apply computer skills to process analysis, automated control systems, and statistical quality control.

Chemical engineers held about 33,000 jobs in 2000. Manufacturing industries employed 73 percent of all chemical engineers, primarily in the chemicals, electronics, petroleum refining, paper, and related industries. Most others worked for engineering services, research and testing services, or consulting firms that design chemical plants. Some worked on a contract basis for government agencies or as independent consultants.

Civil

Civil engineers design and supervise the construction of roads, buildings, airports, tunnels, dams, bridges, and water supply and sewage systems. Civil engineering, considered one of the oldest engineering disciplines, encompasses structural, water resources, environmental, construction, transportation, and geotechnical engineering.

Many civil engineers hold supervisory or administrative positions, from supervisor of a construction site to city engineer. Others may work in design, construction, research, and teaching.

Civil engineers held about 232,000 jobs in 2000. A little over half were employed by firms providing engineering consulting services, primarily developing designs for construction projects. Almost one third of the jobs were in federal, state, and local government agencies. The construction and manufacturing industries accounted for most of the remaining employment. About 12,000 civil engineers were self-employed, many as consultants.

Civil engineers usually work near major industrial and commercial centers, often at construction sites. Some projects are in remote areas or foreign countries. In some jobs, civil engineers must move to work on different projects.

Computer Hardware

Computer hardware engineers research, design, develop, and test computer hardware and supervise its manufacture and installation. Hardware refers to computer chips, circuit boards, computer systems, and related peripherals. Computer software engineers—often called computer engineers—design and develop the software systems that control computers. These workers are covered elsewhere in the *Handbook*. The work of computer hardware engineers is similar to electronics engineer work, but unlike electronics engineers, computer hardware engineers work exclusively with computers and computer-related equipment. In addition to design and development, computer hardware engineers may supervise the manufacturing and installation of computers and computer-related equipment. The rapid advances in computer technology are because of the research, development, and design efforts of computer hardware engineers. To keep up with technology change, these engineers must continually update their knowledge.

The number of computer hardware engineers is relatively small compared with the number of other computer-related workers who work with software or computer applications. Computer hardware engineers held about 60,000 jobs in 2000. About 25 percent were employed in computer and data processing services. About 10% worked in computer and office equipment manufacturing, but many were employed in communications industries and engineering consulting firms.

Construction management

Construction managers plan and coordinate construction projects. They may have job titles such as constructor, construction superintendent, general superintendent, project engineer, project manager, general construction manager, or executive construction manager. Managers who work in the construction industry, such as general managers, project engineers, and others, increasingly are called *constructors.* Constructors manage, coordinate, and supervise the construction process from the conceptual development stage through final construction on a timely and economical basis. Given designs for buildings, roads, bridges, or other projects, constructors oversee the organization, scheduling, and implementation of the project to execute those designs. They are responsible for coordinating and managing people, materials, and equipment; budgets, schedules, and contracts; and safety of employees and the general public.

Construction managers held 389,000 jobs in 2002. Almost half were self-employed. Most of the rest were employed in the construction industry, 15 percent by specialty trade contractors—for example, plumbing, heating and air-conditioning, and electrical contractors—and 21 percent by general building contractors. Architectural, engineering, and related services firms, as well as local governments, employed others.

Electrical and Electronics

From geographical information systems that continuously provide the location of a vehicle to giant electric power generators, electrical and electronics engineers are responsible for a wide range of technologies. Electrical and electronics engineers design, develop, test, and supervise the manufacture of electrical and electronic equipment. Some of this equipment includes power generating, controlling, and transmission devices used by electric utilities; and electric motors, machinery controls, lighting, and wiring in buildings, automobiles, aircraft, radar and navigation systems, and broadcast and communications systems. Many electrical and electronics engineers work in areas closely related to computers. However, engineers whose work is related exclusively to computer hardware are considered computer hardware engineers, an occupation covered elsewhere in the *Handbook.*

Electrical and electronics engineers specialize in different areas such as power generation, transmission, and distribution; communications; electrical equipment manufacturing; or a specialty, e.g., industrial robot control systems and aviation electronics. Electrical and electronics engineers design new products, write performance requirements, and develop maintenance schedules. They test equipment, solve operating problems, and estimate engineering project time and cost.

Electrical and electronics engineers held about 288,000 jobs in 2000, making their occupation the largest branch of engineering. Most jobs were in engineering and business consulting firms, government agencies, and manufacturers of electrical and electronic and computer and office equipment, industrial machinery, and professional and scientific instruments. Transportation, communications, and utilities firms as well as personnel supply services and computer and data processing services firms accounted for most of the remaining jobs.

California, Texas, New York, and New Jersey, with many large electronics firms, employ nearly one third of all electrical and electronics engineers.

Engineering Technology

 Engineering technicians use the principles and theories of science, engineering, and mathematics to solve technical problems in research and development, manufacturing, sales, construction, inspection, and maintenance. Their work is more limited in scope and more practically-oriented than that of scientists and engineers. Many engineering technicians assist engineers and scientists, especially in research and development. Others work in quality control—inspecting products and processes, conducting tests, or collecting data. In manufacturing, they may assist in product design, development, or production. Most engineering technicians specialize in certain areas, learning skills and working in the same disciplines as engineers. Occupational titles, therefore, tend to reflect those of engineers.

Engineering technicians held 478,000 jobs in 2002. About 39 percent of all engineering technicians worked in manufacturing, mainly in the computer and electronic equipment, transportation equipment, and machinery manufacturing industries. Another 20 percent worked in professional, scientific, and technical service industries, mostly in engineering or business services companies that do engineering work on contract for government, manufacturing firms, or other organizations.

Environmental

 Using the principles of biology and chemistry, environmental engineers develop methods to solve environment-related problems. They are involved in water and air pollution control, recycling, waste disposal, and public health issues. Environmental engineers conduct hazardous waste management studies, evaluate hazard significance, offer treatment and containment analysis, and develop regulations to prevent mishaps. They design municipal sewage and industrial wastewater systems. They analyze scientific data, research controversial projects, and perform quality control checks.

Environmental engineers are concerned with local and worldwide environmental issues. They study and attempt to minimize the effects of acid rain, global warming, automobile emissions, and ozone depletion. They are involved in wildlife protection.

Many environmental engineers work as consultants, helping their clients comply with regulations and clean-up hazardous sites, including brownfields, which are abandoned urban or industrial sites that may contain environmental hazards.

Environmental engineers held about 52,000 jobs in 2000. More than one third worked in engineering and management services and about 16,000 were employed in federal, state, and local government agencies. The remainder worked in various manufacturing industries.

Industrial

Industrial engineers determine the most effective ways for an organization to use basic production factors—people, machines, materials, information, and energy—to make a product or to provide a service. They are the bridge between management goals and operational performance. They are more concerned with increasing productivity through the personnel management, business organization methods, and technology than are other engineers, who generally work more with products or processes. Although most industrial engineers work in manufacturing industries, they can work in consulting services, healthcare, and communications.

To solve organizational, production, and related problems efficiently, industrial engineers study the product and its requirements, use mathematical methods such as operations research to meet those requirements, and design manufacturing and information systems. They develop management control systems to aid in financial planning and cost analysis, design production planning and control systems to coordinate activities and ensure product quality, and design or improve systems for the physical distribution of goods and services. Industrial engineers determine which plant location has the best combination of raw materials availability, transportation facilities, and costs. Industrial engineers use computers to simulate and control activities and devices, such as assembly lines and robots. They develop wage and salary administration systems and job evaluation programs. Many industrial engineers move into management positions because the work is closely related.

The work of health and safety engineers is similar to industrial engineer work in that they are concerned with the entire production process. They promote worksite or product safety and health by applying knowledge of industrial processes, as well as mechanical, chemical, and psychological principles. They must anticipate and evaluate hazardous conditions as well as develop hazard control methods. They must be familiar with the application of health and safety regulations.

Industrial engineers, including health and safety, held about 198,000 jobs in 2000. More than 65 percent of these jobs were in manufacturing industries. Because they can use their skills in almost any organization, industrial engineers are more widely distributed among manufacturing industries than are other engineers.

Their skills can be readily applied outside manufacturing as well. Some work in engineering and management services, utilities, and business services; others work for government agencies or as independent consultants.

Materials

 Materials engineers are involved in materials extraction, development, processing, and testing used to create products from computer chips and television screens to golf clubs and snow skis. They work with metals, ceramics, plastics, semiconductors, and composites (materials combinations) to create materials that meet certain mechanical, electrical, and chemical requirements. They select materials for new applications.

Numerous developments within materials engineering make manipulating and using materials possible. For example, materials engineers can create and then study materials at an atomic level using advanced processes, electrons, neutrons, or x-rays and to replicate the characteristics of materials and their components with computers.

Materials engineers specializing in metals are metallurgical engineers, and those in ceramics are ceramic engineers. Most metallurgical engineers work in one of three main metallurgy branches: extractive or chemical, physical, and process. Extractive metallurgists are concerned with removing metals from ores and refining and alloying them to obtain useful metal. Physical metallurgists study the nature, structure, and physical properties of metals and their alloys, and relate them to the methods for processing them into final products. Process metallurgists develop and improve metal working processes such as casting, forging, rolling, and drawing. Ceramic engineers develop ceramic materials and the processes for making ceramic materials into useful products. Ceramics include all nonmetallic, inorganic materials that require high processing temperatures. Ceramic engineers work on products as diverse as glassware, automobile and aircraft engine components, fiber optic communication lines, tile, and electric insulators.

Materials engineers held about 33,000 jobs in 2000. Because materials are building blocks for other goods, materials engineers are widely distributed among manufacturing industries. In fact, 84 percent of materials engineers worked in manufacturing industries, primarily metal production and processing, electronic and electrical equipment, transportation equipment, and industrial machinery and equipment. They worked in services industries such as engineering and management and research and testing services. Most remaining materials engineers worked for federal and state governments.

Mechanical

 Mechanical engineers research, develop, design, manufacture, and test tools, engines, machines, and other mechanical devices. They work on power-producing machines such as electric generators, internal combustion engines, and steam and gas turbines. They develop power-using machines such as refrigeration and air conditioning equipment, machine tools, material handling systems, elevators and escalators, industrial production equipment, and robots used in manufacturing. Mechanical engineers design tools needed by other engineers. The field of nanotechnology, which involves creating high-performance materials and components by integrating atoms and molecules, is introducing entirely new principles to the design process.

Computers assist mechanical engineers by performing computations efficiently and by aiding the design process by permitting the modeling and simulation of designs. Computer-Aided Design (CAD) and Computer-Aided Manufacturing (CAM) are used for design data processing and for developing alternative designs.

Mechanical engineers work in many industries, and their work varies by industry and function. Some specialties include applied mechanics, CAD and CAM, energy systems, pressure vessels and piping, and heating, refrigeration, and air conditioning systems. Mechanical engineering is one of the broadest engineering disciplines. Mechanical engineers may work in production operations in manufacturing or agriculture, maintenance, or technical sales though many are administrators or managers.

Mechanical engineers held about 221,000 jobs in 2000. More than 50% of the jobs were in manufacturing, mostly in machinery, transportation equipment, electrical equipment, instruments, and fabricated metal products industries. Engineering and management services, business services, and the federal government provided most of the remaining jobs.

Mining and Geological

 Mining and geological engineers find, extract, and prepare coal, metals, and minerals for use by manufacturing industries and utilities. They design open pit and underground mines, supervise the construction of mine shafts and tunnels in underground operations, and devise methods for transporting minerals to processing plants. Mining engineers are responsible for the safe, economical, and environmentally sound operation of mines. Some mining engineers work with geologists and metallurgical engineers to locate and appraise ore deposits. Others develop mining equipment or direct mineral processing operations to separate minerals from the dirt, rock, and other mixed materials. Mining engineers frequently specialize in the mining of one mineral or metal, such as coal or gold. With increased emphasis on protecting the environment, many mining engineers work to solve problems related to land reclamation and water and air pollution.

Mining safety engineers use their knowledge of mine design and practices to ensure the safety of workers and to comply with state and federal safety regulations. They inspect walls and roof surfaces, test air samples, and examine mining equipment for compliance with safety practices.

Mining and geological engineers, including mining safety engineers, held about 6,500 jobs in 2000. One half worked in the mining industry, and other mining engineers worked in government agencies or engineering consulting firms.

Mining engineers usually are employed at the natural deposit location, often near small communities, and sometimes outside the United States. Those in research and development, management, consulting, or sales, however, are often located in metropolitan areas.

Nuclear

 Nuclear engineers research and develop the processes, instruments, and systems used to benefit from nuclear energy and radiation. They design, develop, monitor, and operate nuclear plants to generate power. They may work on the nuclear fuel cycle, i.e., the production, handling, and use of nuclear fuel and the safe disposal of waste produced by nuclear energy. They may work on fusion energy. Some specialize in nuclear power source development for spacecraft; others find industrial and medical uses for radioactive materials, such as in medical diagnostic and treatment equipment.

Nuclear engineers held about 14,000 jobs in 2000. About 58 percent were in utilities, 26 percent in engineering consulting firms, and 14 percent in the federal government. More than half of all federally employed nuclear engineers were civilian employees of the Navy, and most of the rest worked for the Department of Energy. Most non-federally employed nuclear engineers worked for public utilities or engineering consulting companies. Some worked for defense manufacturers or nuclear power equipment manufacturers.

Petroleum

 Petroleum engineers search the world for reservoirs containing oil or natural gas. Once discovered, petroleum engineers work with geologists and other specialists to understand the geologic formation and properties of the rock containing the reservoir, determine the drilling methods, and monitor drilling and production operations. They design equipment and processes to achieve the maximum profitable oil and gas recovery. Petroleum engineers rely on computer models to simulate reservoir performance using recovery techniques. They use computer models for simulations of the effects of drilling options.

Because only a small proportion of oil and gas in a reservoir will flow out under natural forces, petroleum engineers develop and use enhanced recovery methods. These include injecting water, chemicals, gases, or steam into an oil reservoir to force out the oil, and using computercontrolled drilling or fracturing to con-

nect a larger reservoir area to a single well. Because today's best techniques recover a portion of the reservoir oil and gas, petroleum engineers research and develop technology and methods to increase recovery and lower drilling and production operations cost.

Petroleum engineers held about 9,000 jobs in 2000, mostly in oil and gas extraction, petroleum refining, and engineering and architectural services. Employers include major oil companies and hundreds of smaller, independent oil exploration, production, and service companies. Engineering consulting firms and
government agencies employ many petroleum engineers.

Most petroleum engineers work where oil and gas are found. Large numbers are
employed in Texas, Louisiana, Oklahoma, and California, including off-shore sites.
Many American petroleum engineers work overseas in oil-producing countries.

> *Never doubt that a thoughtful group of committed citizens can change
> the world. Indeed, it's the only thing that ever has.*
>   —Margaret Mead

Now that you have information on the engineering professions, we will examine service-learning projects and how they fit into these disciplines.

2.3 SERVICE-LEARNING AND THE ENGINEERING PROFESSIONS

Service-learning has been used by engineering students to accomplish many
goals that serve society and the profession. The following list of completed
service-learning projects in engineering is intended to illustrate the ways in which
you could use service-learning in your education. The engineering disciplines that
would work on such projects are listed in parentheses after each project. Keep in
mind that most engineers can work on projects in which they are not specifically
listed; the list is intended to show projects that specific engineering disciplines
tend to work on.

Engineering projects are made stronger by working in teams with people outside engineering disciplines. For example, community parks usually require the
expertise of a landscape architect. Community expertise must be included in all
phases of a service-learning project. You are encouraged to look at the service-
learning project profiles in Chapter 9 of this text, or to consult http://epics.ecn
.purdue.edu/projects/teams_nationwide.htm for more specific information on service-learning projects in engineering.

Service-learning has been used in Colleges of Engineering to do the following:

- Provide training in math, science, engineering, and technology for K–12 science and math teachers (all engineering disciplines)
- Design structures and floor plans to minimize home construction and energy costs for Habitat for Humanity (civil and mechanical)
- Design a community park with a bicycle trail (civil and environmental)
- Design communications devices for people with disabilities (electrical, computer, biological, biomedical)

- Develop computer-controlled toys for children with physical disabilities (electrical, computer, biological, biomedical)
- Design a multimedia center and animal habitats for local zoos (electrical, computer, mechanical, civil, environmental, biological)
- Design and construct a climbing wall for a Girl Scout troop challenge course (mechanical and aerospace)
- Design and build bird sanctuaries, butterfly gardens, and playgrounds for public elementary schools (biological, environmental)
- Create a site plan, report, and recommendations for a community wanting the optimal landfill location (agricultural, biological, environmental)
- Reducing flow time of emergency room patients in a non-profit hospital (industrial, biomedical)
- Design and construct a wetland for treating dairy waste at a university (agricultural, biological, environmental)
- Design and implement a confidential database for non-profit agencies to coordinate services and track clients (electrical and computer)
- Write successful grant proposals to fund service-learning projects (all engineering disciplines)

Exercise

Can you think of a service-learning project that would integrate your engineering discipline with a community need? Expand on your idea by answering the following questions:

- What is the community need?
- What are the historical, cultural, political, and ethical aspects of this community need?
- What are the engineering aspects of this community need?
- Who in the community is currently working on this problem?
- How might you work with the community to address this community need?

2.4 NATIONAL SOCIETY OF PROFESSIONAL ENGINEERS (NSPE) CODE OF ETHICS[2]

Ethics is centrally important to the engineering profession; to be a successful engineer, you must know how principles of engineering ethics relate to your work and how to abide by these principles. Several engineering disciplines have their own specific ethics codes, including chemical[3], civil[4], mechanical[5], and electrical[6].

---

[2] Code is reprinted with permission of NSPE.
[3] Through AiChE, the American Institute of Chemical Engineers
[4] Through ASCE, the American Society of Civil Engineers
[5] Through ASME, the American Society of Mechanical Engineers
[6] Through the Institute of Electrical and Electronics Engineers

While codes of ethics are very important for providing guidelines for ethical practice, they do not fully encompass the important topic of ethics in engineering. Ethical issues involving service-learning in engineering are contained in chapter eight. Readers are encouraged to consult the following reference for a more detailed examination of engineering ethics:

Schinzinger, R. and M. Martin. 2000. *Introduction to Engineering Ethics.* New York: McGraw-Hill. 260 pp.

The NSPE has developed a code of ethics that applies to all engineering disciplines. It is presented here in its entirety so that you can become familiar with the fundamental canons, rules of practice, and professional obligations of all engineers.

NSPE Code of Ethics for Engineers

Preamble

Engineering is an important and learned profession. As members of this profession, engineers are expected to exhibit the highest standards of honesty and integrity. Engineering has a direct and vital impact on the quality of life for all people. Accordingly, the services provided by engineers require honesty, impartiality, fairness, and equity, and must be dedicated to the protection of the public health, safety, and welfare. Engineers must perform under a standard of professional behavior that requires adherence to the highest principles of ethical conduct.

I. Fundamental Canons

Engineers, in the fulfillment of their professional duties, shall:

1. Hold paramount the safety, health and welfare of the public.
2. Perform services only in areas of their competence.
3. Issue public statements only in an objective and truthful manner.
4. Act for each employer or client as faithful agents or trustees.
5. Avoid deceptive acts.
6. Conduct themselves honorably, responsibly, ethically, and lawfully so as to enhance the honor, reputation, and usefulness of the profession.

II. Rules of Practice

1. Engineers shall hold paramount the safety, health, and welfare of the public.
   a. If engineers' judgment is overruled under circumstances that endanger life or property, they shall notify their employer or client and such other authority as may be appropriate.
   b. Engineers shall approve only those engineering documents in conformity with applicable standards.

     c.   Engineers shall not reveal facts, data, or information without the prior consent of the client or employer except as authorized or required by law or this Code.

     d.   Engineers shall not permit the use of their name or associate in business ventures with any person or firm that they believe are engaged in fraudulent or dishonest enterprise.

     e.   Engineers shall not aid or abet the unlawful practice of engineering by a person or firm.

     f.   Engineers having knowledge of any alleged violation of this Code shall report thereon to appropriate professional bodies and, when relevant, to public authorities, and cooperate with the proper authorities in furnishing such information or assistance as may be required.

2. Engineers shall perform services only in the areas of their competence.

     a.   Engineers shall undertake assignments only when qualified by education or experience in the specific technical fields involved.

     b.   Engineers shall not affix their signatures to any plans or documents dealing with subject matter in which they lack competence, nor to any plan or document not prepared under their direction and control.

     c.   Engineers may accept assignments and assume responsibility for coordination of an entire project and sign and seal the engineering documents for the entire project, provided each technical segment is signed and sealed only by the qualified engineers who prepared the segment.

3. Engineers shall issue public statements only in an objective and truthful manner.

     a.   Engineers shall be objective and truthful in professional reports, statements, or testimony. They shall include all relevant and pertinent information in such reports, statements, or testimony, which should bear the date indicating when it was current.

     b.   Engineers may express publicly technical opinions founded upon knowledge of the facts and competence in the subject matter.

     c.   Engineers shall issue no statements, criticisms, or arguments on technical matters that are inspired or paid for by interested parties unless they have prefaced their comments by explicitly identifying the interested parties on whose behalf they are speaking, and by revealing the existence of any interest the engineers may have in the matters.

4. Engineers shall act for each employer or client as faithful agents or trustees.

     a.   Engineers shall disclose all known or potential conflicts of interest that could influence or appear to influence their judgment or the quality of their services.

     b.   Engineers shall not accept compensation, financial or otherwise, from more than one party for services on the same project, or for services pertaining to the same project, unless the circumstances are fully disclosed and agreed to by all interested parties.

     c.   Engineers shall not solicit or accept financial or other valuable consideration, directly or indirectly, from outside agents in connection with the work for which they are responsible.

d.   Engineers in public service as members, advisors, or employees of a governmental or quasi-governmental body or department shall not participate in decisions with respect to services solicited or provided by them or their organizations in private or public engineering practice.

e.   Engineers shall not solicit or accept a contract from a governmental body on which a principal or officer of their organization serves as a member.

5.   Engineers shall avoid deceptive acts.

a.   Engineers shall not falsify their qualifications or permit misrepresentation of their or their associates' qualifications. They shall not misrepresent or exaggerate their responsibility in or for the subject matter of prior assignments. Brochures or other presentations incident to the solicitation of employment shall not misrepresent pertinent facts concerning employers, employees, associates, joint ventures, or past accomplishments.

b.   Engineers shall not offer, give, solicit or receive, directly or indirectly, any contribution to influence the award of a contract by public authority, or which may be reasonably construed by the public as having the effect of intent to influencing the awarding of a contract. They shall not offer any gift or other valuable consideration in order to secure work. They shall not pay a commission, percentage, or brokerage fee in order to secure work, except to a bona fide employee or bona fide established commercial or marketing agencies retained by them.

III. Professional Obligations

1.   Engineers shall be guided in all their relations by the highest standards of honesty and integrity.

a.   Engineers shall acknowledge their errors and shall not distort or alter the facts.

b.   Engineers shall advise their clients or employers when they believe a project will not be successful.

c.   Engineers shall not accept outside employment to the detriment of their regular work or interest. Before accepting any outside engineering employment, they will notify their employers.

d.   Engineers shall not attempt to attract an engineer from another employer by false or misleading pretenses.

e.   Engineers shall not promote their own interest at the expense of the dignity and integrity of the profession.

2.   Engineers shall, at all times, strive to serve the public interest.

a.   Engineers shall seek opportunities to participate in civic affairs; career guidance for youths; and work for the advancement of the safety, health, and well-being of their community.

b.   Engineers shall not complete, sign, or seal plans and/or specifications not in conformity with applicable engineering standards. If the client or employer insists on such unprofessional conduct, engineers shall notify the proper authorities and withdraw from further service on the project.

    c.   Engineers shall endeavor to extend public knowledge and appreciation of engineering and its achievements.

3. Engineers shall avoid all conduct or practice that deceives the public.

    a.   Engineers shall avoid the use of statements containing a material misrepresentation of fact or omitting a material fact.

    b.   Consistent with the foregoing, engineers may advertise for recruitment of personnel.

    c.   Consistent with the foregoing, engineers may prepare articles for the lay or technical press, but such articles shall not imply credit to the author for work performed by others.

4. Engineers shall not disclose, without consent, confidential information concerning the business affairs or technical processes of any present or former client or employer, or public body on which they serve.

    a.   Engineers shall not, without the consent of all interested parties, promote or arrange for new employment or practice in connection with a specific project for which the engineer has gained particular and specialized knowledge.

    b.   Engineers shall not, without the consent of all interested parties, participate in or represent an adversary interest in connection with a specific project or proceeding in which the engineer has gained particular specialized knowledge on behalf of a former client or employer.

5. Engineers shall not be influenced in their professional duties by conflicting interests.

    a.   Engineers shall not accept financial or other considerations, including free engineering designs, from material or equipment suppliers for specifying their product.

    b.   Engineers shall not accept commissions or allowances, directly or indirectly, from contractors or other parties dealing with clients or employers of the engineer in connection with work for which the engineer is responsible.

6. Engineers shall not attempt to obtain employment or advancement or professional engagements by untruthfully criticizing other engineers, or by other improper or questionable methods.

    a.   Engineers shall not request, propose, or accept a commission on a contingent basis under circumstances in which their judgment may be compromised.

    b.   Engineers in salaried positions shall accept part-time engineering work only to the extent consistent with policies of the employer and in accordance with ethical considerations.

    c.   Engineers shall not, without consent, use equipment, supplies, laboratory, or office facilities of an employer to carry on outside private practice.

7. Engineers shall not attempt to injure, maliciously or falsely, directly or indirectly, the professional reputation, prospects, practice, or employment of

other engineers. Engineers who believe others are guilty of unethical or illegal practice shall present such information to the proper authority for action.

   a.   Engineers in private practice shall not review the work of another engineer for the same client, except with the knowledge of such engineer, or unless the connection of such engineer with the work has been terminated.

   b.   Engineers in governmental, industrial, or educational employ are entitled to review and evaluate the work of other engineers when so required by their employment duties.

   c.   Engineers in sales or industrial employ are entitled to make engineering comparisons of represented products with products of other suppliers.

8. Engineers shall accept personal responsibility for their professional activities provided, however, that engineers may seek indemnification for services arising out of their practice for other than gross negligence, where the engineer's interests cannot otherwise be protected.

   a.   Engineers shall conform with state registration laws in the practice of engineering.

   b.   Engineers shall not use association with a non-engineer, a corporation, or partnership as a "cloak" for unethical acts.

9. Engineers shall give credit for engineering work to those to whom credit is due, and will recognize the proprietary interests of others.

   a.   Engineers shall, whenever possible, name the person or persons who may be individually responsible for designs, inventions, writings, or other accomplishments.

   b.   Engineers using designs supplied by a client recognize that the designs remain the property of the client and may not be duplicated by the engineer for others without express permission.

   c.   Engineers, before undertaking work for others in connection with which the engineer may make improvements, plans, designs, inventions, or other records that may justify copyrights or patents, should enter into a positive agreement regarding ownership.

   d.   Engineers' designs, data, records, and notes referring exclusively to an employer's work are the employer's property. The employer should indemnify the engineer for use of the information for any purpose other than the original purpose.

   e.   Engineers shall continue their professional development throughout their careers and should keep current in their specialty fields by engaging in professional practice, participating in continuing education courses, reading in the technical literature, and attending professional meetings and seminars.

—*As Revised January 2003*

Ethics is a critically important area of study in engineering, and pervades every situation in which an engineer is involved. We presented the Code of Ethics so that you could think about ethical aspects of engineering and service learning throughout your course and project. In the next section, we will discuss what we mean by socially responsible engineering. Ethics is an important part of this concept.

2.5 THE LINK BETWEEN SOCIETAL IMPLICATIONS AND ENGINEERING: SOCIALLY RESPONSIBLE ENGINEERING

2.5.1. Background

Remember the definition of engineering from earlier this chapter:

Engineering is the profession in which a knowledge of the mathematical and natural sciences gained by study, experience, and practice is applied with judgment to develop ways to utilize, economically, the materials and forces of nature for the benefit of humankind.

The idea that engineers behave in socially responsible ways is taken for granted in this definition, and in most definitions of engineering. However, this is not always the case. History provides us with numerous examples of engineering practiced in socially responsible ways, and engineering practiced in ways that created more problems. The focus of this section is to illustrate examples, to discuss some of the methods that engineers are using to be socially responsible, and to provide tips for ways in which you can practice socially responsible engineering.

Most engineers do not plan to solve problems in ways that cause more problems than they initially addressed. Because we continue to learn over time, our practices change to reflect the things we have learned. Thus, something that was designed according to all laws and recommendations twenty years ago may be considered an irresponsible design using today's laws and recommendations. It's important to realize that the state of the art, or most up-to-date engineering instructions and data, will change over time. You need to be aware of the most up-to-date information to be an effective engineer. You should also remember a few concepts regarding social responsibility and engineering. We will examine several examples to illustrate these points and then talk about these principles explicitly.

One example of engineering in a socially irresponsible way was described by Langdon Winner (1986, 1993). Winner studied the New York City planner Robert Moses, and the way in which Moses built overpasses (bridges) on the Long Island Expressway. The overpasses were placed low to the ground on purpose, so that buses would not be able to pass under them. This resulted in portions of Long Island, particularly beaches, being inaccessible by public transportation. Because people with less money depended on public transportation to go to the beach, the

The history and philosophy of technology is extremely important, and being well informed of the relationship between society and technology from these standpoints is ideal for creating well-designed solutions to societal problems. The following references offer excellent information in this regard:

Dorf, R. 2001. Technology, Humans, and Society: Toward a Sustainable World. Academic Press, San Diego.

Boyte, H. and N. Kari. 1996. Building America: The democratic promise of public work. Temple University Press, Philadelphia.

Sclove, R. 1995. Democracy and Technology. Guilford Press. ISBN: 089862861

Tenner, E. 1997. Why things bite back: technology and the revenge of unintended consequences. Vintage Books. ISBN: 0679747567

We encourage taking a course on the history of technology, science, and society, or a course on the philosophy of technology if offered.

bridges stopped these people from accessing the beach. Winner (1986) says, "Thus, the height of the bridge was a political statement—inequality in built form—that became an enduring part of both the physical infrastructure and social landscape of New York." This is an example in which engineering was deliberately used to promote class and race segregation.

Another example that contains irresponsible engineering theories by today's standards is contained in the passage below. This statement came from a book by Billy Vaughn Koen called *Definition of the Engineering Method*, published in 1951 as follows:

"We immediately run into three practical difficulties when we consider the engineer's change: the engineer doesn't know where he is going, how he is going to get there or if anyone will care when he does. . . . An example will make this point clear. The Aswan Dam in Egypt has increased the salinity of the Nile by ten percent, has led to the collapse of the sardine industry in the Delta, has caused coastal erosion and has forced the 100,000 Nubians displaced by the reservoir to try to adapt to life as farmers on the newly created arable land. These liabilities have been offset—some would say more than offset—by other assets, such as the generation of enough hydroelectric power to furnish half of Egypt's electrical needs. Our interest, however, is not to critique this spectacular engineering project or to reconcile conflicting opinions as to its net worth, but to emphasize that before construction, the engineer could not predict the exact change in salinity and erosion or the exact human costs to the sardine fisherman and the Nubians. The final state always has a reality the initial state lacks."

Thanks to vast improvements in computing, prediction and analysis of engineering situations is much better than it was in 1951. Thus, it is no longer true that an engineer does not know where he or she is going and how to get there. Accountability to stakeholders and the public has developed to the point that we care about what happens when the engineer reaches the conclusion of his or her project. Although the final state does have a reality that the initial state lacks, our picture of the virtual state before construction is now close to the actual picture after construction.

This passage states that our interest should not be in weighing the pros and cons of the spectacular engineering project, but rather on the engineering process of change itself. This traditional view of engineering has evolved; engineering decisions are made by carefully weighing the pros and cons of an engineering project and the effects it will have on the environment and society. The communities directly affected have a say in the design process. Service learning in engineering reinforces this concept of community-based design.

Henry Ford's accomplishment represent one example of an engineering approach ahead of its time. Ford (1863–1947) worked as the Chief Engineer for the Edison Illuminating Company in Detroit before starting the Ford Motor Company in 1903. As the Vice President and Chief Engineer of the Ford Motor Company, he worked to produce a car that was efficient, reliable, and cheap so that everyone could afford one. Ford's engineering innovations included the creation of an efficient assembly line and the design of programs such as Village Industries for the workers in his company such that they could live and work harmoniously. Ford provided innovations in the use of agricultural products in industrial production, for example, soybean-based plastics were used to make automobile trunks.

In 1936, Ford and his son Edsel started the Ford Foundation, a statewide philanthropic organization with the mission "to promote human welfare." The Ford Foundation branched out from Michigan to international stature in 1950. Today, the Ford Foundation has thirteen offices worldwide, which work locally and globally to advocate for the following goals:

- Strengthen democratic values
- Reduce poverty and injustice
- Promote international cooperation
- Advance human achievement

There is controversy regarding Henry Ford. Though his life and work provide an excellent example of socially responsible engineering and how engineering can bridge with public life, Ford himself is a study in contradictions. He was a pacifist and contributed to and was involved in world peace efforts at the same time he owned a newspaper that routinely published anti-Semitic articles. Ford was an anti-Semite. Though he actively worked to make the lives of his employees better, Ford was fiercely opposed to labor unions and was the last manufacturer of automobiles to unionize. These seeming contradictions remind us of the complexities of individuals.

More recently, engineering approaches have been considered within the framework of sustainable development. "Sustainable development is development that meets the needs of the present without compromising the ability of future generations to meet their own needs" (Brundtland Commission Report, 1987). This approach involves a triple bottom line: environmental quality, economic health, and social equity. The concept of sustainable development was agreed upon at the Earth Summit sponsored by the United Nations in Rio de Janeiro in 1992, and leaves the technology and policies that develop to each nation.

Now let's look at some of the guiding principles in terms of engineering in a socially responsible manner.

2.5.2 Green Engineering and Lifecycle Design

In May 2003, the San Destin Conference on Green Engineering was held in Destin, Florida. Engineers from numerous disciplines worked together to define and discuss this subject. The information given below was taken from the conference proceedings (excerpted from http://www.enviro.utoledo.edu/Green/index.htm).

> "Green engineering is the design, commercialization, and use of processes and products, which are feasible and economical while minimizing 1) generation of pollution at the source, and 2) risk to human health and the environment. The discipline embraces the concept that decisions to protect human health and the environment can have the greatest impact and cost effectiveness when applied early to the design and development phase of a process or product."
>
> Green engineering transforms existing engineering disciplines and practices to those that promote sustainability. Green engineering incorporates development and implementation of technologically and economically viable products, processes, and systems that promote human welfare while protecting human health and elevating the protection of the biosphere as a criterion in engineering solutions.

The following are the principles of green engineering:

1. Engineer processes and products holistically, use systems analysis, and integrate environmental impact assessment tools
2. Conserve and improve natural ecosystems while protecting human health and well-being
3. Use lifecycle thinking in all engineering activities
4. Ensure that all material and energy inputs and outputs are as inherently safe and benign as possible
5. Minimize depletion of natural resources
6. Prevent waste
7. Develop and apply engineering solutions, while being cognizant of local geography, aspirations, and cultures
8. Create engineering solutions beyond current or dominant technologies; improve, innovate, and invent (technologies) to achieve sustainability
9. Actively engage communities and stakeholders in development of engineering solutions
10. There is a duty to inform society of the practice of green engineering.

Lifecycle design is a concept closely related to green engineering. It involves careful planning through the design, construction, life, and "death" of the product, process, device or system in an effort to minimize environmental impact. The Pacific Northwest Pollution Prevention Resource Center has published a checklist for lifecycle design and design for the environment. Parts of this checklist[7] are

---

[7] Prepared by the Pacific Northwest Pollution Prevention Resource Center, www.pprc.org, with funding from the U.S. Environmental Protection Agency / Region 10. Originally published October 2001.

presented here to illustrate how to incorporate the concept of lifecycle design into engineering design methods:

Design Considerations Before Manufacturing

- Minimize ecological (soil, water, air, etc.) disturbance for all product parts and manufacturing
- Design for easy disassembly of product parts
  - Use the fewest materials and numbers of parts possible
  - Use interchangeable parts; identify materials
  - Make hazardous parts easily detachable
  - Make disassembly easy and efficient
  - Minimize disposable components
- Minimize weight and volume
- Incorporate recovered materials
- Use low-energy materials and processes
- Avoid hazardous or toxic materials
- Consider transportation implications of supplies, raw materials, the product, and packaging (minimize weight and volume and buy locally if possible)
- Design the product for use and maintenance that minimizes environmental impact (minimizing energy and water use, operation without oil, battery, chemicals, or other consumables, etc.)

Design Considerations During Manufacturing

- Minimize the use of toxic chemicals, emissions, water, and energy (especially heavy metals and chemicals linked to global warming and ozone depletion)
- Minimize surface treatments of parts; use water and vegetable based coatings
- Minimize energy and water intensive manufacturing processes
- Maximize energy and water recovery
- Minimize and/or reclaim process discharge or "waste streams"
- Minimize and/or reuse scrap parts
- Follow spill prevention and secondary containment procedures

Design Considerations During Product Distribution and Packaging

- Use environmental packaging and materials, especially reusable and non-hazardous materials
- Ask suppliers to minimize packaging
- Minimize volume, weight, and material types
- Organize and use efficient means of transportation
- Prevent hazardous spills during transport

Design Considerations at the End of Useful Life of the Product

- Maximize material and part recovery opportunities
- Avoid gaseous, liquid, or leachable releases from any portion of the product that requires disposal

Many companies are already practicing green engineering. Xerox buys back equipment at the end of its useful life, remanufactures the original components, re-assembles the components into new machines, and sells these machines. Most of the fabrics made by the sports clothing company Patagonia are created with organic cotton and recycled plastic beverage bottles. Approximately three-quarters of automobiles at the end of their useful lives are recycled to create new products. Most companies recognize the importance of this green engineering in terms of being economically viable in a global economy.

> *Technology is a queer thing. It brings you great gifts with one hand, and it stabs you in the back with the other.*
> —Carrie P. Snow

2.5.3 Socially Responsible Engineering: Putting it all Together

You now have information on the engineering discipline, the types of engineering, and the role of engineering in society. You have examples, good and bad, of the ways in which engineering can have an impact on society. Finally, you have the principles of green engineering and lifecycle design. How can you put all this together into socially responsible engineering? What does it mean to be a socially responsible engineer?

Remember that doing engineering design takes skill in math and science, but to be effective you need to work with community groups and the public through all stages of the design process, communicate or disseminate your design to technical and non-technical audiences, and understand the culture into which your design will integrate.

The following set of tips are intended to assist you in integrating all the information in this chapter into an approach to engineering that is socially responsive and responsible.

Think hard about how your problems are defined or framed. Engineers tend to remove the social and political aspects from problem solving to make the process easier and more efficient. The major setback with this approach is that your solution may not be the best one because social and political aspects were not part of the way in which the problem was originally defined. This process can be deliberate (e.g., not enough time, we need to make assumptions, get on with things as quickly as possible) or accidental (oh yeah, we didn't think about that!). Bringing the community and the public into your engineering design methods and decision making from the start of your project will assist you in solving a correctly defined problem.

Realize that engineering and technology decisions are value-laden. Engineering decisions have consequences that are political, social, ethical, and moral. Engineers acknowledge this, yet many engineers do not play a pivotal role in making value decisions because such subjects are not in their area of expertise. Engineers do not need college degrees in social studies, political science, or philosophy to make value decisions. The tendency to avoid these issues leaves other groups to make value decisions without our input. The point is not who is the most qualified; the point is that we all need to be at the table to make these decisions, especially the public.

Art Kaplan, at the Center for Bioethics at Penn State, explains that the United States is the world's most advanced nation technologically, with the least amount of regulation and oversight. People tend to think that the study of ethics lags behind the issues created by technologies, but this is not true. The ethicists keep up with the technology, but politics are slow. In effect, this leaves the marketplace, and to some extent, the law, in charge of where the technology goes (in other words, who is paying for it). This approach puzzles the rest of the world.[8]

Realize that engineering itself is value-laden. In addition to the decision-making in engineering being closely linked with values, the entire engineering profession in our society is value-laden. In our society, people tend to think that society and technology are separable (this is why engineers sometimes think, "We'll leave the society part to the liberal arts people") and that technological professions are more valuable than non-technical professions. This can be seen in salaries (engineers make more money than people engaged in professions that involve the liberal arts) and in prestige.

Remember that these values are dependent on culture. Being a medical doctor in Russia was considered a highly valued profession until women entered the field in large numbers. Medicine has become a devalued profession in Russia, salaries have dropped drastically, and many men have left the profession (can you think of the value judgment at work in this example?). Education is highly valued in Japanese culture; teachers are more revered than any other profession and are paid accordingly. Getting into school to become a teacher in Japan is difficult because of the extreme competition in this profession. These examples illustrate the way in which culture values professional disciplines.

No area of study is better than another. Many professions are needed to have a rich and diverse society; all are equally important for addressing and solving problems.

In engineering, use systems thinking instead of linear thinking. Linear thinking essentially means that you have a cause-effect relationship (if I do A, then B will happen). Systems thinking means that your cause can have many effects, some of which will not be immediately evident (if I do A, then B, C, and D will happen; in addition, B and D will cause E, which will affect A and C, etc.). History is full of examples of linear thinking that resulted in multiple problems later because systems thinking was not used. This approach can be difficult to ac-

---

[8] Interview with Terry Gross on Fresh Air, aired July 11, 2001

complish because it can be hard to predict consequences removed from the immediate situation. For example, one unintended consequence of the Aswan dam involves the increased incidence of schistosomiasis, a parasitic disease caused by flatworms that breed in snails that live in the Nile river. Before the dam was constructed, the natural dry season killed the snails and controlled the disease. With canals from the dam filled with water year round, the snails proliferate and so does the disease. Schistosomiasis causes weakness and lethargy, and causes bladder cancer in long-term, untreated cases.

Several methods for conducting systems thinking in engineering are available. Two include environmental lifecycle assessment, and material flows and cycles. Environmental lifecycle assessment accounts for all the environmental effects and resource needs of a process or product throughout its lifecycle. The objective of this method is to quantify these effects and needs and to minimize them through engineering design or other means. Lifecycle assessment provides a comprehensive estimation of environmental effects. Material flows and cycles is a method that involves tracking material use and location as a function of time. Though not as comprehensive as environmental lifecycle assessment, this method provides information on how components can be used, reused, and disposed of; this can lead to decisions made at the systems (entire process) level.

Engineering and technical decisions should be democratic. Democracy means, "by the people, for the people, and of the people." Ultimately, engineering serves society and the people in society. As such, people should be involved in the engineering process. You should always know your community partner, your stakeholders (which people or groups of people will have a relationship with your engineering project), and their needs and desires. Frame your engineering project within these parameters, and work with these groups throughout the project. Additionally, you should understand the problem or situation from multiple perspectives, including the following:

- Historical
- Cultural
- Ethical
- Societal (local and global)
- Democratic
- Minimizes negative impacts
- Environmental (local effects)
- Ecological (global effects)
- Educational
- Technical

These perspectives will give you insight into how to approach and solve engineering problems. For an example of this approach, see the case study of a playground design in Chapter 8. For information on working with community partners and team members, see section 7.4.

2.6 CONCLUSIONS

In this chapter, you learned about the engineering disciplines and service-learning projects conducted within each discipline. You were introduced to the Code of Ethics for Engineers, which defines the fundamental canons, rules of practice, and professional obligations of all engineers. You learned about socially responsible engineering practices and how to put these concepts into action in an engineering capacity.

In the next chapter, you will learn about the engineering method, which is the engineer's road map; the engineering method is a set of steps that every engineer follows to create solutions to an engineering problem or situation. The engineering method is one of the most important things that you will learn and use as an engineer.

REFERENCES

Winner, L. Do artifacts have politics? In *The Whale and the Reactor.* Chicago: University of Chicago Press, 1986.

Winner, L. Upon Opening the Black Box and Finding It Empty: Social Constructivism and the Philosophy of Technology. *Journal of Science, Technology, & Human Values.* 18(3): 362–378, 1993.

EXERCISES

1. Interview an engineer working in the specific engineering discipline in which you are interested. Ask this engineer the following questions and complete a written summary of this interview:
   - What made you want to become an engineer?
   - Describe your educational background
   - What experiences inside and outside the classroom have helped you in your professional career?
   - What are your job activities?
   - What are the things you like best about your job and the things you find most challenging in your job?
   - How do you use engineering in a service capacity (service to society and/or community)
   - Do you have any advice for me as a future engineer?
2. Write a research based career report on a discipline of engineering in which you are interested. Your report should include the following sections:
   - A description of the types of projects and job activities you envision yourself doing in an engineering career.
   - A description seven to ten projects that represent recent engineering research in your area of interest. Also identify technical research trends based on this survey of projects.

- A description of your engineering curriculum, including electives that you can take. Examine course descriptions for the required and elective courses in your major to help you prepare this section.
- An analysis section: based on your interests, your engineering research, and your curriculum information, are you confident in your choice of engineering major? Why or why not?
- A reflection section: Will a degree in your current discipline help you to get where you want to go professionally? Why or why not? Create a plan of action that you believe will help you to meet your career goals.

3. Choose a product, device, process or system. Discuss the implications of green engineering and lifecycle design on the design, manufacture, useful life, and disposal of this entity.

4. Examine the excerpted paragraph on the Aswan Dam from Billy Vaughn Koen's book presented in this chapter. The dam has been the subject of a lot of literature; eventually, two dams were built. Research the dam(s) and prepare a paper on the advantages and disadvantages of the Aswan. Your paper should also discuss unintended consequences and how they were addressed. If a new change in the Aswan dam were proposed today, how would you proceed in terms of socially responsible engineering (see section 2.5.3)?

5. Think about your service-learning project. How might you approach this service-learning project using the principles of socially responsible engineering? Prepare a one page essay or a short presentation to answer this question.

Chapter 3

The Engineering Design Method
for Service-Learning

Engineering is the art or science of making practical.

—Samuel C. Florman.

3.1 INTRODUCTION

Design is one of the defining characteristics of engineering. Engineering as a profession has been called "design under constraint" as it deals with competing variables and criteria to create the best result or product to meet our society's needs. Engineering is distinguished from the sciences by the solutions sought to the investigated problems. While scientists seek answers to basic questions about the physical world, engineers seek the best possible solution among diverse alternatives with conflicting goals. Engineers participate in "an innovative and methodical application of scientific knowledge and technology to produce a device, system or process that is intended to satisfy human need(s)" (Voland, 2004).

The practice that engineers employ to develop and select from alternative solutions is the engineering design process, which is used by all engineering disciplines. The general set of steps or tasks enable effective and efficient generation and evaluation of solutions to design problems that are the "most complex and ill-structured of all problems" (Jonassen, 2000).

Specific steps must be taken during the design process to optimize the design and to reduce problems and redesign efforts and costs. The design process is a cyclic process, which may be repeated many times over the product's life. While most agree the design process is highly interactive and cyclic, the names and descriptions of each step vary from reference to reference. Commonalities do exist between different definitions. For this text, we will divide the design process into seven distinct phases:

Phase 1: Problem identification
Phase 2: Specification development/planning
Phase 3: Conceptual design
Phase 4: Detailed design
Phase 5: Production
Phase 6: Service and maintenance
Phase 7: Redesign or retirement and disposal

In service-learning, there is no difference between the design process and the principles that are applied. The earlier steps that help to define the problem are critical since many of the problems presented in service-learning are not as well-defined or as easily applied to technical solutions. Design process optimization is part of the value you are providing to the community. If you neglect to identify key design issues, it may require a redesign or modification that may extend past your course and make delivery difficult or impossible within your academic program. As with other aspects of service-learning, there is a premium placed on quality and products that will work because you are delivering things to be used beyond your class.

3.2 THE DESIGN CYCLE

While the seven phases are presented as a linear list, the process is a cycle as shown in Figure 3.1. The cycle may repeat during the part's life as a product is fielded, redesigned, and refined. Within each phase, smaller cycles may repeat. Within the design cycle itself, repeats and smaller cycles may occur. For example, when the detailed design begins, a problem might be identified that requires a re-examination of the specifications, which brings the team back to that phase. A miscommunication between your design team and your community partner may result in revisiting the problem identification and specifications. Iterations are a normal part of the design cycle and process.

In addition to iterations, each phase has a divergent component and a convergent component as shown in Figure 3.2. In the divergent component, options are considered. One of the techniques used in this part of the cycle is brainstorming

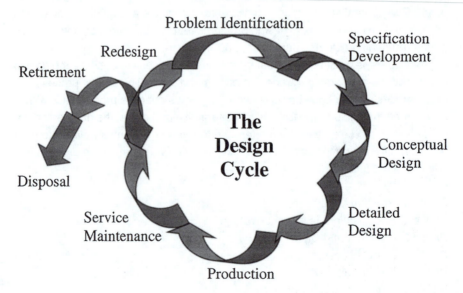

Figure 3.1 This process is a cyclic process.

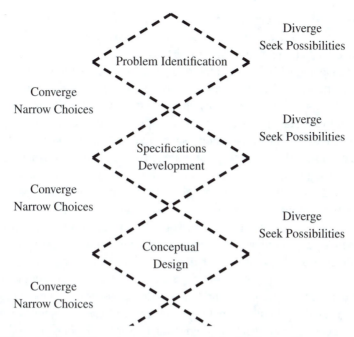

Diverge
Seek Possibilities

Problem Identification

Converge
Narrow Choices

Diverge
Seek Possibilities

Specifications
Development

Converge
Narrow Choices

Diverge
Seek Possibilities

Conceptual
Design

Converge
Narrow Choices

Figure 3.2 Divergent and Convergent Components in the Design Process

and other techniques outlined in the Engineering Analysis Skills Chapter of this text. Ideas are generated for consideration. Many student teams use brainstorming or other techniques in the conceptual design phase but not in others. Students should use these techniques during all phases of the design process to ensure maximal possibilities and ideas. The second component is the convergent component where ideas are sorted out and choices are narrowed. In this chapter, we will review tools for narrowing choices in systematic ways. While elements may be eliminated, keep a record of the ideas at each phase. As we stated before, design is cyclic and each phase may repeat. Having a map of ideas and considerations at each phase can make redesigns easier.

Going Slow to Go Fast

As children, many of us read the fable of the tortoise and the hare. The story illustrated how a slow and steady pace can be more effective in the long run than a quick start. This lesson applies directly to the design process. Good design teams practice the concept of going slow initially to go fast later. The early parts of the design process may seem to slow a design team down but they are important. Student design teams are always in a rush to get building. Taking a methodical approach is most efficient and will lead to better designs. Approaching your designs in a methodical manner will eliminate the need to repeat the processes later. An analogy would be taking a few minutes before leaving on a trip to verify that you have everything you need. The alternative is to do the check once you are on the road. If you discovered you forgot something, you can go back to get it which delays your trip or you can continue with the trip without the forgotten piece. The design process works the same way. If an initial design is laid out and an issue is identified, the choices are to go back and redesign, delaying the final result or continuing while knowing the design is missing an important element.

A systematic approach ensures that your community partner's needs are being addressed to your best ability and that you are applying your technical skills and tools to the design development. This process includes modeling your designs before things are constructed. Many student design teams fall into a trap of what is called a hobbyist design approach. In this approach, a design is built and tweaked until it works and seems to meet the project's intent. This is costly and takes longer to complete. Simple calculations can help in the design process and computer models can be used to make design decisions before artifacts or prototypes are built. For software projects, block diagrams, flowcharts, and/or pseudocode can be manipulated more easily than actual programming code.

Depending on the year in your engineering program, you will have different tools available. Modern engineering practice integrates all the engineering science tools to predict behavior and to make design decisions early in the process based on calculations and computer predictions. Today's tools help organize the design process and predict how the eventual design will function before it is built. The expectation of today's engineering teams is that by the time a prototype is built, it works. Analytic models verify its behavior and design decisions were made based on the models. These tools have reduced the development time of a new design. Integrating analysis tools will provide a better solution for your community partner and will provide you and your design team a better experience for your careers.

Document As You Go

At each phase of the design process, material will have to be documented for future reference. Decisions made at each phase will lay the groundwork for future decisions. Record what went into these decisions. The data examined, constraints considered, assumptions made and rationale for the decisions have to be summarized so your team or later teams can reconstruct your decisions. The design process is cyclic; almost every successful design is revisited to improve and adapt it to new environments or to address a problem encountered after it enters service. Well documented summaries will make the process of redesigning much easier and faster.

Your team should document as you go and not leave documentation efforts until the end of the project. Set deadlines for your team so that each phase gets documented as it is completed. Waiting until the end of the class makes documentation difficult and sometimes accurately reconstructing the important details becomes impossible.

If you are successful in your design, the results of your work will last well beyond your class time. Solving any future problems will depend upon the documentation you leave behind for your community partners or future classes.

3.3 THE DESIGN PROCESS

The seven steps in the design process are outlined below. At each phase, we have provided suggestions for your teams to follow to improve the results of your work.

1. Problem Identification

The first phase of the design process is to identify the problem. This may appear trivial, but it is crucial, and if done improperly, can result in disaster for the remaining design process.

Problem identification may require a slightly different way of thinking than you are accustomed to. You may be starting the process with a problem statement given to you by your professor or your community partner, but you should revisit the problem identification phase periodically to verify that you are fully identifying the real problem. In most classes, the instructor is considered the expert; anything she or he says must be right and there is no reason to go further. When addressing designs for community needs, no single expert may be available. The community partners may not fully understand all the available technologies. The partners may have asked for something based on their understanding of what is possible. They may have asked for a database management system for part of their organization but not for other parts because they did not realize how the different parts could be integrated so easily. Additionally, your instructor may or may not fully understand the context and issues facing the community partner.

Needs versus Wants

One of the questions to ask your design team is, Do we know what our community partner needs or are we just relying on what they said they want?

Talk to any engineering firm and ask if it understands this difference. The reaction will most likely be that this is the difference between staying in or out of business. A high-level manager of aerospace products once told a service-learning class that this is one of the biggest distinctions that kept them in business. He said that if they only relied on what their customers said they wanted, they would be out of business quickly. They had learned to move past the wants to identify what their customers needed and what would provide value. The same applies to community-based projects. Many community partners do not understand the available technology so they do not know what to ask for. You and your team may not understand what their needs are in order to effectively identify potential solutions. You cannot rely solely on the community partner to define your specifications and potential solutions. You and your design team must develop a clear problem statement and this requires an understanding of the community context for your design.

Community Context

Understanding the larger issues and the context for your designs is a critical step in the design process. The issues you address are usually new to you and your

Examples of Rushing to The Problem Statement

One group of first-year engineering students were working on an assignment to bring improved technology into the classrooms of their local Head Start program. They originally developed plans before visiting a Head Start classroom. When they returned from their first session with the students, they reported to their professor that none of their concepts were going to work. They did not understand what was needed for the children until they had spent time with them. The professor was not surprised and the team needed to return to the beginning of the process.

Other examples are less obvious at first. Another team that learned this lesson worked with their local affiliate of Habitat for Humanity. A team of senior engineering students took on the task of improving the energy efficiency of new Habitat homes and had special interests in alternative building materials. They found materials that were produced from recycled materials and much more environmentally friendly. They found ways to integrate the materials into the designs of the new homes that Habitat was building to improve the homes' energy efficiency. They did not understand two other components of the Habitat affiliates mission and operation. Their materials were more expensive than the ones they would replace. The energy savings was not enough to offset the increased costs for the homeowners. Habitat's mission is to provide affordable and decent housing and the alternative materials, though they had technical benefits, did not reduce the cost to the homeowners. The second piece they missed, which was less obvious, was that the materials they would have replaced were donated to Habitat by the local supplier. The cost increase to purchase the alternative material compared to the donated insulation would have resulted in an even more expensive home for the homeowners. The students learned that they should have spent more time understanding the larger issues and how Habitat worked locally.

A third example comes from another team that worked with a local Habitat for Humanity affiliate. Habitat had requested a database to help with their Restore operation, where they sold donated items that Habitat could not put directly into homes. The specifications seemed straightforward until the team dug deeper. They thought that they were designing a database that would serve Restore and had started the coding for the database. During a design review, they discovered that the larger problem was the affiliate's data management strategy. The items that came into the Restore were donated. The donors were tracked by hand using a separate system, but Restore's operation could improve by linking this functionality to its database. If the donors were included, that database part would need to be designed to track the donors and to manage thank you letters, tax statements, and solicitations. Decisions on what donated items went to Restore and

(box continues)

(*continued*)

> what went to home construction were handled by a third system and done by hand. Another database was needed to manage what items had been donated and what would be needed for home construction. What the team realized was that they were building the first piece in a larger data management project and that their piece needed to fit into the overall operation. This changed how they approached their design. If they had not taken the time to ask larger questions and get to know their community partner, they would have designed a stand alone product that might not have been integrated into the larger systems.

team and the technical solutions are often new to your community partners. Students need to spend some time with the community organizations and/or researching the needs they must address with their design work.

Spending time understanding the issues related to your community partner and the needs they are addressing is a valuable part of your education and will make your designs more effective and increase the likelihood that they will be used. Taking the time up front will allow you to go faster later, make fewer mistakes, and increase your value to the community. See section 7.4 for recommendations on communicating with community partners.

2. Specifications Development

Once you have identified the problem, you need to address the solution. The first step in generating a solution is identifying the constraints and boundaries of your problem. Constraints include who will use the product, cost, ease of use, safety, and environmental impact. What is the scope of the solution? What part of the larger community issues will your design seek to meet? If you are working with Habitat for Humanity (addressing poverty housing globally), that is the larger issue you are addressing. Your design, however, will not solve this whole problem on a global or even local scale. Your team needs to identify which parts of this larger problem your design will address.

The answers to these questions are specifications and their development is the second phase of the design process. In this phase, you will generate a set of measurable specification or goals so you know when your design is successful. These specifications become the goals for the rest of the design process. A well-developed set of specifications will ensure your design usage and will address the problem you identified in phase one. Specifications should be shared with your community partner and other technical advisors, including your instructor, to ensure that the goals for the design are appropriate and complete.

Make the specifications quantifiable and measurable whenever possible. Setting targets for your specifications that you can measure them will allow your team to determine if you have met them and by how much, e.g., how close you came to your specifications. Your design team may need research to define the specifications, including the issues facing the community partner. Just as the team that worked with the database with Habitat for Humanity in the earlier example, you may provide additional value to your community partner and this should be reflected in your specifications. In service-learning, you are looking to add value by maximizing community impact, and establishing a good set of specifications is important.

Who Will Use the Product and Who Will Benefit From It?

The first set in developing the specifications is to identify all the design users and beneficiaries. For example, you might be working with a technical resource person for a local school, but other teachers who are not as technically savvy may be using your product, and your specifications should include them. Understanding who will use your product will allow you to define the environment for your design. Will clients for the agency you are working with be using the product? Will the users be fluent in English?

One way to summarize users and beneficiaries is to list them as shown in Table 3.1. Each design user or beneficiary (in other applications, we could call them customers) is listed along with appropriate capabilities, backgrounds, and expertise. What is their level of technical knowledge and capabilities? Then think of how each could benefit from the work you are doing. This can help identify the customer requirements.

The next step in setting specifications is to look at the users or customer requirements. These requirements can fall under several categories and include the following:

- Functional performance, i.e., what do they need it to do?
- Human factors
- Physical, e.g., weight, size, color
- Time, reliability, how long does it need to last, how long between servicing
- Cost
- Standards
- Test Method
- Service and maintenance

The list of categories for customer/user requirements can change depending on the design you are creating. A complete list of requirement can be generated

Table 3.1   Users and Beneficiaries of The Design

Design User or Beneficiary	Backgrounds and Capabilities	Benefit Description

Table 3.2   Define Your Customer Requirements

Customer/User Requirements	User #1	User #2	User #3	User #4
Functional Requirements				
Human Factors				
Physical Requirements				

and placed in a column in a table as shown in Table 3.2. Each user or beneficiary can be listed in a separate column. This grid is useful as the team looks for the most important solution or design characteristics. Each square in the matrix matches a requirement with a user. The importance of each requirement for each user can be entered in the table using a five point scale.

Use a five-point scale:

5 = important
4 = somewhat important
3 = neutral
2 = not important
1 = does not matter to this user

The completed chart will help your team visualize the most important requirements. Finding the critical requirement is not always as simple as summing each row. Some of the users or beneficiaries may be more important than others. One technique is to rank each user's importance, e.g., on a scale from one to ten. You can multiply these rankings by the importance scale to get a weighted average.

Finding the most important requirements is one of the areas that needs engineering judgment. Your team should work with the data that these tables provide and discuss their implications before continuing with the process. Presenting your conclusions to your instructor, technical advisor, and community partners will help develop the most effective specification set.

Defining the customer requirements is not the end of this phase; you must develop engineering specifications related to the customer requirements. Engineering specifications are quantitative specifications that address each customer requirement your team felt was important to the design.

For instance, a product might need to be "light" in your requirements. In an engineering specification, this would translate to a weight target. In your requirements for a web page, a set of resources might need to be easily found. Your engineering specifications would define how many mouse clicks are needed from the main page. Your requirements might say that a web page needs to be accessible, but specific accessibility guidelines can be met. Each engineering specification should be phrased in terms of measurable quantity.

The reason for being quantitative is because you can measure progress toward design targets. Later in the design process, your team may discover that not all of the targets can be met simultaneously. At that point, you may need to make trade offs. By using quantitative targets, your team can determine how close you can come to your intended targets and decide which specifications to optimize.

The second reason that quantifiable engineering specifications are useful is when comparing competing products. A question your team needs to ask is what other competitive or alternative products are available to your design problem. To answer this question, your team should take time to perform a market analysis to assess commercial product availability and to ensure that your designs will not infringe upon existing patents or copyrights.

In service-learning, your goal is to meet a community need. If commercial products are available, finding them will provide community value and could fill the need you are addressing. Usually, commercial products do not meet the exact needs that you are addressing. They may be too expensive or are missing the customized traits your team can provide. However, you can use the existing products as benchmarks to help your design team identify the value you can provide to your community partner.

Finding benchmark products can be done using web searches and discussions with the community partners and your instructors. Some students have found useful leads by talking with community organizations with a similar mission in their hometowns.

Patent searches are useful and we recommend that each student learn how to read a patent. Patents can identify alternatives and you must know if your design will infringe upon any existing patents. Accessing patent databases can be done over the Web using the US Patent and Trademark Office's website (www.uspto.gov) or through the Community of Science Patent Search (http://www.cos.com). This site has parts that require a login but by selecting *services* and then *patents* you can search the database without a login. Detailed patent searches take a long time, usually more than ten hours. Plan for this time input accordingly.

In a commercial design process, the market research will end with an analysis of whether existing products meet your needs and if a market opportunity exists for your design. If no market opportunity exists, your team does not need to continue with the design process. Comparing the benchmarked products with your proposed design will allow your team to evaluate your design potential. Table 3.3 shows how the benchmarked products can be identified. The bottom line of Table

Table 3.3   Comparing Alternatives

	Engr. Spec. 1	Engr. Spec. 2	Engr. 3	Engr. 4
Benchmark #1				
Benchmark #2				
Benchmark #3				
Design Targets				

3-3 represents your team's design targets. Your team needs to meet these engineering specifications for improvement upon the existing products to meet the needs you are addressing. The table allows you see how much of an improvement your new design is over existing products.

In service-learning, you will follow the same process as a corporation, except that the decision to go to market is motivated by different criteria. In a commercial venture, the question pivots around the issue of return on investment, i.e., how much money can be made? In your context, the question is does your design meet the community need more effectively and economically?

Your community partner should review the specifications document as well as the comparison of benchmarked products. They should have an opportunity to review and comment on it before your team proceeds to the next phase. The specifications document is a living document, so as the design process continues, changes may (and probably will) be needed. All of the design team members and your community partner must be able to access the document's latest version as it matures.

3. Conceptual Design

The conceptual design phase begins your design team's generation of solutions. In this phase, you will develop ideas to meet your community partner's needs using the developed specifications. As with all phases, this phase starts with a divergent component where ideas are generated using techniques including brainstorming methods.

Functional Decomposition: A common mistake for design teams is to look at the design as a whole and begin brainstorming on solving the whole problem. Though this can lead to good solutions, dissecting the project to the smallest pieces using functional decomposition is more effective. In functional decomposition, your team identifies the functions your design must accomplish. Start with your overall design purpose and label that the primary function. Ask if this function can be broken into components or sub-functions. If it can, develop a diagram as shown in Figure 3.3. As each sub-function is identified, ask if it can be dissected further into simpler tasks or sub-functions. Continue until each task or function is at the most basic level.

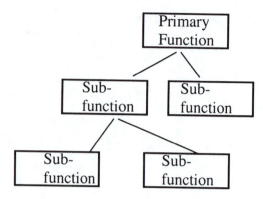

Figure 3.3 Functional Decomposition

To illustrate this method, examine the functional decomposition of a mechanical pencil. The primary function of a mechanical pencil is to write. This primary function can be broken down into sub-functions, e.g., applying graphite to paper and removing or erasing it. The application of graphite can be broken down further:

1. Storage of the lead or graphite
2. Extending the lead so that is exposed and applied to the paper
3. Holding the lead in place
4. Retracting the lead after use

The mechanical pencil example has generated four sub-functions just for the lead application. Other sub-functions can be identified and added to the list. Your design team can brainstorm how to meet each of the basic sub-functions. This method is a systematic way to look at all the smaller design details and provide a way to integrate ideas from different people and sources into the design.

If a team were to generate ideas at the system or whole product level, they would likely miss ideas from parts of the team. By using the functional decomposition, you can take the best ideas from each component and integrate them into a whole system.

Once you have identified possibilities, you will need to select the best ideas. Comparing has several possibilities including relative and absolute comparisons is shown in Figure 3.4. It may not be possible to take all the best ideas because some may integrate with others. In these cases, the team may need to evaluate different sets of systems. When you do that, a decision matrix is an excellent method.

Decision Matrix

One systematic way to evaluate alternatives is a decision matrix, illustrated in Table 3.4. In a decision matrix, criteria are developed to evaluate alternatives.

Type of Comparison	Technique	Basis for Comparison
Absolute	Engineering Models Research Data Feasibility Study	Engineering Judgement Gut Feel State of the Art
	Test Data Technology Availability	Customer Attributes
Relative	Decision Matrix	Specifications

Figure 3.4 Ways to make decisions

Table 3.4   Decision Matrix

	Weights	Ideas to be Compared
Criteria for Comparison		

These criteria can come from your engineering specifications. Each criterion is given a weight and each idea is evaluated on how well it meets that criterion.

A sample decision matrix is shown for a student weighing offers for an internship. She has identified the criteria for the position along with relative weighting factors for each. She has listed her current offers in columns. To complete the table, she needs to rate how well each company meets the criteria. A five-point scale with five (being excellent) and one or zero (being poor or not at all) is commonly used. The ratings can be multiplied by the weighting factors and a total score found for each company.

This method should be used cautiously. Though the tool is useful, a team can get carried away with its accuracy. After the ratings are applied and the totals found, the team should evaluate the results to see if they make sense. For example, in the criteria in Table 3.5, is the Boss twice as important as the salary? Perhaps not. The decision matrix is useful but needs accurate engineering judgment to yield valid results.

4. Detailed Design and Development

Once the concept is defined, the details must be determined. We have a saying that design is done by top-down specifications, bottom-up implementation. When we started defining the problem, we asked about what the broader issues were and worked down to the details. In the detailed design phase, we will begin with the specific details and work them into the overall system. For a physical design, detailed drawings will be made for all components. Computer-aided design (CAD) software packages are used to make component drawings that can be compiled into assembly drawings.

Table 3.5   Sample Decision Matrix Comparing Companies To Work For

Criteria	Wts.	Company A	Company B	Company C	Company D
Location	5				
Salary	2				
Bonus	1				
Job	3				
Training	2				
Boss	4				
Totals					

Freezing interfaces: In large designs, some decisions must be made early in the process to allow the designers responsible for components to finalize their individual parts of the overall design. As we noted, the implementation of the detailed design begins with the individual components. When one sub-team makes changes, problems can occur that affect the other sub-teams as they work on their own components. One method for managing these changes is to create interface drawings or protocols. Each sub-team agrees to interface configurations or protocols where the components will interact or come together. Three examples of interfaces are below:

- In a mechanical design, the first created drawing is an interface drawing that only shows where the parts will be connected, such as flanges. Each major connection point is specified by a size (e.g., diameter), number and size of bolts, and a distance from the other flanges. All the details in between are left for the sub-team's detailed design.
- In a software project, the protocols for passing data between parts of the code are defined. Flowcharts or block diagrams are used to specify inputs and outputs to and from each component. The variables are defined in terms of the numbers of variables, the order of variables, and the format for the variables to be passed. The sub-teams generate the output details.
- In an electrical system, numbers of inputs and outputs are defined as well as signals, voltages, or current ranges. The number of signals and configuration of inputs and outputs are specified, such as the connectors, number of pins in a connector, and the function of each pin. Details of how the signals or power comes to those connectors are left to the individuals or teams responsible for that part.

If your team has a large project, identifying the interfaces allows one part of the team to work with and not adversely affect the other parts of the team. Each sub-team can work on the components' details knowing that they will come together

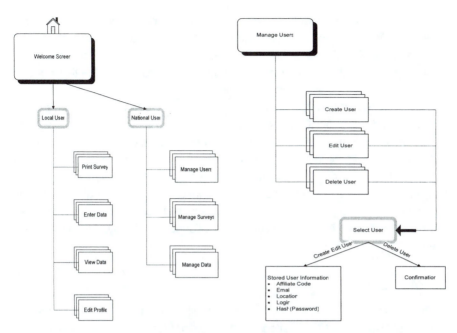

Figure 3.5 Schematics for a software project for Habitat for Humanity to survey their homeowners.

in a system that will meet the specifications developed in the earlier design process phases.

Engineering Analysis: Earlier we talked about a rigorous engineering design methodology versus a hobbyist design approach. Analysis is the key feature that distinguishes engineering design and is a major component to a rigorous design process. Analysis can occur at different parts of the design process, but may be most useful at the start of the detailed design phase. As components are defined, analyses will ensure that each component will effectively withstand its environment throughout its useful life. The components' durability and useful life will be calculated to ensure safe and reliable operation once the design is fielded. Mathematical and computational models will allow the design team to make trade-off decisions without having to build multiple prototypes and test them.

As details are designed, decisions need to be made for the components' thickness, materials, and sizes. Analysis tools help guide the designers in these decisions and allow for trade-off studies without building prototypes. It is much less expensive and faster to generate and examine a model for a design than to build multiple prototypes and test them. Modern design teams model their work and expect the first prototype to work.

Design for Failure Mode and Effect Analysis (DFMEA) is what process designers can use to avoid failure scenarios when the design is fielded. Upon completing the initial design, design teams go through this systematic process to analyze potential failure modes and make design adjustments to prevent failures or to minimize the failure's impact.

DFMEA's first step identifies potential failures. These can be components breaking or users improperly using the final design. Your design team can brainstorm on possible failure scenarios. The second process step is to determine the failures' impact on the entire system. The third step is to look at the likelihood of each failure scenario and the impact it will have.

The team should then take the failure scenarios and ask if the design can be modified to address how the failures could be avoided or minimized. Warning systems can be put into place to warn users of impending failures. Systems could be redesigned to mitigate failure scenarios, especially from user interactions.

The DFMEA is useful, especially as your design teams complete subsystems. Having the entire team systematically identify failure scenarios for all subsystems will improve the design integrity and can serve as a check for the team's work. Focusing on the subsystems and missing failure scenarios on a system or user level is easy.

Bill of Materials

A bill of materials or comprehensive listing of all components needed for the design should be created as detailed design decisions are made. The bill of materials calculates costs and ensures that all the materials are on hand when construction begins. Spreadsheets track bills of materials since they can sort data and calculate unit prices and quantities. Many design teams appoint one person to manage the bill of materials and keep an accounting of the design costs.

As the detailed design is developed, changes to the original concept will occur. Results of analysis may show that conceptual combinations are not feasible. Costs may rise beyond specifications limits. The DFMEA may show failure modes that could become catastrophic. These and other scenarios can result in the detailed design changing. In every case, the changes should be made in keeping with the specifications from the earlier phases. When trade offs are needed, the specifications documents should be the guide for the direction to proceed. Documenting the changes and the rationales well will assist future teams that might redesign or upgrade the original design.

5. Production

In the production phase, the design is built. For physical products, materials are purchased, parts are manufactured, and the design is assembled. For software designs, the full code is written and debugged. In a commercial design process, the development (or prototyping) phase and the full-scale production phase would occur. For most service-learning applications, the prototype is the final design and delivered product.

In some cases, the prototype is a model to evaluate for a future production run. In a larger production run, manufacturability is a key design constraint and factor in the product cost. Design choices can affect how costly a product will be and the manufactured pieces' reliability.

In service-learning projects, production costs may not be the most important design aspect since student labor reduces these costs. The real costs may, therefore, be hidden in the design. If your design is setting the stage for a later pro-duction version of your product, these costs need to be considered and factored into the design to meet the specifications.

Good designers learn to get input from experienced manufacturing engineers and technicians during the detailed design to improve the manufacturability of their components and the assembly of the product. Making components easier to manufacture makes them less expensive and increases the quality of the finished parts. Rules of thumb for manufacturing include using standard sizes for compo-nents whenever possible and minimizing how many times a part has to be set up on a machine or handled by operators during manufacture and assembly. Keep-ing the number of unique parts to a minimum and using standard sizes for all components are good practices that can reduce manufacturing and inventory costs. Entire texts and courses are devoted to manufacturing. As an engineering student or as a practicing engineer, one of the best ways to learn is to talk to ex-perienced practitioners, like machinists. They can pass along many lessons they have learned. In community work, you may run across individuals who have ex-perience and you should be ready to learn from them.

Testing the Product in Real Field Conditions

You should test the product before delivering it to your community partner. If pos-sible, test critical components for durability and life expectancy in conditions that simulate the true operating conditions. You can release beta software versions to a controlled number of community partners; this is a good way to gather data on the design's effectiveness. Physical designs can follow similar patterns through trials and simulations with community members. Data from these tests should be collected systematically and the results documented. You should share results with the design team to identify places of improvement.

Delivery of the Finished Product

The ultimate goal of a service-learning design is for the product to be delivered to the community partner at the end of the production phase. Your design team needs to understand the delivery conditions. Do you need to follow a procedure before product delivery? In most companies, a formal review is done before any product delivery. Some service-learning programs model this process. A sample delivery checklist used by the Purdue University EPICS team is shown on page 68.

All documentation, user manuals, maintenance guides, etc., should accom-pany the delivered product to answer any questions the community partners may have. Often a training session is needed upon product delivery so the users can get comfortable with all delivered items and have their initial questions answered.

Deliver a product to the community before the end of your class. A team should leave class time for problems to be identified and addressed before leaving cam-pus. A common mistake that can leave bad feelings in the community is to deliver a project right at the end of the quarter or semester. If a problem arises, the stu-dents are gone and the community partner is left without a working product. A

Delivery Checklist

Team: _____ Community Partner: _____
Project: _____

Prior to Delivery Review	Date Completed
Test project to make sure it is functioning	
Complete user manuals and troubleshooting guides	
Verify the project is identified as an EPICS project (has sticker or other appropriate signage)	

During Delivery Review (Completed by reviewers)	Acceptable?
Have the customer's requirements been adequately addressed by the project?	
Is the project appearance quality acceptable for delivery?	
Have appropriate safety issues been addressed?	
Is the project identifiable as an EPICS project (has sticker or other appropriate signage)?	
Does the team have appropriate technical documentation to provide project support/maintenance?	
Would you recommend project deployment?	
Names of reviewers (or attach appropriate Design Review forms):	

Prior to or During Delivery	Date Completed
Make appointment with project partner for project delivery	
Obtain signature on Hold Harmless Agreement by project partner	
Give a project demo, which explains project functions to the project partner	
Deliver user manuals and troubleshooting guides	
Provide contact information to project partner for project assistance/maintenance	

After Delivery	Date Completed
Turn Signed Hold Harmless into EPICS Program Coordinator within one week of delivery	
Post PDF version of Hold Harmless Agreement to team website within one week of delivery	
Contact project partner two weeks after delivery for any questions/problems	

minimum of two weeks is recommended for delivery, which could include the last week of classes and exam week.

6. Service

Service and management of delivered products have become important in many company's design and production plans. Medical equipment manufacturers, for example, contract with hospitals to maintain and manage the hospitals' equipment. Service agreements like these reduce the customer burden and obligation. How a product will be serviced is an essential part of the design and needs to be considered early in the design process, whether your team will be responsible for the service or not.

In service-learning, the servicing of a delivered product is often handled by the community partner's staff/volunteers. These people may not have a strong technical background, so servicing and maintaining your design needs to be accessible and easy to understand. Unlike companies with help lines, once students graduate, no one may be around to call for follow up questions if the servicing materials are confusing and incomplete. Therefore, the documentation your team leaves behind becomes an even more critical part of the design process. Service and operating manuals need to be delivered with the finished design and be clear enough for the people who will maintain the products. These manuals should explain how to operate the product and how to diagnosis problems. A service manual should include how to fix simple things on the design, how to troubleshoot, and how to identify simple problems. When possible, spare parts should be included with the delivered product along with clear instructions for replacement. You should include a complete bill of materials along with contact information on where to order parts.

Your team can add significant value to your design by identifying how your product will be serviced and by whom. Community resources can be tapped to address service and maintenance issues. Perhaps student organizations could be responsible for future maintenance. Are there groups of retirees, professional or trade organizations, or unions that might handle this as a community service? Training the staff to perform maintenance goes a long way to adding design value. Service is a critical design phase, and for community-based projects it is often the difference between a student project that was dumped onto the community and a project that added value to the community.

7. Redesign or Retirement and Disposal

Redesign

A natural part of the design cycle is redesign. Almost any product that has been in service for a significant amount of time has undergone a redesign of some sort. Redesigns might be small in nature and involve small components or they may be major and associated with a new product version released to production. The software industry has established a system to identify how significant a redesign is by the digit that is changed with new versions.

For a version 1.00, redesigns would be classified in this way:

1.01 = A minor redesign involving small aspects of the design
1.10 = A redesign that is more significant but integrated into the same overall design
2.00 = A redesign that changes the fundamentals of the overall design or add significantly new features

Redesigns in service-learning projects may be additions or fixes to keep a fielded project in operation, or they may involve a new prototype to replace a defective or obsolete project.

When a project is redesigned, all of the design process steps should be re-evaluated and followed. Each step is revisited to determine the validity and sufficiency of the previous information and decisions. Since a redesign is needed, asking what problem is being solved becomes necessary. Is the objective to keep the existing product in the field and quickly fix it, or is a new and improved design needed? Has new information come to light to change the specifications? Have materials become available to make alternative design options possible? New techniques and information may be available to improve the designs and more recent benchmarks may be available for comparison.

The enormous advantage of a redesign cycle is that many of the steps are revisited but not necessarily totally recreated. Documentation and decisions from the previous cycle may still be valid and appropriate and can be reused. Many of the components from earlier designs can be used, reducing the time and expense of the design. In many industries, derivative designs, which are redesigns and upgrades based on previous designs, are the most common development form. These designs save significant costs and resources by building on previous designs. These designs can be leveraged similarly in service-learning and can build upon the lessons that have been learned from prior work.

Retirement/Disposal

Redesigning is not always the best solution for an existing design. After analysis of a product and the costs and resources needed to maintain the current design or to replace it, your team may conclude that the existing product needs to be retired from service. This is a natural part of the product life cycle. The decision to retire a piece should be made in conjunction with the community partner and be based on the value the piece is adding and the costs to maintain the current version. When service-learning students take a product out of service that was deployed by other students, the success and value that the product provided should be celebrated.

Taking something out of service brings up disposal questions. Many products are made with materials that cannot be easily recycled and/or are not suitable for landfill disposal. How a product will be retired is an important design constraint and is becoming more of a design issue. Modern companies are being held accountable for what happens to their products after they have exceeded their useful lives.

When one considers the philosophy of service-learning, it is important that a product delivered to the community should not present a toxic waste hazard or environmental concern. Not everything can be recycled, but a design can be implemented that integrates as many recyclable materials and components as possible. The parts that are non-recyclable should be designed so that they can be taken care of at the local waste disposal facility rather than requiring special handling. At some point, the product will complete its useful life and need to be disposed. Planning for this during design will provide value to the community partner and show that you are being a good environmental steward.

If the design works well, the student designers will have finished college when this occurs so the community partners will be left with the decision to retire the product. Leaving guidelines and instructions for the disposal and/or recycling of the design provides a valuable service. In the commercial world, the end of the product cycle is gaining attention during the initial design phase as corporations are being held accountable for environmental problems their products create. Litigation related to these problems has prompted a renewed attention level to the product's life in the early design cycle stages. Service-learning students who are adding value to communities should ensure that their products are not time bombs that will create headaches for the community or the community partners.

SUMMARY

In this chapter, the design process was presented as a cycle and described as if a design team moved through the cycle one stage at a time. An older method of design followed this linear path. Each phase was dealt with in sequence. So, for example, if a design characteristic created a manufacturing problem, it was identified in the production phase. This model is referred to as an over-the-wall approach. Each phase is completed in a larger firm by a different team, and is passed over the wall to the next team for the next phase. If a problem was identified that required redesign, it was passed back to that team.

Modern design philosophy employs a concurrent design philosophy. During each phase's description, comments arose that later parts of the cycle should be

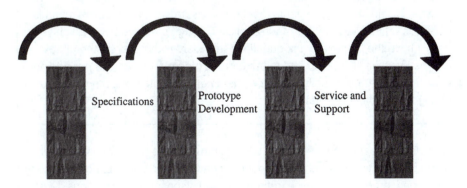

Specifications   Prototype Development   Service and Support

Figure 3.6 Avoid the "over-the-wall" mindset for design

Thinking Like An Engineer When Beginning A New Project: Advice From An Experienced Software Engineer.

Contributed by Jon Reid, CTO, Savitar Corporation

Most of us have heard the old joke: Does the engineer think the glass is half-full or half-empty? The answer: The engineer thinks the glass is twice as big as it needs to be. When approaching a new design, the first step is to find out exactly how big the glass needs to be. With software engineering projects, that means spending time with the users of the software, not only talking about the requirements but also observing the users at work. A great many of the design issues that involve later software use arise from a misunderstanding about how the software is to be used and what components are most important. Take every opportunity to interact with the customer even if it is inconvenient for your schedule so that both the developer and the customer will realize the benefits at the end of the project. Plan interaction as a regular part of the schedule, with time allotted on the project schedule for it.

Understand which parts of the application are important to the user. How much time do they spend doing data entry versus running reports or queries? Do they use the reports? Do they use the keyboard or the mouse? I have seen projects where the developers spent all their time on an elaborate user interface for data entry and ignored the reports that output the data entered into the system. The users were not at all happy with the resulting system. With no way to get the data out, they saw no benefit from easier or faster data entry.

Spend time with all the users of the system, not just one or two. Find out the important features for each type of user. The data entry personnel and the department manager naturally focus on different parts of the system. What is the key benefit for each stakeholder and how can the technology support that benefit for each user?

When you do have a more formal requirements discussion, use the understanding gained through observation and informal interaction to interpret the stated requirements in a more informed context. Recognize that what is said in a requirements meeting only scratches the surface; much is assumed that needs to be made explicit. Through previous observation you will have the context to ask questions that clarify what the customer says. Then you will be able to make an informed judgment as to whether adding a certain feature actually helps the customer or simply makes the glass too big for what it will contain.

considered in earlier phases; this is what **concurrent design** means. Each phase of the design cycle is taken into account at each phase. When specifications are developed, production, service, retirement, and disposal should be considered. In large companies, this is done by placing people with skills and responsibilities in these different areas onto a design team. In a service-learning experience, this can be done by asking members of your team to play the role of an advocate for these other phases in the design process. Each team member can take the lead in a different phase; when you are not in that phase, you can be an advocate for that phase. If your team does not have seven people, some will have responsibility for multiple phases. Each person will need to understand that process phase and will become more of an expert and a resource to the rest of the team. Sharing the responsibility and gaining insight to the others' ideas and viewpoints will produce a better design on a shorter timeline and provide more value to the community partner, which is the goal of the service-learning experience.

Designing real products for real needs is difficult. Breaking the design process into phases and smaller steps allows large problems to be manageable. By following the sound design practices presented in this chapter, engineering students at all levels can provide local or global community value. Practicing good design techniques will provide experiences that students can build upon as they enter their own careers.

REFERENCES

ABET. *Criteria for Accrediting Programs in Engineering.* Accreditation Board for Engineering and Technology, Baltimore, MD, 2002. (www.abet.org)

Adams, RS, Turns J, and Atman, CJ. What Would Design Learning Look Like? *Proceedings of Expertise in Design.* Sydney, Australia, 2003.

Hyman, B. *Fundamentals of Engineering Design.* Upper Saddle River, NJ: Prentice Hall, 1998.

Jonassesn, D. H. Toward a design theory of problem solving. *Educational Technology: Research & Development*, 48(4), 63–85, 2000.

Lesh, R and Doerr, HM. *Beyond Constructivism: Models and Modeling Perspectives on Mathematics Teaching, Learning, and Problem Solving.* Mahwah, NJ: Lawrence Erlbaum Associates, 2003.

National Academy of Engineering. Center for the Advancement of Scholarship in Engineering Education, NAE Engineering Projects, 2002. (http://www.nae .edu/nae/caseecomnew.nsf)

Petrosky, H. *To Engineer is Human, The Role of Failure in Successful Design.* New York: Vintage Books, 1992.

Ullman, DG. *The Mechanical Design Process,* 3rd Ed. New York: McGraw-Hill, 2003.

Voland, G. *Engineering by Design*, 2nd Ed. Upper Saddle River, NJ: Prentice Hall, 2004.

Wulf, WA. and Fisher, GMC. A Makeover for Engineering Education, *Issues in Science and Technology*, Spring, 2002. www.nap.edu/issues/18.3/p_wulf.html.

EXERCISES

1. Write a letter to your grandmother describing the engineering design process.

2. Prepare an oral discussion for your grandparents that explains the engineering design process.

3. Find a product from your own field and prepare a presentation on how the design process was used in the development of this product.

4. Interview a practicing design engineer about her or his use of the design process in their job. Prepare an oral presentation on your findings.

5. Interview a practicing design engineer about her or his use of the design process in their job. Summarize on your findings in a written report.

6. Prepare an outline of the design process and identify tasks related to your project in each stage.

7. Prepare a decision matrix for you and your friends to determine what to do this coming weekend.

8. Prepare a memo which summarizes the anticipated failure modes for your design. For each failure mode, identify the implications of the failure and how this failure could be (if possible) avoided (include proposed design changes)

9. Write an outline for a maintenance or user manual for your design.

10. Prepare a section to be inserted in a maintenance manual on proper disposal of your project after it has expended its useful life.

11. Interview a production engineer or technician and ask them what advice they would have for a design engineer. Prepare a short oral presentation on this topic.

12. Create a flow chart or diagram on how you and your classmates will progress through the design process during your project. Be prepared to share your results with the rest of your class.

13. Research and identify one product that failed, at least initially (failure could mean it broke or that it didn't sell). Identify what in the design contributed to the failure and how similar failures could be avoided.

14. Write an essay comparing and contrasting the scientific method and the engineering design process.

15. Divide your class into six groups with each group taking one of the first six steps in the design process. Each group should prepare an oral argument on why their step is the most important step in the design process.

16. Find three patents on products that address similar issue to the ones you are addressing. Prepare a memo summarizing the attributes of these products and identify how your design will meet a need that these do not fully address.

Chapter 4

Engineering Analysis Skills

Not everything that counts can be counted, and not everything that can be counted counts.

—Einstein

4.1 INTRODUCTION

Seven-year-old Dan could build all kinds of things: toy cars, ramps, and simple mechanical gadgets. Even more amazing was that he could do all this with four simple tools: scissors, hammer, screwdriver, and duct tape. One Christmas, his father asked if he'd like more tools. "No thanks, Dad" was his response. "If I can't make it with these, it's not worth making." It wasn't long, however, before Dan realized that the cool stuff he could create or the problems he could solve were dependent on the tools he had. So he began gathering more tools and learning how to use them. Today, he still solves problems and makes a lot of cool stuff, like real cars, furniture, playgrounds, and even houses. His tools fill a van, a workshop and a garage. Having the right tools and knowing how to use them are critical components of his success.

Likewise, most people, when they are children, learn a few reliable ways to solve problems. Most fifth graders in math class know common problem-solving methods like "draw a picture," "work backwards," or the ever-popular "guess and check" (check in the back of the textbook for the correct answer, that is). Unfortunately, many people choose to stop adding new problem-solving tools to their mental toolbox. "If I don't know how to solve it, it's probably not worth solving anyway," they may think. Or, "I'll skip this problem for now and get back to my usual tasks." This severely limits them. Engineers, by definition, need to be good at solving problems and making things. Therefore, filling your toolbox with the right tools and knowing how to use them are critical components to becoming a successful engineer.

> "To invent, you need a good imagination and a pile of junk."
> —Thomas Edison

The goal of this chapter is to increase the number of problem-solving strategies and techniques you commonly use, and to enhance your ability to apply them creatively in various problem-solving settings. Hopefully, this will be only the beginning of a lifelong process of gaining new mental tools and learning how to use them.

4.2 GENERAL STRATEGIES FOR ANALYTIC AND CREATIVE PROBLEM SOLVING

The toolbox analogy is very appropriate for engineering students. Practicing engineers are employed to solve a very wide variety of problems. These roles can require very different problem-solving abilities. Problem solving can be broken into Analytic and Creative methods. Most students are more familiar with analytic problem solving where there is one correct answer. In creative problem solving there is no single right answer. Your analytic tools represent what's in your toolbox. Your creative skills represent how you handle your tools.

To better understand the difference between these two kinds of problem solving, let's examine the one function that is common to all engineers: design. In the Design chapter, we detailed a design process with seven phases as follows:

Phase 1: Problem Identification
Phase 2: Specification Development/Planning
Phase 3: Conceptual Design
Phase 4: Detailed Design
Phase 5: Production
Phase 6: Service and Maintenance
Phase 7: Redesign or Retirement and Disposal

By definition, design is open-ended and has many different solutions. The automobile is a good example. Some time when you are riding in a car, count the number of different designs you see while on the road. All of these designs were the result of engineers solving a series of problems involved in producing an automobile. The design process as a whole is a **creative problem-solving process**.

> *In creative problem solving, there is no single right answer.*

The other method, **analytic problem solving**, is also part of the design process. When analyzing a design concept, there is only one answer to the question "Will it fail?" A civil engineer designing a bridge might employ a host of design concepts, though at some point he or she must accurately assess the loads that the bridge can support.

Most engineering curricula provide many opportunities to develop analytic problem-solving abilities, especially in the first few years. This is an important skill. Improper engineering decisions can put the public at risk. For this reason, it is imperative that proper analytical skills be developed.

As an engineering student you will be learning math, science and computer skills that will allow you to tackle very complex problems later in your career. These are critical, and are part of the problem-solving skill set for analysis. However, other tools are equally necessary.

Engineers also can find that technical solutions applied correctly can become outmoded or prove dangerous if they aren't applied with the right judgment. Our creative skills can help greatly in big-picture evaluation, which can determine the long-term success of a solution. The solution of one problem can cause others if foresight is neglected, and this is not easily avoided in all cases. For instance, the guilt that the developers of dynamite and atomic fission have publicly expressed relates to a regret for lack of foresight. Early Greek engineers invented many devices and processes which they refused to disclose because they knew they would be misused. The foresight to see how technically correct solutions can malfunction or be misapplied takes creative skill to develop. What about fertilizers which boost crops but poison water supplies? Modern engineers need to learn how to apply the right solution at the right time in the right way for the right reason with the right customer.

Most people rely on two or three methods to solve problems. If these methods don't yield a successful answer, they become stuck. Truly exceptional problem solvers learn to use multiple problem-solving techniques to find the optimum solution. The following is a list of possible tools or strategies that can help solve simple problems:

1. Look for a pattern
2. Construct a table
3. Consider possibilities systematically
4. Act it out
5. Make a model
6. Make a figure, graph or drawing
7. Work backwards
8. Select appropriate notation
9. Restate the problem in your own words
10. Identify necessary, desired and given information
11. Write an open-ended sentence
12. Identify a sub-goal
13. First solve a simpler problem

14. Change your point of view
15. Check for hidden assumptions
16. Use a resource
17. Generalize
18. Check the solution; validate it
19. Find another way to solve the problem
20. Find another solution
21. Study the solution process
22. Discuss limitations
23. Get a bigger hammer
24. Get a smaller hammer
25. Sleep on it
26. Brainstorm
27. Involve others

In both analytic and creative problem solving, there are different methods for tackling problems. Have you ever experienced being stuck on a difficult math or science problem? Developing additional tools or methods will allow you to tackle more of these problems effectively, making you a better engineer.

The rest of this chapter is a presentation of different ways of solving problems. These are some of the techniques that have been shown to be effective. Each person has a unique set of talents and will be drawn naturally to certain problem-solving tools. Others will find a different set useful. The important thing as an engineering student is to experiment and find as many useful tools as you can. This will equip you to tackle the wide range of challenges which tomorrow's engineers will face.

4.3 ANALYTIC PROBLEM SOLVING

Given the importance of proper analysis in engineering and the design process, it is important to develop a disciplined way of approaching engineering problems. Solving analytic problems has been the subject of a great deal of research, which has resulted in several models. One of the most important analytic problem-solving methods that students are exposed to is the Scientific Method. The steps in the Scientific Method are as follows:

1. Define the problem
2. Gather the facts
3. Develop a hypothesis
4. Perform a test
5. Evaluate the results

In the Scientific Method, the steps can be repeated if the desired results are not achieved. The process ends when an acceptable understanding of the phenomenon under study is achieved.

In the analysis of engineering applications, a similar process can be developed to answer problems. The advantage of developing a set method for solving analytic problems is that it provides a framework to help young engineers when they are presented with larger and more complex problems. Just like a musician practices basic scales in order to set the foundation for complex pieces to be played later, an engineer should develop a sound fundamental way to approach problems. Fortunately, early in your engineering studies you will be taking many science and math courses that will be suited to this methodology.

The Analytic Method we will discuss has six steps:

1. Define the problem and make a problem statement
2. Diagram and describe
3. Apply theory and equations
4. Simplify the assumptions
5. Solve the necessary problems
6. Verify accuracy to required level

Following these steps will help you better understand the problem you are solving and allow you to identify areas where inaccuracies might occur.

Step 1: Problem Statement

It is important to restate the problem you are solving in your own words. In textbook problems, this helps you understand what you need to solve. In real life situations, this helps to ensure that you are solving the correct problem. Write down your summary, then double-check that your impression of the problem is the one that actually matches the original problem. Putting the problem in your own words is also an excellent way to focus on the part of the problem you need to solve. Often, engineering challenges are large and complex, and the critical task is to understand what part of the problem you need to solve.

Step 2: Description

The next step is to describe the problem and list all that is known. In addition to restating the problem, list the information given and what needs to be found. This is shown in Example 4.2, which follows this section. Typically, in textbook problems, all the information given is actually needed for the problem. In real problems, more information is typically available than is needed to do the calculations. In other cases, information may be missing. Formally writing out what you need and what is required helps you to clearly sort this out.

It is also helpful to draw a diagram or sketch of the problem you are solving to be able to understand the problem. Pictures help many people to clarify the problem and what is needed. They are also a great aid when explaining the problem to someone else. The old saying could be restated as "A picture is worth a thousand calculations."

Step 3: Theory

State explicitly the theory or equations needed to solve the problem. It is important that you write this out completely at this step. You will find that most real problems and those you are asked to solve as an undergraduate student will not require exact solutions to complete equations. Understanding the parts of the equations that ought to be neglected is vital to your success.

It is not uncommon to get into a routine of solving a simplified version of equations. These may be fine under certain conditions. An example can be seen in the flow of air over a body, like a car or airplane wing. At low speeds, the density of the air is considered a constant. At higher speeds this is not the case, and if the density were considered a constant, errors would result. Starting with full equations and then simplifying reduces the likelihood that important factors will be overlooked.

Step 4: Simplifying Assumptions

As mentioned above, engineering and scientific applications often cannot be solved precisely. Even if they are solvable, determining the solution might be cost prohibitive. For instance, an exact solution might require a high-speed computer to calculate for a year to get an answer, and this would not be an effective use of resources. Weather prediction at locations of interest is such an example.

To solve the problem presented in a timely and cost-effective manner, simplifying assumptions are usually required. Simplifying assumptions can make the problem easier to solve and still provide an accurate result. It is important to write the assumptions down along with how they simplify the problem. This documents the assumptions and allows the final result to be interpreted in terms of these assumptions.

While estimation and approximation are useful tools, engineers also are concerned with the accuracy and reliability of their results. Approximations are often possible if assumptions are made to simplify the problem at hand. An important concept for engineers to understand in such situations is the Conservative Assumption.

In engineering problem solving, "conservative" has a non-political meaning. A conservative assumption is one that introduces errors on the safe side. We mentioned that estimations can be used to determine the bounds of a solution. An engineer should be able to look at those bounds and determine which end of the spectrum yields the safer solution. By selecting the safer condition, you are assuring that your calculation will result in a responsible conclusion.

Consider the example of a materials engineer selecting a metal alloy for an engine. Stress level and temperature are two of the parameters the engineer must consider. At the early stages of a design, these may not be known. What he or she could do is estimate the parameters. This could be done with a simplified analysis. It could also be done using prior experience. Often, products evolve from earlier designs for which there are data. If such data exist, ask how the new design will affect the parameters you are interested in. Will the stress increase? Will it double? Perhaps a conservative assumption would be to double the stress level of a previous design.

After taking the conservative case, a material can be selected. A question the engineer should ask is: "If a more precise answer were known, could I use a cheaper or lighter material?" If the answer is No, then the simple analysis might be sufficient. If Yes, the engineer could build a case for why a more detailed analysis is justified.

Another example of conservatism can be seen in the design of a swingset (see Fig. 4.1). In most sets, there is a horizontal piece from which the swings hang, and an inverted V-shaped support on each end. If you were the design engineer, you might have to size these supports.

One of the first questions to ask is, "For what weight do we size the swingset?" One way to answer this question is to do a research project on the weight distribution of children, followed by doing research into the use of swings by children at different ages, and then analyzing those data to determine typical weights of children that would use such swings. You might even need to observe playground activity to see if several children pile on a swing or load the set in different ways-say, by climbing on it. This might take weeks to do, but you would have excellent data.

On the other hand, you could just assume a heavy load that would exceed anything the children would produce. For this case, say, 500 pounds per swing. That would assume the equivalent of two large adults on each swing. Make the calculation to determine the needed supports, and then ask if it makes sense to be more detailed.

To answer this, one has to answer the question "What problem am I solving?" Do I need the most precise answer I can get? Am I after a safe and reliable answer regardless of other concerns?

In engineering, the "other concerns" include such things as cost and availability. In the current example, the supports would most likely be made of common

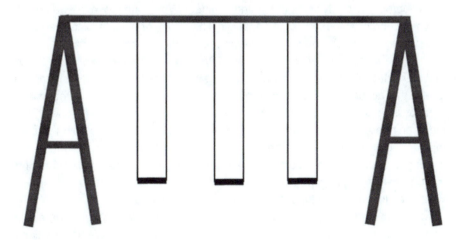

Figure 4.1 Simple swing set.

materials. Swingsets are typically made of wood or steel tubing. So, one way to answer the above questions is to quickly check and see if making a more detailed analysis would be justified. Check the prices of the materials needed for your conservative assumption against potential materials based on a more detailed analysis. Does the price difference justify a more detailed analysis? Another way to ask this is, "Does the price difference justify spending time to do the analysis?" Remember, as an engineer, your time costs money.

The answer may be, "It depends." It would depend on how much the difference is and how many you are going to produce. It wouldn't make sense to spend a week analyzing or researching the answer if it saves you or your company only $500. If your company was producing a million sets and you could save $5 per set, it would justify more detailed work on your part.

Approximation can improve decision-making indirectly as well. By using it to quickly resolve minor aspects of a problem, you can focus on the more pressing aspects.

Engineers are faced with these types of decisions every day in design and analysis. They must accurately determine what problem is to be solved and how to solve it. Safety of the public is of paramount concern in the engineering profession. You might be faced with a short-term safety emergency where you need to quickly prioritize solutions. Or you might be designing a consumer product where you have to take the long-term view. Swing-sets are often used for generations, after all.

As an engineer, you will need to develop the ability to answer, "What problem am I really solving?" and, "How do I get the solution I need most efficiently?"

Example 4.1

A manager for an aerospace firm had a method for "breaking in" young engineers. Shortly after the new engineer came to work in his group, the manager would look for an appropriate analysis for the young engineer. When one arose, he would ask the young engineer to perform the analysis. The engineer would typically embark on a path to construct a huge computer model requiring lengthy input and output files that would take a few weeks to complete. The manager would return to the engineer's desk the following morning, asking for the results. After hearing the response that all that was really accomplished was to map out the next three weeks worth of work, the manager would erupt and explain in a loud voice that he or she had been hired as an engineer and what they were supposed to be doing was an engineering analysis, not a "science project". He would then show the young engineer how to do a simplified analysis that would take an afternoon to perform and would answer the question given the appropriate conservative assumptions. He would then leave the engineer to the new analysis method.

While his methods were questionable, his point was well taken. There are always time and cost concerns as well as accuracy. If conservative assumptions are made, safe and reliable design and analysis decision can often be made quickly.

Step 5: Problem Solution

Now the problem is set up for you actually to perform the calculations. This might be done by hand or by using the computer. It is important to learn how to perform simple hand calculations; however, computer applications make complex and repetitive calculations much easier. When using computer simulations, develop a means to document what you have done in deriving the solution. This will allow you to find errors faster, as well as to show others what you have done.

Step 6: Accuracy Verification

Engineers work on solutions that can affect the livelihood and safety of people. It is important that the solution an engineer develops is accurate.

> *When you have mastered numbers, you will in fact no longer be read-
> ing numbers, any more than you read words when reading books. You
> will be reading meanings.*   —W. E. B. Du Bois p.83

The author had a student once whom I challenged on this very topic. He seemed to take a cavalier attitude about the accuracy of his work. Getting all the problems mostly correct would get him a B or a C in the class. I tried to explain the importance of accuracy and how people's safety might depend on his work. He told me that in class I caught his mistakes, and on the job someone would check his work. This is not necessarily the case! Companies do not hire some engineers to check other engineers' work. In most systems, there are checks in place. However, engineers are responsible for verifying that their own solutions are accurate. Therefore, it is important for the student to develop skills to meet any required standard.

A fascinating aspect of engineering is that the degree of accuracy needed is a variable under constant consideration. A problem or project may be properly solved within a tenth of an inch, but accuracy to a hundredth might be unneeded and difficult to control, rendering that kind of accuracy incorrect. But the next step of the solution might even require accuracy to the thousandth. Be sure of standards!

There are many different ways to verify a result. Some of these ways are:

- Estimate the answer.
- Simplify the problem and solve the simpler problem. Are the answers consistent?
- Compare with similar solutions. In many cases, other problems were solved similarly to the one currently in question.
- Compare to previous work.
- Ask a more experienced engineer to review the result.
- Compare to published literature on similar problems.
- Ask yourself if it makes sense.
- Compare to your own experience.
- Repeat the calculation.
- Run a computer simulation or model.
- Redo the calculation backwards.

It may be difficult to tell if your answer is exactly correct, but you should be able to tell if it is close or within a factor of 10. This will often flag any systematic error. Being able to back up your confidence in your answer will help you make better decisions on how your results will be used.

The following example will illustrate the analytic method.

Example 4.2

Problem: A ball is projected from the top of a 35 m tower at an angle 25° from horizontal with an initial velocity $v_0 = 80$ m/s. What is the time it takes to reach the ground, and what is the horizontal distance from the tower to the point of impact?

Problem Statement: Given: Initial velocity $v_0 = 80$ m/s
Initial trajectory = 25° from horizontal
Ball is launched from a height of 35 m
Find: 1) Time to impact
2) Distance of impact from the tower

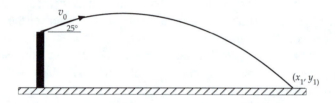

Equations: Found in a physics text:

$$x_1 = x_0 + v_0 t \cos \theta + \frac{1}{2} a_x t^2 \tag{a}$$

$$y_1 = y_0 + v_0 t \cos \theta + \frac{1}{2} a_y t^2 \tag{b}$$

Assumptions: Neglect air resistance
Acceleration $a_y = -9.81$ m/s² is constant in the vertical direction
Acceleration is zero in the horizontal direction, $a_x = 0$
Ground is level and impact occurs at $y = -35$ m
Solution: Begin with equation (b):

$$-35 = 0 + 80t \sin 25° - \frac{1}{2} 9.8t^2 \text{ or } t^2 - 6.90t - 7.14 = 0$$

$$\therefore t = \frac{-b \pm \sqrt{b^2 - 4ac}}{2a} = \frac{6.9 \pm \sqrt{6.9^2 + 4 \times 1 \times 7.14}}{2} = 7.81 \text{ sec}$$

The solution must be 7.81 sec, since time must be positive.

The distance is found using equation (a):

$$x_1 = 0 + 80 \times 7.81 \times \cos 25° = 566 \text{ m}$$

Estimation

Estimation is a problem solving tool that engineers need to develop. It can provide quick answers to problems and to verify complicated analyses. Young engineers are invariably amazed when they begin their careers at how the older, more experienced engineers can estimate so closely to problems before the analysis is even done.

While estimation or approximation may not yield the precision you require for an engineering analysis, it is a very useful tool. One thing that is can do is to help you check your analysis. Estimation can provide bounds for potential answers. This is especially critical in today's dependence on computer solutions. Your method may be correct, but one character mistyped will throw your results off. It is important to be able to have confidence in your results by developing tools to verify accuracy.

Estimation can also be used to help decide if a detailed analysis is needed. Estimating using a best case and worst case scenario can yield an upper an lower bound on the problem. If the entire range of potential solutions is acceptable, why do the detailed analysis? What if for our case, the whole range of temperatures met our design constraints? It would not have justified a month of our work. In this

---

The author was amazed at one such case that he experienced first hand. He was responsible for doing a detailed temperature analysis on a gas turbine engine that was to go on a new commercial aircraft. They presented plan to some managers and people from the Chief Engineers Office. The plan called for two engineers working full time for a month on the analysis.

One of the more senior engineers who had attended the presentation sent him some numbers the next day. He had gone back to his office and made some approximate calculations and sent me the results. His note told him to check his results against his numbers.

After the month long analysis, which involved making a detailed computer model of the components, he checked our results with his "back of the envelope" calculations. He was very close to the result! His answers were not exactly the same, but they were very close. The detailed analysis did provide a higher degree of precision. However, the senior engineer was very close.

What he had done was simply use suggestion #13 from the problem solving methods. He solved a simpler problem. He used simple shapes with known solutions to approximate the behavior of the complex shapes of the jet engine's components.

case, the added precision was needed and did lead to a design benefit. As engineers, you will be asked to decide when a detailed analysis is required and when it is not.

Example 4.3

With all of today's sophisticated analytical tools, it may be hard to imagine that accurate measurements could be made with out them. Take the size of a molecule. Today's technology makes this measurement possible. Could you have made this measurement in the 18th century? Benjamin Franklin did.

He found the size of an oil molecule. He took a known volume of oil and poured it slowly into a still pool of water. The oil spread out in a circular pattern. He measured the circle and calculated the surface area. Since the volume of the oil remained the same, he calculated the height of the oil slick and assumed that was the molecular thickness, which turned out to be true. His result was close to the correct value.

Do we have more accurate measurements now? Certainly we do. However, Benjamin Franklin's measurement was certainly better than no value. As engineers, there will be times when no data exists and you will need to make a judgment. Having an approximate result is much better than no data.

Back of the Envelope Calculations

> "Everything should be made as simple as possible, but no simpler."
>
> —Einstein

Back of the envelope calculations are a method of estimation and can provide a rough estimate of parameters in engineering problem solving. They are used throughout the design process and may indicate an idea's feasibility in a design situation. As an engineering design evolves, back of the envelope calculations may be replaced by more exact, more time-consuming methods.

Back of the envelope calculations contain simple formulas for calculating parameters. Often, you estimate formula variables. Additionally, you make several assumptions to enable you to use the formula and estimates. The next two examples illustrate a few of the many ways in which to use back of the envelope calculations.

Example 4.4

Estimate how much mulch[1] surfacing will cost for a playground that is 2500 ft^2 (50′ × 50′). Surfacing is a soft material placed under and around playground equipment to break falls and thus prevent serious injury.

---

[1] Double shredded bark mulch

According to *The Dictionary of Jargon,* by Jonathan Greene, back of the envelope calculations are a set of simple and speedy calculations. The expression comes from the popular image of a genius/absent minded professor scribbling great notations on a scrap of paper.

Back of the Envelope Calculations

You need a volume of playground surfacing. The area is specified, but the surfacing depth is a function of the critical height, which is defined as the play equipment's highest elevation from which a child can reasonably be expected to fall. Because you do not know the critical height, you will have to assume it. From Table 1 of the CPSC[2] Handbook for Public Playground Safety, you estimate the depth of mulch surfacing to be 9 inches (0.75 feet). This means that you are guessing your critical height to be ten feet or less.

The volume of surfacing is $50' \times 50' \times 0.75' = 1875$ ft^3

Suppose that you visit a hardware store and find that 2 ft^3 of mulch is selling for $1.99. The estimated cost is then

$$1875 \text{ ft}^3 \text{ mulch} \times \frac{\$1.99}{2 \text{ ft}^3 \text{ mulch}} = \$1865.63 \text{ or } \$1866$$

If sales tax in your area is 6%, then the cost is $1866 \times 1.06 = \$1978$.

Specific Calculation

Specific calculations for surfacing the playground would be completed toward the end of the design process with the completed specifications. At this point, you would know the critical height and could fully specify the surfacing depth. Additionally, you would identify a specific company that would deliver the mulch, probably by the truckload. The cost would be exact, and would include any sales tax, shipping and handling, and volume discounts that apply. When you have the exact volume of surfacing and the exact cost, you no longer need a back of the envelope calculation.

Example 4.5

Find the volume of an egg.

Although an egg's shape is beautiful (at least the authors think so), it is irregular and difficult to calculate directly. You can use a back of the envelope calculation to estimate the volume of an egg by saying that an egg is approximately spherical. The volume of a sphere is

---

[2] Consumer Product Safety Commission

$$\frac{4\pi}{3} r^3,$$

where *r* is the radius of the egg. You have to estimate the radius of the egg, per-haps by averaging the radius of the long side and short side of the egg. (You could measure this with a ruler.) Another back of the envelope calculation would involve considering the egg to approximate the volume of an ellipsoid (this is a three-dimensional ellipse).

The volume of an ellipsoid is

$$\frac{4\pi}{3} abc.$$

A third way to find the volume of an egg involves volume displacement. If you place a known volume of water inside a beaker, measure it, and place the egg in-side the beaker and measure the volume with the egg. The volume of the egg will be the difference between these two values.

The exact volume could be determined using a computer program that would measure the egg's dimensions at every point in space and would use calculus to determine the egg's volume.

Why would you care about the volume of an egg?

Although this may seem like a trivial example, determining the egg's volume can be important. Engineers need to design refrigeration systems to keep eggs fresh, packages to hold them, and transport methods that do not break them. All of these designs require knowing the egg's volume. The volume of a batch of eggs will vary (hence the sizing system for eggs, for example, grade A large, or grade A extra large).

Estimation can be a very powerful tool to check accuracy and make analysis decisions. Senior engineers in industry often comment that current graduates lack the ability to do an approximation. This has become more important with the de-pendence of computer tools and solutions. Computer analyses lend themselves to typos on inputs or arithmetic errors. Being able to predict the ballpark of the ex-pected results can head off potentially disastrous results.

4.4 CREATIVE PROBLEM SOLVING

Creativity is at the heart of engineering design. Much literature exists on creativ-ity, and if it can be taught. Everyone agrees on this: Each person is innately cre-ative, and is more or less in touch with this part of themselves. In the first part of this section, we will examine ways for you to develop your creative self. In the sec-ond part of the section, we will present creative problem-solving strategies.

Developing Your Creativity

Most of this section is adapted from Michael Gelb's book *How to Think like Leonardo da Vinci: Seven Steps to Genius Every Day.* This book describes the

> The definition of create comes from the Latin words creatus and crescere, meaning to grow. It means to bring into existence, to produce or bring about by a course of action or behavior, or to produce through imaginative skill (adapted from merriamwebster.com).

famous artist and inventor, and suggests that seven da Vincian principles have to do with being creative. The book presents numerous exercises for developing each creative principle. We will present each of the seven, and things to think about when developing these principles from an engineering standpoint.

> *If anthropologists were fish, the last thing they would discover is water.*
> —Margaret Mead.

1. **Curiosita** is defined as an insatiably curious approach to life and an unrelenting quest for continuous learning. Keeping a journal (or several) around you at all times is a great way to record questions, observations, dreams, and ideas, and will enhance your curiosita.

As applied to engineering, think about finding illustrative metaphors in nature for things that have been designed:

- Leonardo da Vinci designed musical pipes based on the human larynx
- Alexander Graham Bell modeled the telephone after the human ear
- The idea for Velcro came from the inventor observing the burrs that stick to clothing
- The pull tab for soda cans was invented by asking the following question: What in nature opens easily? The answer was peeling a banana.

Other metaphors in nature include the following:

- The way a hummingbird and a helicopter fly
- Snake fangs and hypodermic needles
- The large ears of a jackrabbit and a heat exchanger

One example for developing curiosita included in the da Vinci book involves finding the question. This exercise can be useful as applied to an engineering situation. Think about your design project with regard to the following set of questions:

- What is the problem?
  - Underlying issues?
  - Preconceptions, prejudices, or paradigms that may be influencing my perception?
- When did it start?
- Who cares about it?
  - Is affected by it?

- ◦ Created it?
- ◦ Can help solve it?
- How does it happen?
- Where does it happen?
- Why is it important? Why?

When thinking about your service-learning project, ask the following questions with regard to curiosita:

- Am I asking the right questions?
- What do I need to do in order to design a great (your device, system, or process)?

2. **Dimostrazione** is a commitment to test knowledge through experience, persistence, and a willingness to learn from mistakes. This quality is best summed up by Ziggy, who stated, "Good judgment comes from experience. Experience comes from poor judgment."

Because engineering involves judgment, you must develop your dimostrazione. Write down your answers to the following questions while thinking about dimostrazione:

- Are you ever deceived by your own opinions?
- Are your opinions and beliefs your own?
- Who is the most independent, original thinker you know? What makes that person an original?
- Do you make the most of your mistakes?

Another important concept involved in dimostrazione is perspective. Looking at the same issue from different perspectives can yield new information and insight into ways to look at a problem or conceive of solutions. Think about the following:

Would your belief, thought, or idea change if you

- Lived in a different country?
- Came from another religious, racial, economic, or class background?
- Were twenty years older or younger?
- Were a member of the opposite gender?

In terms of engineering design, ask the following questions to develop dimostrazione:

- How can I improve my ability to learn from my mistakes and experiences?
- How can I develop independence of thought?
- How have my experiences with my project (as a participant, with community partners, with stakeholders, from observation, from collected knowledge and information) influenced the way I think about [the device or system you're designing])?

3. **Sensazione** is defined as the continual refinement of the senses as a means to enliven experience. Gelb suggests that the more in touch you are with all your senses, the more likely you are to be creative. The book contains numerous exercises to help develop all of your senses. For most of us, sight and sound are the most developed. Think about how your service-learning project might change if you concentrated on your senses, especially smell, touch, and taste. Can you design your device or system to enhance the senses?

4. **Sfumato** is a willingness to embrace ambiguity, paradox, and uncertainty (Sfumato means "going up in smoke"). Although this can be difficult, the idea is to make friends using ambiguity and anxiety. When multiple solutions exist for an engineering problem, this technique can be useful. The trick is to examine the different perspectives (dimostrazione) and to create a design and/or make recommendations that best meet the different perspectives. For your service-learning project, does your design have paradoxes? Why and how might you address those?

> *It is the mark of an educated mind to be able to entertain a thought without accepting it.*   —Aristotle

For example, in playground design, many experts believe that the increased emphasis placed on safety has resulted in diminished challenges for children on playgrounds and less creativity involving playground designs. The paradox is that a safer playground has resulted in a more boring environment. Can you use other creative qualities in this section to expand on this idea?

5. **Arte/Scienza** is the development of the balance between art and science, imagination and logic. One established concept with regard to whole-brain thinking is the idea that if you mostly use the left half of your brain, then you excel at logical and analytical thinking. If you are right brained, you excel at imaginative, big picture thinking. Engineers and scientists use their left brain more, and artists use their right brain more.

Gelb poses the following question: Are you a scientist who studies art, or an artist who studies science? The bottom line is to BE BOTH. The separation is artificial. As an engineer, your designs must be logical, but the best designs speak to social context, aesthetics, and address multiple needs. If applicable, what activities can you provide with regard to your service-learning project to enhance left-brain and right-brain thinking?

6. **Corporalita** is the cultivation of grace, ambidexterity, fitness, and poise. Gelb suggests areas of interest for this principle, including balance, diet, listening to your body, and the reciprocal relationship between attitude and physical state. When thinking about engineering design, think about how you can nurture the body and mind balance. How will this translate into the engineering design approach you take, and into the actual device, system, or process you create?

7. **Connessione** is a recognition and appreciation for the interconnectedness of all things and phenomena, or systems thinking. Systems thinking is already a important concept in engineering (see Chapter 2 for details). Remember that acting on one thing in a system will cause many responses, some of which are obvious, and some of which are not, some of which are immediate, and some of which are not. Your challenge as an engineer is to try to see how things fit together and to anticipate and address any unintended consequences from your service-learning or other engineering projects.

One example of an unintended consequence requiring systems thinking occurred when students were designing a playground for children with hearing impairments and/or deafness. Hard plastic is commonly used for slides, and initial playground designs for this group contained these slides. After completing extensive research, students discovered that children with cochlear implants, devices surgically implanted into a child's ear canal to facilitate hearing, could not use plastic slides. Sliding on plastic produces static electricity, which would destroy the electrodes in the cochlear implant, which in turn would require surgery to repair. These concepts were not evident when thinking about designing playgrounds. Further research revealed that cochlear implants could be removed before the students entered the playground, so that these students could use plastic slides as long as they removed the implants before entering the playground.

Now that you have an idea of the principles of being a creative person, let's look at creative problem-solving strategies that you can apply in engineering situations.

CREATIVE PROBLEM SOLVING STRATEGIES

Many engineering problems are open-ended and complex. Such problems require creative problem solving. To maximize the creative problem-solving process, a systematic approach is recommended. Just as with analytic problem solving, developing a systematic approach to using creativity will pay dividends in better solutions.

> *Dividing the process into steps allows you to break a large, complex problem into simpler problems where your various skills can be used.*

Revisiting our toolbox analogy, the creative method provides the solid judgment needed to use your analytic tools. Individual thinking skills are your basics here. The method we'll outline now will help you to apply these skills and choose solution strategies effectively.

There are numerous ways to look at the creative problem-solving process. We will present a method which focuses on answering these five questions:

1. What is wrong?
2. What do we know?

3. What is the real problem?
4. What is the best solution?
5. How do we implement the solution?

By dividing the process into steps, you are more likely to follow a complete and careful problem-solving procedure, and more effective solutions are going to result. This also allows you to break a large, complex problem into simpler problems where your various skills can be used. Using such a strategy, the sky is the limit on the complexity of projects which an engineer can complete. It's astonishing and satisfying to see what can be done.

Divergence and Convergence

At each phase of the process, there is both a divergent and a convergent part of the process, as shown in Figure 4.2. In the divergent process, you start at one point and reach for as many ideas as possible. Quantity is important. Identifying possibilities is the goal of the divergent phase of each step. In this portion of the process (indicated by the outward pointing arrows, $\leftarrow \rightarrow$) use the brainstorming and idea-generating techniques described in subsequent sections. Look for as many possibilities as you can. Often, the best solutions come from different ideas.

In the convergence phase (indicated by inward pointing arrows, $\rightarrow \leftarrow$) use analytical and evaluative tools to narrow the possibilities to the one(s) most likely to yield results. Quality is most important, and finding the best possibility to move the process to the next phase is the goal. One common method is to use a matrix to rate ideas based on defined criteria.) If one choice fails to produce satisfactory results, go back to the idea lists for another method to tackle the problem.

In order to illustrate the creative problem-solving process, let's consider an example of a problem and work through the process. The problem we will use for illustration is a student who is getting low grades. This certainly is a problem that needs a solution. Let's see how the process works.

What's Wrong?

In the first step of the problem-solving process, an issue is identified. This can be something stated for you by a supervisor or a professor, or something you determine on your own. This is the stage where entrepreneurs thrive—looking for an opportunity to meet a need. Similarly, engineers look to find solutions to meet a need. This may involve optimizing a process, improving customer satisfaction, or addressing reliability issues.

To illustrate the process, let's take our example of the difficulty that beginning engineering students can have with grades. Most students were proficient in high school and didn't need to study much. The demands of engineering programs can catch some students off guard. Improving grades is the problem we will tackle.

At this stage, we need to identify that there is a problem that is worth our effort in solving. A good start would be to identify whether it truly is a problem. How

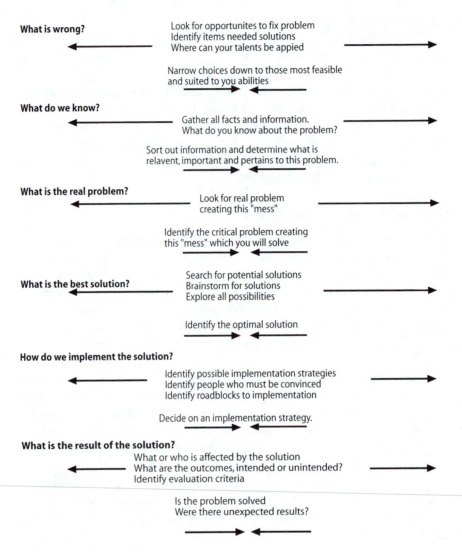

What is wrong?

Look for opportunites to fix problem
Identify items needed solutions
Where can your talents be appied

Narrow choices down to those most feasible
and suited to you abilities

What do we know?

Gather all facts and information.
What do you know about the problem?

Sort out information and determine what is
relavent, important and pertains to this problem.

What is the real problem?

Look for real problem
creating this "mess"

Identify the critical problem creating
this "mess" which you will solve

What is the best solution?

Search for potential solutions
Brainstorm for solutions
Explore all possibilities

Identify the optimal solution

How do we implement the solution?

Identify possible implementation strategies
Identify people who must be convinced
Identify roadblocks to implementation

Decide on an implementation strategy.

What is the result of the solution?

What or who is affected by the solution
What are the outcomes, intended or unintended?
Identify evaluation criteria

Is the problem solved
Were there unexpected results?

Figure 4.2 Problem-solving process.

could you do this? Total your scores thus far in your classes and compare them with the possible scores listed in your syllabus. Talk with your professor(s) to find out where you are in the classes and if grades will be given on a curve. Talk to an advisor about realistic grade expectations (complete the "finding the question" exercise in page 87 of this book). At the end of this process, you should know if you have a grade problem.

What Do We Know?

The second step in problem solving is the gathering of facts. All facts and information related to the problem identified in the first step are gathered. In this initial information gathering stage, do not try to evaluate whether the data are central to the problem. As will be explained in the brainstorming and idea generating sections to follow, premature evaluation can be a hindrance to generating adequate information.

With our example of the student questioning his grades, the information we generate might include:

1. Current test grades in each course
2. Current homework and quiz grades in each course
3. Percent of the semester's grade already determined in each course
4. Class average in each course
5. Professors' grading policies
6. Homework assignments behind
7. Current study times
8. Current study places
9. Effective time spent on each course
10. Time spent doing homework in each course
11. Performance of your friends
12. Your high school grades
13. Your high school study routine
14. Your college grades
15. Your college study routine

Part of this process is to list the facts that you know. To be thorough, you should request assistance from someone with a different point of view. This could be a friend, an advisor, a parent or a professor. They might come up with a critical factor you have overlooked.

What Is the Real Problem?

This stage is one that is often skipped, but it is critical to effective solutions. The difference between this stage and the first is that this step of the process answers the question *why*. Identifying the initial problem answers the question of *what*, or what is wrong. To effectively fix the problem, a problem solver needs to understand *why* the problem exists. The danger is that only symptoms of the problem will be addressed, rather than root causes.

In our example, we are problem solving low class grades. That is the *what* question. To really understand a problem, the *why* must be answered. Why are the grades low? Answering this question will identify the cause of the problem. The cause is what must be dealt with for a problem to be effectively addressed.

In our case, we must understand why the class grades are low. Let us assume that poor test scores result in the low grades. But this doesn't tell us why the test scores are low. This is a great opportunity for brainstorming potential causes. In this divergent phase of problem definition, don't worry about evaluating the potential causes. Wait until the list is generated.

Possible causes may include:

- Poor test-taking skills
- Incomplete or insufficient notes
- Poor class attendance
- Not understanding the required reading
- Not spending enough time studying
- Studying the wrong material
- Attending the wrong class
- Studying ineffectively (e.g., trying to cram the night before tests)
- Failing to understand the material (*note*: might reveal need for tutor or study group)
- Using solution manuals or friends as a crutch to do homework
- Not at physical peak at test time (i.e., up all night before the test)
- Didn't work enough problems from the book

After you have created the list of potential causes, evaluate each as to its validity. In our example, there may be more than one cause contributing to the low grades. If so, make a rank-ordered list and rank the causes in order of their impact on class performance.

Assume the original list is reduced to:

- Poor class attendance
- Studying ineffectively
- Not spending enough time studying
- Not understanding the material

Rank the former list in order of their impact on grades. You may be able to do this yourself or you may need help. An effective problem solver will seek input from others when it is appropriate. In this case, a professor or academic advisor might be able to help you rank the causes and help determine which ones will provide the greatest impact. For this example, say the rank order was:

1. Not understanding the material
2. Studying ineffectively
3. Not spending enough time studying
4. Poor class attendance

We determined that while class attendance was important, it was not the key factor in the poor performance. The key item was not understanding the material. This goes with ineffective studying and insufficient time.

Identifying key causes of problems is vital, so let's look at another example.

What Is the Best Solution?

Once the problem has been defined, potential solutions need to be generated. This can be done by yourself or with the help of friends. In an engineering application, it is wise to confer with experienced experts about the problem's solution. This may be most productive after you have begun a list of causes. The expert can comment on your list and offer his or her own suggestions as well. This is a great way to get your ideas critiqued. After you gain more experience, you will find that technical experts help you narrow down the choices rather than providing more. Also, go to more than one source. This may provide more ideas as well as help with the next step.

In our example, the technical expert may be a professor or advisor who is knowledgeable about studying. Let's assume that the following list of potential solutions has been generated.

- Get a tutor
- Visit your professors during office hours
- Make outside appointments with professors
- Visit help rooms
- Form a study group
- Use study methods ideal for your learning type (see www.cas.lsu.edu for details)
- Outline books
- Get old exams
- Get old sets of notes
- Outline lecture notes
- Review notes with professors
- Do extra problems
- Get additional references
- Make a time schedule
- Drop classes
- Retake the classes in the summer
- Go to review sessions

The list now must be evaluated and the best solution decided upon. This convergent phase of the problem-solving process is best done with the input of others. It is especially helpful to get the opinions of those who have experience and/or expertise in the area you are investigating. In an engineering application, this may be a lead engineer. In our case, it could be an academic advisor, a teaching assistant, or a professor. These experts can be consulted individually or asked to participate as a group.

When refining solutions, an effective tool is to ask yourself which of them will make the biggest impact and which will require the least effort. Each solution gets ranked high or low as to impact and effort. Ideal solutions are those that have a high impact yet require a low level of effort. A visual tool which helps make this process easier is the problem-solving matrix shown in Figure 4.3. Solutions that fall in quadrant B should be avoided. These solutions require a great deal of effort for marginal payoff. Solutions that are the most effective are those in quadrant C. These are the ones that are easy to implement and will produce significant results. It may be necessary to include solutions in quadrant D, requiring high effort and yielding high impact. These should be carefully evaluated to ensure that the investment is worth the reward.

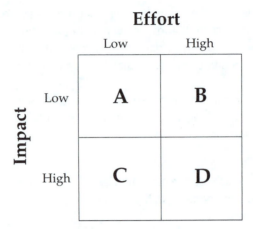

Figure 4.3 A Problem-Solving Matrix.

Implementing the Solution

Implementing the solution is a step that may seem trivial and not worth discussion. This step, however, is a critical phase of the problem solving process. In our scenario, the solution selected may have been:

- **Do extra problems

To accomplish this solution, appropriate additional problems must be selected, completed, and corrected. Implementation probably requires the assistance of the instructor to help select appropriate problems. To randomly pick additional practice problems could move the effort from quadrant C to D and even B. To have the greatest chances of success, you would want to gain the assistance of your instructor. Other sources of assistance could come from a study group which poses the challenges of encouraging the group to do extra problems with you.

As with all the other steps, a divergent phase begins the step including such activities as brainstorming. The convergent phase of the step culminates with the selection of the implementation plan.

In engineering applications, implementation can be a very critical phase of the process. Most of the solutions to problems either require additional resources including money or the cooperation of other groups that are either not directly affected by the problem or not under your control. Especially early in your career, you will not have control over the people who need to implement solutions so you will need to sell your ideas to the managers who do. An effective implementation plan will be critical to getting your solutions accomplished.

President Jimmy Carter was educated as an engineer and was one of the most respected presidents as a strong moral person. During his presidency, the country was in an energy crisis and action was needed to address this problem. He summoned Tip O'Neal, the speaker of the House of Representatives, to the White House to explain his plan. Mr. O'Neal responded by giving the President a list of people that would need to be sold on the plan before it went public. President Carter was new to Washington and was going to skip the development of an implementation plan before enacting it. He believed that with the country in an energy crisis, it was obvious what was needed and cooperation was a given. Tip O'Neal was very experienced in the Washington political system and understood that they needed to spend time gaining acceptance of their plan before it could be implemented.

Engineering situations can be very similar. While most are not as political as Washington D.C., most require gaining acceptance of others to implement a solution. In all of these cases, gaining the recognition of those involved is a critical part of the problem solving process.

Example 4.6

Engineers are trained problem solvers. Many engineers move into other careers where their problem-solving abilities are valued. One such case is Greg Smith, who was called into the ministry after becoming a mechanical engineer.

"As soon as people discover that I have a degree in mechanical engineering and am in the ministry, they always ask me the same question, 'So, do you still plan on using your engineering degree some day?' It is difficult for people to understand that I use my engineering training every day as a full time minister.

"One of the greatest skills I learned at Purdue was problem solving. Professors in mechanical engineering were notorious for giving us more information than we would need to solve the problem. Our job was to sift through all the facts and only use what was needed to reach a solution. I find myself using this very skill whenever I am involved in personal counseling. For example, just this week I was listening to someone unload about all the stress he was experiencing from life. He listed his job, a second business at home, family and finances as the primary sources of stress. After further conversation, I was able to "solve" his problem by showing that most of his stress was related to only one of the four sources he listed. The root issue was that this person was basing much of his self-image on his success in this one area of life. I helped him regain his sense of balance in seeing his self-worth not in job performance, but in who he was as a whole person."

Example 4.7

"What was the confusion?" Defining the real problem is often the most critical stage of the problem-solving process and the one most often skipped. In engineering, this can be the difference between a successful design and a failure.

An example of this occurred with an engine maker. A new model engine was introduced and began selling quickly. A problem developed, however, and failures started to happen. Cracks initiating from a series of bolt holes were causing the engines to fail. A team of engineers was assembled and the part was redesigned. They determined that the cause of failure was high stress in the area of the bolt hole. Embossments were added to strengthen the area. It was a success, until the redesigned engines accumulated enough time in the field to crack again. A new team of engineers looked at the problem and quickly determined that the cause was a three-dimensional coupling of stress concentrations created by the embossments, resulting in too high a stress near the hole where the crack started. The part was redesigned and introduced into the field. It was a success—until the redesigned engines accumulated enough time in the field to crack yet again.

A third team of engineers was assembled. This time, they stepped back and asked what the real cause was. Part of the team ran sophisticated stress models of the part, just like the other two teams had done. The new team members looked for other causes. They found that the machine creating the hole introduced microcracks into the surface of the bolt holes. The stress models predicted that further stresses would start a crack. However, if a crack were intentionally introduced, the allowable stresses were much lower and the part would not fail. The cause wasn't with cracking but with the wrong kind of cracking. The third team was a success because it had looked for the real problem. Identifying the root cause initially, which in this case involved the machining process, would have saved the company millions of dollars and spared customers the grief of the engine failures.

Evaluating the Solution

Implementation does not necessarily end the problem solving process. Just as the design process is a circular process with each design leading to possible new designs, problem solving can also be cyclic. Once a solution has been found and implemented, an evaluation should be performed. As with the other steps in the problems solving process, this step begins with a divergence phase as the problem solver asks what makes a successful solution and how it will be evaluated. To effectively evaluate a solution, criteria for success must be established. Sometimes there are objective criteria for evaluation, but in many circumstances the criteria for success are more subjective.

Once the criteria have been established, the evaluation process should be defined including who will evaluate the solution. Often it is desirable to get a neutral view of someone who was not involved in the formulation of the solution process to be the evaluator.

If the solution is a success, the process may be done. Often in engineering applications, solutions are intermediate and lead to other opportunities. The software industry is a prime example. Software is written to utilize the current computer technologies to address issues. Almost as soon as it is completed, new technologies are available which open up new opportunities or require new solutions.

Some times a "success" does not address the true problem as was the case of the turbine disk failures described earlier. In these cases, the evaluation process may need time to deem the solution a true success. In other cases, solutions have unintended outcomes that require a new solution even if the initial solution was deemed a success.

Whether a solution is effective or not, there is value in taking time to reflect on the solution and its implications. This allows you as a problem solver to learn from the process and the solution. Critically evaluating solutions and opportunities is a skill that is extremely valuable as an engineer and is discussed further in the critical thinking section of this chapter.

4.5 PERSONAL PROBLEM SOLVING STYLES

The creative problem solving model presented previously is one of the models that can be used to solve the open-ended problems engineers face in every day situations. You may find yourself in an organization that uses another model. There are many models for problem solving and each describes the process in slightly different steps. Isaken and Treffinger, for example, break the creative problem solving process into six linear steps [Isaken and Treffinger]. These six steps are:

1. Mess Finding
2. Data Finding
3. Problem Finding
4. Idea Finding
5. Solution Finding
6. Acceptance Finding

Dr. Min Basadur of McMaster University developed another model, a circular one, which he calls Simplex, based on his experience as a product development engineer with the Procter and Gamble Company. This model separates the problem solving process into eight different steps that are listed below [Basadur]

1. Problem finding
2. Fact finding
3. Problem defining
4. Idea finding
5. Evaluating and selecting
6. Action planning
7. Gaining acceptance
8. Taking action

All these problem solving processes provide a systematic approach to problem solving. Each process has divergent phases where options need to be generated along with convergent phases when best options need to be selected.

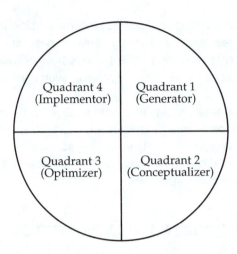

Figure 4.4 The four quadrants of Basadur's Simplex Creative Problem Solving Process (with permission from the Center for Research in Applied Creativity).

Basadur has created and patented a unique method of helping individuals participating in the creative problem solving process identify which parts of the process they are more comfortable in than others. This method, called the Basadur Simplex Creative Problem Solving Profile, reflects your personal creative problem solving style. Everyone has a different creative problem solving style. Your particular style reflects your relative preferences for the different parts of the problem solving process.

Basadur's Creative Problem Solving Profile method identifies four styles and each style correlates with two of the eight problem solving steps in the eight step circular model of creative problem solving above. Thus the eight problem solving steps are grouped into four quadrants or stages of the complete problem solving process.

These four steps are shown as quadrants in Figure 4.4. The Basadur Creative Problem Solving Process begins with quadrant one, the generation of new problems and opportunities. It cycles through quadrant two, the conceptualization of the problem or opportunity and of new, potentially useful ideas, and quadrant three, the optimization of new solutions. It ends with quadrant four, the implementation of new solutions. Each quadrant requires different kinds of thinking and problem solving skills.

Basadur describes the four different quadrants or stages as follows.

Generating

Generating involves getting the problem solving process rolling. Generative thinking involves gathering information through direct experience, questioning, imagining possibilities, sensing new problems and opportunities, and viewing situations from different perspectives. People and organizations strong in generating skills prefer to come up with options or diverge rather than evaluate and select, or converge. They see relevance in almost everything and think of good and bad sides to almost any fact, idea or issue. They dislike becoming too organized or delegating the complete problem, but are willing to let others take care of the details. They enjoy ambiguity and are hard to pin down. They delight in juggling many new projects simultaneously. Every solution they explore suggests several new problems to be solved. Thinking in this quadrant includes problem finding and fact finding.

Conceptualizing

Conceptualizing keeps the innovation process going. Like generating, it involves divergence. But rather than gaining understanding by direct experience, it favors gaining understanding by abstract thinking. It results in putting new ideas together, discovering insights that help define problems, and creating theoretical models to explain things. People and organizations strong in conceptualizing skills enjoy taking information scattered all over the map from the generator phase and making sense of it. Conceptualizers need to 'understand'; to them, a theory must be logically sound and precise. They prefer to proceed only with a clear grasp of a situation and when the problem or main idea is well defined. They dislike having to prioritize, implement or agonize over poorly understood alternatives. They like to play with ideas and are not overly concerned with moving to action. Thinking in this quadrant includes problem defining and idea finding.

Optimizing

Optimizing moves the innovation process further. Like conceptualizing, it favors gaining understanding by abstract thinking. But rather than diverge, an individual with this thinking style prefers to converge. This results in converting abstract ideas and alternatives into practical solutions and plans. Individuals rely on mentally testing ideas rather than on trying things out. People who favor the optimizing style prefer to create optimal solutions to a few well-defined problems or issues. They prefer to focus on specific problems and sort through large amounts of information to pinpoint 'what's wrong' in a given situation. They are usually confident in their ability to make a sound logical evaluation and to select the best option or solution to a problem. They often lack patience with ambiguity and dislike 'dreaming' about additional ideas, points of view, or relations among problems. They believe they 'know' what the problem is. Thinking in this quadrant includes idea evaluation and selection and action planning.

Implenting

Implementing completes the innovation process. Like optimizing, it favors converging. However, it favors learning by direct experience rather than by abstract thinking. This results in getting things done. Individuals rely on trying things out rather than mentally testing them. People and organizations strong in implementing prefer situations in which they must somehow make things work. They do not need complete understanding in order to proceed and adapt quickly to immediate changing circumstances. When a theory does not appear to fit the facts they will readily discard it. Others perceive them as enthusiastic about getting the job done but also as impatient or even pushy as they try to turn plans and ideas into action. They will try as many different approaches as necessary and follow up or 'bird dog' as needed to ensure that the new procedure will stick. Thinking in this quadrant includes gaining acceptance and implementing.

Your Creative Problem Solving Style

Basadur's research with thousands of engineers, managers and others has shown that everyone has a different creative problem solving style. Your particular style reflects your relative preferences for each of the four quadrants of the creative problem solving process: generating/initiating, conceptualizing, optimizing and implementing. Your behavior and thinking processes can not be pigeonholed in any single quadrant. Rather they're a combination or blend of quadrants: you prefer one quadrant in particular, but you also have secondary preferences for one or two adjacent quadrants. Your blend of styles is called the creative problem solving style. Stated another way, your creative problem solving style shows which particular steps of the process you gravitate toward.

Typically as an engineer, you will be working as part of a team or larger organization. Basadur's research has shown that entire organizations also have their own problem solving process profiles. An organization's profile reflects such things as the kinds of people it hires, its culture and its values. For example, if an organization focuses almost entirely on short term results, it may be overloaded with implementers but have no conceptualizers or generators. The organization will show strengths in processes that deliver its current products and services efficiently. But it will show weaknesses in processes of long-term planning and product development that would help it stay ahead of change. Rushing to solve problems, this organization will continually find itself reworking failed solutions without pausing to conduct adequate fact finding and problem definition. By contrast, an organization with too many generators or conceptualizers and no implementers will continually find good problems to solve and great ideas for products and processes to develop. But it will never carry them to their conclusion. You can likely think of many examples of companies showing this imbalances in innovation process profiles.

Basadur suggests that in order to succeed in creative problem solving, a team requires strengths in all four quadrants. Teams must appreciate the importance of all four quadrants and find ways to fit together their members' styles. Team members must learn to use their differing styles in complementary ways. For example, generating ideas for new products and methods must start somewhere with some individuals scanning the environment picking up data and cues from customers and suggesting possible opportunities for changes and improvement. Thus, the generator raises new information and possibilities—usually not fully developed, but in the form of starting points for new projects. Then the conceptualizer pulls together the facts and idea fragments from the generator phase into well-defined problems and challenges and more clearly developed ideas worth further evaluation. Good conceptualizers give sound structure to fledgling ideas and opportunities. The optimizer then takes these well-defined ideas and finds a practical best solution and well-detailed efficient plans for proceeding. Finally, implementers must carry forward the practical solutions and plans to make them fit real-life situations and conditions.

Skills in all four quadrants are equally valuable. As an engineering student, you will find yourself working on group projects. Often, these projects involve designs that are open-ended and are well suited for creative problem solving. Use these opportunities to practice utilizing your problem solving skills and preferences as well as those of your team members.

Why Are We Different?

What causes the main differences in people's approaches to problem-solving? Basadur's research suggests that they usually stem from inevitable differences in how knowledge and understanding—"learning"—are gained and used. No two individuals, teams or organizations learn in the same way. Nor do they use what they learn in the same way. As shown in Figure 4.5, some individuals and organizations prefer to learn through direct, concrete experiencing (doing). They gain understanding by physical processing. Others prefer to learn through more detached abstract thinking (analyzing). They gain understanding by mental processing. All individuals and organizations gain knowledge and understanding in both ways but to differing degrees. Similarly, while some individual and organizations prefer to use their knowledge for ideation, others prefer to use their knowl-

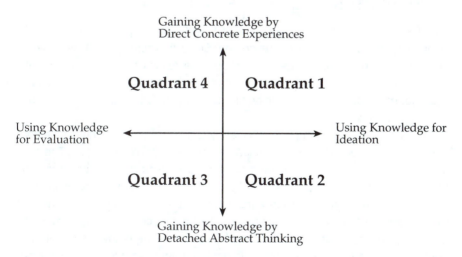

Figure 4.5 The two dimensions of the Basadur Simplex Creative Problem Solving Profile. (The Basadur Problem Solving Model and Profile are copyrighted and are used with the permission of Dr. Min Basadur.)

edge for evaluation. Again, all individuals and organizations use their knowledge in both ways but to differing degrees.

How an individual or organization combines these different ways of gaining and using knowledge determines their problem solving process profile. When you understand these differences, you can shift your own orientation in order to complement the problem solving process preferences of others. Equally important, you can take various approaches to working with people. You can decide on the optimum strategy for helping someone else to learn something. And you can decide whom to turn to for help in ideation or evaluation. Understanding these differences also helps you interact with other people to help them make the best use of the creative problem solving process. For example, you can help strong optimizers discover new problems and facts or present new problems and facts to them. You can help strong implementers better define challenges or present well defined challenges to them. You can help strong generators/initiators evaluate and select from among solutions and make plans, or present to them evaluated solutions and ready-made plans. You can help strong conceptualizer, to convince others of the value of their ideas and push them to act on them, or push their ideas through to acceptance and implementation [Basadur].

> *The goal of brainstorming is to stimulate your mind to trigger concepts or ideas that normal problem solving might miss.*

4.6 BRAINSTORMING STRATEGIES

Alex Osborn, an advertising executive in the 1930s, devised the technique of stimulating ideas known as *brainstorming*. Since that time, countless business and engineering solutions have come about as a result of his method. Basically, brainstorming is a technique used to stimulate as many innovative solutions as possible. These solutions can then be used in both analytic and creative problem-solving practices.

The goal of brainstorming is to stimulate your mind to trigger concepts or ideas that normal problem solving might miss. This has a physiological basis. The mind stores information in a network. Memories are accessed in the brain by remembering the address of the memory. When asked about ideas for potential solutions, some would come just by thinking about the problem. A portion of your brain will be stimulated and ideas will be brought to the surface. However, there will be areas of your brain that will not be searched because the pathways to get there are not stimulated. In brainstorming, we get the brain to search as many regions of the brain as possible.

At times it may seem difficult to generate ideas. Isakssen and Treffinger suggest using the method of idea lists. The concept is simple. Write down the ideas you have currently. Then, use these ideas to branch out into new ideas. To help

> *Let your mind wander and write down any ideas that come into your head.*

stimulate your thinking in new directions, a set of key words was developed by Alex Osborn. These words include:

Adapt—What else is like this? What other ideas does this suggest? Are there any ideas from the past that could be copied or adapted? Whom could I emulate?

Put to other uses—Are there new ways to use the object as is? Are there other uses if modified?

Modify—Could you change the meaning, color, motion, sound, odor, taste, form or shape? What other changes could you make? Can you give it a new twist?

Magnify—What can you add to it? Can you give it a greater frequency? Make it stronger, larger, higher, longer, or thicker? Can you add extra value? Could you add another ingredient? Could you multiply or exaggerate it?

Minify—What could you subtract or eliminate? Could you make it smaller, lighter, or slower? Could you split it up? Could you condense it? Could you reduce the frequency, miniaturize it, or streamline it?

Substitute—What if I used a different ingredient, material, person, process, power source, place, approach or tone of voice? Who else instead? What else instead? What if you put it in another place or in another time?

Rearrange—Could you interchange the pieces? Could you use an alternate layout, sequence, or pattern? Could you change the pace or schedule? What if you transpose the cause and effect?

Reverse—What if you tried opposite roles? Could you turn it backwards, upside down, or inside out? Could you reverse it or see it through a mirror? What if you transpose the positive and negative?

Combine—Could you use a blend, an assortment, an alloy, or an ensemble? Could you combine purposes, units, ideas, functions, or appeals?

Creativity expert Bob Eberle took Osborn's list and created an easy-to-remember word by adding "eliminate" to the list. Eberle's word is SCAMPER. The words used to form SCAMPER are:

Substitute?
Combine?
Adapt?
Modify? Minify? Magnify?
Put to other uses?
Eliminate?
Reverse? Rearrange?

Using the SCAMPER list may help to generate new ideas.

Individual Brainstorming

Brainstorming can be done either individually or in a group. Brainstorming individually has the advantage of privacy. There may be times when you deal with a professional or personal problem that you don't want to share with a group.

Some research shows that individuals may generate more ideas by working by themselves. Edward de Bono attributes this to the concept that "individuals on their own can pursue many different directions. There is no need to talk and no need to listen. An individual on his or her own can pursue an idea that seems 'mad' at first and can stay with the idea until it makes sense. This is almost impossible with a group."

When brainstorming individually, select a place that is free from distraction and interruption. Begin by writing down your initial idea. Now you will want to generate as many other ideas as possible. Let your mind wander and write down any ideas that come into your head. Don't evaluate your ideas; just keep writing them down. If you start to lose momentum, refer to the SCAMPER questions and see if these lead to any other ideas.

There are different formats for recording your ideas when brainstorming. Some find that generating in ordered lists works best for them. Others will write all over a sheet of paper, or in patterns. Kinesthetic (hands-on) learners often find that putting ideas on small pieces of paper, which allows them to move them around, helps the creative process. Auditory (hearing) learners might say the ideas out loud as they are generated.

Group Brainstorming

The goal of group brainstorming is the same as with individual brainstorming—to generate as many potential solutions as possible without judging any of them. The power of the group comes when each member of the group is involved in a way that uses their creativity to good advantage.

There are a few advantages to group brainstorming. The first is simply that the additional people will look at a problem differently and bring fresh perspectives. When brainstorming is done correctly, these different views trigger ideas that you would not have come up with on your own.

Another advantage to group brainstorming is that it gets others involved in the problem-solving process early. As you will see in the following section, a key component in problem solving is implementing your solution. If people whose cooperation you need are in the brainstorming group, they will be much more agreeable to your final solutions. After all, it was partly their idea.

To run an effective group brainstorming session, it helps to use basic guidelines. Those outlined in this section have been proven effective in engineering applications. They are also very helpful for use in student organizations and the committees that engineering students are encouraged to join. This process not only covers the generation of ideas, but also provides a quick way to evaluate and converge on a solution. In some situations, you may want to stop after the ideas are generated and evaluate them later.

The guidelines for this process include:

1. Pick a facilitator
2. Define the problem
3. Select a small group
4. Explain the process
5. Record ideas
6. Involve everyone
7. No evaluating
8. Eliminate duplicates
9. Pick three

Pick a Facilitator

The first step is to select a facilitator who will record the ideas and keep the group focused. The facilitator is also responsible for making sure the group obeys the ground rules of brainstorming.

Define the Problem

It is important that all the participants understand the problem you are looking to solve before generating solutions. Once you start generating ideas, distractions can bring the definition process to a grinding halt. Idea generation would be hampered if the group tried to define the problem they are trying to solve at the wrong time. The definition discussion should happen before the solution idea generating phase.

Small Group

The group size should be kept manageable. Professor Goldschmidt from Purdue University recommends groups of six to 12 members. Groups smaller than that can work, but with less benefit from the group process. Groups larger than 12 become unwieldy and people won't feel as involved. If you need to brainstorm with a larger group, break it into smaller subgroups and reconvene after the groups have come up with separate ideas.

Explain the Process

Providing the details of the process that the group will follow is important. It gives the participants a feeling of comfort to know what they are getting into. Once the process begins, it is counterproductive to go back and discuss ground rules. This can stymie idea generation just like a mis-timed definition of the problem.

Record Ideas

Record ideas in a way that is visible to the whole group. Preferably, arrange the group in a semicircle around the person recording. A chalkboard, flip chart, white-

> *The power of group brainstorming lies in taking advantage of the creative minds of every member of the group, not just the ones who could dominate the discussion.*

board, or newsprint taped to a wall all work well. It is important to record all ideas, even if they seem silly. Often the best ideas come from a silly suggestion that triggers a good idea. By writing the suggestions in a way that is visible to all, the participants can use their sight as well as hearing to absorb ideas which may trigger additional ideas. The use of multiple senses helps to stimulate more ideas. Also, having all the ideas in front of the participants guarantees recollection and allows for new ideas, triggered by earlier ideas. Using the SCAMPER questions is a great way to keep ideas flowing.

Involve Everyone

Start with one idea from the facilitator or another volunteer and write it down. It is easier to get going once the paper or writing surface is no longer completely blank. Go around the group, allowing each person to add one idea per round. If a person doesn't have an idea, let them say "pass," and move on. It is more important to keep moving quickly than to have the participants feel like they must provide an idea every time.

By taking turns, all the participants are ensured an equal opportunity to participate. If the suggestions were taken in a free-flowing way, some participants might monopolize the discussion. The power of group brainstorming lies in taking advantage of the creative minds of every member of the group, not just the ones who could dominate the discussion. Often, the best ideas come from the people who are quiet and would get pushed out of the discussion in a free-flowing setting. It matters not when or how the ideas come, as long as they are allowed to surface.

Continue the process until everyone has "passed" at least once. Even if only one person is still generating ideas, keep everyone involved and keep asking everyone in turn. The one person who is generating ideas might stimulate an idea in someone else at any point. Give everyone the opportunity to come up with a last idea. The last idea may very well be the one that you use.

No Evaluating

This may be hard for the facilitator or some participants. Telling someone that their suggestion is dumb, ridiculous, out-in-left-field, or making any other negative judgment makes that person (and the rest of the group) less likely to speak up. The genius of brainstorming is the free generation of ideas without deciding if they are good until the correct stage. There are countless times when the wackiest ideas are brought up right before the best ideas. Wacky suggestions can trigger ideas that end up being the final solution. Write each idea down, as crazy as some may be. This makes participants feel at ease. They will feel more comfortable making way-out suggestions and will not fear being made fun of or censored.

Avoiding negative comments is one thing, but if you are facilitating, you need to watch for more subtle signals. You might be communicating indirectly to someone that his or her ideas are not good. If you are writing the ideas down, it is natural to say "good idea" or "great idea." What happens, however, if one person gets "great idea" comments and the others don't? Or what if it is just one person who doesn't get the "great idea" comments?

The participants need to feel completely at ease during brainstorming. Providing negative feedback in the form of laughter, sarcastic remarks, or even the absence of praise will work to dampen the comfort level and therefore, the creativity. It is safest not to make any value judgments about any ideas at this point. If you are facilitating, try to respond to each idea the same way and to keep "order in your court," so to speak. If you are a participant, try not to make value statements or jokes about other ideas.

Eliminate Duplicates

After generating ideas, you may want to study the suggestions. In some cases, it is to your advantage to sort out a solution or the top several solutions. Doing this at the end of group brainstorming can be very easy and also serves to involve the group members in the decision process.

The first step is to examine the list of ideas and eliminate duplicates. There is a fine line between eliminating duplicates and creating limiting categories. This step is designed to eliminate repeated ideas. Ask if they really are the same. If they are similar, leave both. Creating categories only reduces the possible solutions and defeats the purpose of brainstorming.

The next step is to allow the group to ask clarifying questions about suggestions. This is still not the time for evaluation-only clarification. Don't let this become a discussion of merits. Clarification may help in eliminating and identifying duplicates.

Pick Three

Once everyone understands all ideas as best they can, have them evaluate the suggestions. This can be done quickly and simply. First, ask everyone to pick their three top choices. (Each person can select more if you need more possibilities or solutions.) After each member has determined these in their own minds, let each member vote "out loud" by marking their choices. Do this with a dot or other mark, but not a 1, 2 and 3. The top ideas are selected based on the total number of marked votes they receive. The winners then can be forwarded to the problem-solving phases to see if any survive as the final solution.

Note that with this method of voting, the group's valuable time is optimized. Time is not wasted determining whether an idea deserves a "1" or a "3." Also, no time is spent on the ideas that no one liked. If all ideas are discussed throughout the process, the ideas that are not chosen by anyone or which are least preferred often occupy discussion for quite a while. It's best to eliminate these likely time sinkholes as soon as possible.

Another benefit of not ranking choices at first is that each member could think that their ideas were the fourth on everyone's list, which might frustrate them. Also, how might it affect someone if their ideas were ranked low by the other members? Such a discouraged person could be one who would have very valuable input the next time it is needed, or it could be that this person will be one whom you need as an ally to implement the group's decision. Either way, there is no need to cast any aspersions on ideas which weren't adopted.

4.7 CRITICAL THINKING

Since engineering is so dominated by systematic problem solving, it is easy to get caught up in the methodologies and look at everything as a problem with a solution. Problem-solving methods teach a systematic manner for analyzing problems which is necessary to tackle engineering problems, but many of life's issues are much more complex and have no one solution.

The author (Oakes) once assigned a project in which students were to design a program using MATLAB® which would predict their financial future and that of a potential spouse. I jokingly suggested that the class use the program when dating to evaluate the impact of a potential spouse on their financial future. ('Sorry, MATLAB says we wouldn't be compatible . . .") The class laughed at the suggestion. Clearly, whom you will marry, or if you will marry, is a complex question and not one that can be solved using some problem-solving methodology or computer algorithm.

Many issues and challenges you will face will have similar complexity and will require a critical perspective. Engineering issues with human, environmental, or ethical impact are among the issues with complex ramifications and require a critical perspective. The issue of poverty is a good example. There have been many programs that have been put into place and many involving engineering-based solutions, but poverty has remained as a pressing social issue. Solutions to the issue of poverty are complex and varying. Though engineers continue to work in this area, programs or solutions are not being brought to bear on an issue that can simply be "solved."

It is easy to get caught up in the processes and methodologies and move quickly to solutions and implementation plans. There will be many times in your career when you will need to critically evaluate what you are doing. It is an important skill to learn to be able to critically evaluate why you are doing something and how you are going about it by taking a step back to gain perspective. At each step, one of the divergent questions that could be asked is "why?"

Sometimes when you critically evaluate what you are doing, you discover deeper meanings or larger issues. An example is the design of toys for children with physical challenges. In the EPICS program (Engineering Projects in Community Service, http://epics.ecn.purdue.edu) students develop engineering-based solutions to community problems. As the students in this program have worked with the children, families, and therapists, they have gained an appreciation for the many complex issues facing the children. When they design toys, they must design them so they can be used within the physical abilities of the children. This is fairly straightforward.

However, what the students have also learned is that there are many other issues, such as socialization issues that they can address. Some of the toys are now designed so that the children with physical challenges can play right along with their peers. They have also learned to design the toys so that the children with physical challenges can control the play. Normally, the children who are not physically challenged control the games and "help" the other children. The engineering students have learned about the socialization of children and its impact on self-esteem.

When working with issues such as people with disabilities, there are often no simple or straightforward answers. They are not simple problems that must be solved, but complex issues that need to be recognized and addressed. By working through the multiple dimensions of these issues, students have become aware of the social and emotional aspects of their work. They have become better designers, but more importantly, they have become better educated about relevant and current issues of the day. When there are discussions about new facilities for people with disabilities, they are able to participate in a meaningful way.

As engineers, you are entrusted with significant responsibility; the fruits of your work have great potential for good, and also potential to harm. While it is vitally important to maintain the highest ethical standards, it is also vital to focus a critical eye on the context and direction of your work. Taking opportunities to step back and evaluate what you are doing and why is as important as the problem-solving methodology we have discussed.

At the beginning of the creative problem-solving process, we discussed how important it was to frame the questions properly. Similarly, when critically evaluating an issue, the question is vitally important. When evaluating an issue, it is important that you become aware of the biases you bring based on your background and experience.

Thomas Edison wanted people around him who would not limit their creative thinking by jumping to conclusions. The story goes that he would take every prospective engineering employee to lunch at his favorite restaurant and recommend the soup. Of course they all ordered the soup unaware that they were being tested. Edison wanted to see if they would salt their soup before tasting it. Salting without tasting, he reasoned, was an indication of someone who jumps to conclusions. He wanted people who were open to questioning and not limited by their preconceptions.

Our own preconceptions make us vulnerable to salting before tasting in many situations. Periodically, ask yourself if you are jumping to conclusions based on your background, personality, or thinking style. Critical thinkers ask the Why and What questions. Why are we approaching the problems this way? What are the implications of the work we are doing? What are the deeper issues? Asking these questions about yourself is a very important part of being a good critical thinker. Why are you studying to become an engineer? What will you do as an engineer to help with your personal fulfillment? Becoming a critical thinker will make you a better problem solver and engineer, and one who is more engaged in and aware of society and its issues.

4.8 CONCLUSIONS

Problem solving is a critical skill within the engineering profession. This chapter introduced numerous techniques and methods for using analytic and creative problem solving. Analytic problem solving strategies are logical and systematic, and tend to yield specific answers. On the other hand, creative problem solving strategies, though they may involve analytic components, are open-ended and complex and tend to yield multiple answers. Estimation, personal problem solving strategies, brainstorming activities, and critical thinking skills involve analytic and creative problem-solving, and represent important attributes that you should develop in preparation for a successful engineering career.

REFERENCES

Basadur, M., *Simplex: A Flight To Creativity*, Creative Education Foundation, Inc., 1994.

Beakley, G. C., Leach, H. W., Hedrick, J. K., *Engineering: An Introduction to a Creative Profession*, 3rd Edition, Macmillan Publishing Co., New York, 1977.

Burghardt, M.D., *Introduction to Engineering Design and Problem Solving*, McGraw-Hill Co., 1999.

Eide, A.R., Jenison, R. D., Mashaw, L. H., Northup, L. L., *Introduction to Engineering Problem Solving,* McGraw-Hill Co., 1998.

Fogler, H. S. and LeBlanc, S. E., *Strategies for Creative Problem Solving*, Prentice Hall, Inc., Englewood Cliffs, New Jersey, 1995.

Gibney, Kate, *Awakening Creativity*, Prism, March 1998, pp. 18–23.

Isaksen, Scott G. and Treffinger, Donald J., *Creative Problem Solving: The Basic Course*, Bearly Limited, Buffalo, New York, 1985.

Lumsdaine, Edward and Lumsdaine, Monika, *Creative Problem Solving—Thinking Skills for a Changing World*, 2nd Edition, McGraw-Hill Co, 1990.

Osborn, A. F., *Applied Imagination: Principles and Procedures of Creative Problem-Solving*, Charles Scriber's Sons, New York, 1963

Panitx, Beth, B*rain Storms*, Prism, March 1998, pp. 24–29.

EXERCISES

1. A new school has exactly 1000 lockers and exactly 1000 students. On the first day of school, the students meet outside the building and agree on the following plan: the first student will enter the school and open all the lockers. The second student will then enter the school and close every locker with an even number (2, 4, 6, 8, etc.). The third student will then 'reverse' every third locker (3, 6, 9, 12, etc.). That is if the locker is closed, he or she will

open it; if it is open, he or she will close it. The fourth student will then reverse every fourth locker, and so on until all 1000 students in turn have entered the building and reversed the proper lockers. Which lockers will finally remain open?

2. You are stalled in a long line of snarled traffic that hasn't moved at all in twenty minutes. You're idly drumming your fingers on the steering wheel, when you accidentally started tapping the horn. Several sharp blasts escaped before you realize it. The driver of the pickup truck in front of you opens his door, gets out and starts to walk menacingly toward your car. He looks big, mean and unhappy. Your car is a convertible and the top is down. What do you do?

3. Your school's team has reached the national championship. Tickets are very difficult to get but you and some friends have managed to get some. You all travel a great distance to the site of the game. The excitement builds on the day of the game until you discover that your tickets are still back in your room on your desk. What do you do? What is the problem that you need to solve?

4. You are a manufacturing engineer working for an aircraft company. The production lines you are responsible for are running at full capacity to keep up with the high demand. One day, you are called into a meeting where you learn that one of your suppliers of bolts has been forging testing results. The tests were never done, so no data exists to tell if the bolts in question meet your standards. You do not know how long the forging of test results has been going on. You are only told that it has been 'a while.' This means that your whole production line including the planes ready to be delivered may be affected. You are asked to develop a plan to manage this crisis. What do you do?

Some background information:
- Bolts are tested as batches or lots. A specified number are taken out of every batch and tested. The testing typically involves loading the bolts until they fail.
- The bolts do not have serial numbers so it is impossible to identify the lot number from which they came.
- The supplier who forged the tests supplies 30% of your inventory of all sizes of bolts.
- Your entire inventory is stored in bins by size. Each bin has a mixture of manufacturers. (To reduce dependence on any one company, you buy bolts from three companies and mix the bolts in the bins sorted by size.)
- Bolts have their manufacturer's symbol stamped on the head of the bolt.
- It takes weeks to assemble or disassemble an aircraft.
- Stopping your assembly line completely to disassemble all aircraft could put your company at financial risk.
- Your customers are waiting on new planes and any delays could cause orders to be lost.
- The FBI has arrested those who forged the test and their business has been closed, at least temporarily.

5. How much of an automobile's tire wears off in one tire rotation?

6. A farmer going on a trip with a squirrel, acorns and a fox had to cross a river in a boat in which he couldn't take more that one of them with him each time he crossed. Since he often had to leave two of them together on one side of the river or the other, how could he plan the crossings so that nothing gets eaten, and they all get across the river safely?

7. Measure the height of your class building using two different methods. Compare your answers and indicate which is more accurate.

8. Pick a grassy area near your class building. Estimate how many blades of grass are in that area. Discuss your methodology.

9. How high do the letters on an expressway sign need to be to be readable?

10. A company has contacted you to design a new kind of amusement park ride. Generate ideas for the new ride. Which idea would you recommend?

11. Estimate the speed of a horse.

12. Estimate the maximum speed of a dog.

13. Estimate the length that a dog has to traverse to go from a sitting position to a full sprint.

14. Estimate the time it takes for a dog to go from a sitting position to a full sprint.

15. Assume that an explosion has occurred in your building. Your room is in tact but the building is in immediate danger of collapsing on you and your classmates. All exits but one (as specified by your instructor) are blocked. The one remaining is nearly blocked. Quickly develop a plan to get your classmates out. Who goes first and who goes last? Why?

16. A child's pool is eight feet in diameter and two feet high. It is filled by a garden hose to a level of one foot. The children complain that it is too cold. Can you heat it up to an acceptable temperature using hot water from the house? How much hot water would you need to add?

17. How else could you heat the water for the children in problem 16?

18. Without referring to a table or book, estimate the melting temperature of aluminum. What are the bounds of potential melting temperatures? Why? What is the actual melting temperature?

19. Select a problem from your calculus class and use the analytic problem solving steps to solve it.

20. Select a problem from your chemistry class and use the analytic problem solving steps to solve it.

21. Select a problem from your physics class and use the analytic problem solving steps to solve it.

22. Write a one to two page paper on a historical figure that had to solve a difficult problem. Provide a description of the problem, solution and the person.

23. Aliens have landed on earth and the come to your class first. They are very frustrated because they can not communicate with you. Develop a plan to break this communication barrier and show them that we are friendly people.

24. You are working on a project that has had many difficulties that are not your fault. However, you are the project leader and your manager has become increasingly frustrated with you and even made a comment that you are the kind of irresponsible person who locks your keys in your car. Your manager is coming into town to see first hand why the project is having problems and you are going to pick her up. You leave early to take time to relax. With the extra time, you decide to take the scenic route and stop the car next to a bubbling stream. Leaving your car, you go over to the stream to just sit and listen. The quiet of the surroundings is just what you needed to calm down before leaving for the airport. Glancing at your watch, you realize that it is time to leave to pick up your manager. Unfortunately, you discover that you indeed have locked your keys in the car. A car passes on the road about every 15 minutes. The nearest house is probably a mile from your location and the nearest town is 15 miles away. The airport is 20 miles away and the flight is due to arrive in 30 minutes. What will you do?

25. You are sitting at your desk in the morning reading your e-mail when your boss bursts into your office. It seems that a local farmer was not happy with your company and has dropped a truckload of potatoes at your plant's entrance. The potatoes are blocking the entrance and must be moved. You have been selected as the lucky engineer to fix this problem. What would you do to move the potatoes and how would you get rid of them? Brainstorm ideas and select the best solution. (Note: You work at a manufacturing plant of some kind that does not use potatoes in its process. The potatoes also appear to be perfectly fine, just in the way.)

26. You work in a rural area that is known for chickens. An epidemic has swept through the area killing thousands of chickens. The EPA has mandated that the chickens may not be put into the landfill nor can they be buried. Develop a plan to get rid of the chickens.

27. A fire has destroyed thousands of acres of forest. Seedlings have been planted in the area but are being destroyed by the local wildlife. Develop a way to reforest the region by preventing the wildlife from eating the seedlings.

28. A survey shows that none of the current high school students in your state are planning to major in engineering when they get to college. Your dean has asked your class to fix this dilemma (with no students, she would be out of a job!). Develop a plan to convince the high school students that engineering is worthwhile.

29. Select a problem from your math book. How many ways can you solve the problem? Demonstrate each method.

30. You and seven of your friends have ordered a round pizza. You need to cut it into eight pieces and are only allowed to make three straight cuts. How can you do this?

31. With which part of the Basadur problem solving process are you most comfortable? Write a one page paper on how your preference affects your problem solving.

32. Take the Basadur problem solving profile test. Report on your scores. How will this information affect your ability to solve problems.

33. You and your classmates have discovered that your funding for college will be withdrawn after this semester. Develop ideas on how you could obtain the money for the rest of your college expenses.

34. Your class has been hired by a new automotive company that wants to produce a brand new car. Their first entry into the market must be truly innovative. Do a preliminary design of this car. What features would it have to set it apart from current vehicles?

35. An alumnus of your engineering program has donated money to build a jogging track that would encircle your campus. The track will be made of a recycled rubberized material. How much of this rubberized material will be needed?

36. Every Christmas season it seems that one toy becomes a "I have to have one" craze. You and some classmates have been hired to come up with next year's toy of the season. What is it?

37. A professional sports team has decided to locate in your town. A local businessperson is going to build a stadium for the team. Unfortunately, the site is contaminated. The project will fall through unless you can devise a way to get rid of the contaminated soil under the new arena. What do you do with the soil?

38. NASA has decided to send astronauts to other planets in the solar system. Psychologists, however, have determined that the astronauts will need something to keep them occupied during the months of travel or they will develop severe mental problems that would threaten the mission. Your job is to devise ways to keep the astronauts occupied for the long journey. Remember that you are limited to what will fit in a space capsule.

39. Landfill space is rapidly running out. Develop a plan to eliminate your city's dependence on the local landfill. The city population is 100,000.

40. An appliance manufacturer has hired you to expand their market. Your job is to develop a new household appliance. What is it and how will it work?

41. College students often have trouble waking up for early classes. Develop a system that will guarantee that the students wake up and attend classes.

42. Select one of your classes. How could that class be more effective in helping your learn?

43. Prepare a one-page report on a significant engineering solution developed in the past five years. Evaluate its effectiveness and report (both intended and unintended) on the outcomes of this solution.

44. Habitat for Humanity International spearheaded an initiative to eliminate substandard housing within the Georgia county in which it is headquartered. One of the first steps was to develop a set of standards to determine if housing was substandard or not. Develop criteria for your own community for determining whether a housing unit is substandard.

45. If your community were to undertake an initiative like the one presented in the previous question, what would need to be done (both from an engineering and community perspective)?

46. Identify one current topic related to engineering or technology that has no single simple solution and write a brief paper discussing issues related to the topic.

47. In the critical thinking section in this chapter, engineers had to pass Edison's "salt test." Identify areas in your own thinking where you might tend to "salt before tasting" (where you might jump to conclusions or use your own biases to overlook potential options).

48. Critically evaluate why you are majoring in engineering. What do you hope to gain by studying engineering?

49. Write a one-page paper on your responsibilities to society as a citizen in your community and as an engineer.

50. Early one morning is starts to snow at a constant rate. Later, at 6:00 A.M., a snow plow sets out to clear a straight street. The plow can remove a fixed volume of snow per unit time. In other words, its speed it inversely proportional to the depth of the snow. If the plow covered twice as much distance in the first hour as the second hour, what time did it start snowing?

51. While three *wise* men are asleep under a tree a mischievous boy paints their foreheads red. Later they all wake up at the same time and all three start laughing. After several minutes suddenly one stops. Why did he stop?

52. Using just a 5-gallon bucket and a 3-gallon bucket, can you put four gallons of water in the 5-gallon bucket? (Assume that you have an unlimited supply of water and that there are no measurement markings of any kind on the buckets.)

53. A bartender has a three-pint glass and a five-pint glass. A customer walks in and orders four pints of beer. Without a measuring cup but with an unlimited supply of beer how does he get a single pint in either glass?

54. You are traveling down a path and come to a fork in the road. A sign lays fallen at the fork indicating that one path leads to a village where everyone tells the truth and the other to a village where everyone tells lies. The sign has been knocked down so you do not know which path leads to which vil-

lage. Then someone from one of the villages (you don't know which one) comes down the path from which you came. You may ask him one question to determine which path goes to which village. What question do you ask?

55. Four mathematicians have the following conversation:
    Alice: I am insane.
    Bob: I am pure.
    Charlie: I am applied.
    Dorothy: I am sane.
    Alice: Charlie is pure.
    Bob: Dorothy is insane.
    Charlie: Bob is applied.
    Dorothy: Charlie is sane.
    You are also given that:
    • Pure mathematicians tell the truth about their beliefs.
    • Applied mathematicians lie about their beliefs.
    • Sane mathematicians beliefs are correct.
    • Insane mathematicians beliefs are incorrect.
    Describe the four mathematicians.

56. Of three men, one man always tells the truth, one always tells lies, and one answers yes or no randomly. Each man knows which man is which. You may ask three yes/no questions to determine who is who. If you ask the same question to more than one person you must count it as a question used for each person asked. What three questions should you ask?

57. Tom is from the census bureau and greets Mary at her door. They have the following conversation:
    | Tom: | I need to know how old your three kids are. |
    | Mary: | The product of their ages is 36. |
    | Tom: | I still don't know their ages. |
    | Mary: | The sum of their ages is the same as my house number. |
    | Tom: | I still don't know their ages. |
    | Mary: | The younger two are twins. |
    | Tom: | Now I know their ages! Thanks! |
    How old are Mary's kids and what is Mary's house number?

58. Choose a device, system, or process of interest. Write a brief description of this entity, and then provide answers to the following questions:
    What aspects of creative problem solving do you think engineers used in the design of this entity? How might the people using it enhance their creativity through its design?

59. Interview a practicing engineer. Find out what types of creative problem solving the engineer does as part of his/her job. What techniques are most useful to the engineer? Under what circumstances is the engineer the most creative? Does the engineer have any advice for you to enhance your creative self?

60. Research an inventor, engineer, or person engaged in creative endeavors whose work you find intriguing. How does/did this person use creativity in their life and work? The following list may be of interest:

Benjamin Bannaker	Thomas Jefferson
Patricia Bath	Margaret Knight
George Washington Carver	Jerome Lemelson
Leonardo da Vinci	Maya Lin
Toshitada Doi	Ellen Ochoa
Charles and Ray Eames	Barbara McClintock
Gertrude Elion	Ralph Teetor
Lillian Moller Gilbreth	Elijah McCoy
Elizabeth Lee Hazen and	Madame C.J. Walker
Rachel Fuller Brown	Mary Walton
Beulah Henry Frank	Lloyd Wright
Grace Hopper	

61. Select an innovative product and research the story of its inventors. Prepare a presentation on how the ideas were formed and the concept generated.

62. Research an organization that has a commitment to innovation. What does this organization do to promote innovation? Why do you think these techniques work?

63. Organizations have problem solving styles. Select an organization and prepare a brief report on their problem solving styles.

64. Brainstorm ideas for toys for children with physical disibilities. Narrow your choices to the top three and identify the benefits of each design. What are the important issues that you would need to consider in your designs?

65. Reverse the direction of the fish image below by moving only three sticks:

66. Think of how things work in the natural world, and how these principles have been integrated into the design of a typical device, for example, an airplane, a filter, or a bird feeder (or another device of your choosing).

67. Use the brainstorming methods discussed in this chapter to generate at least 20 ideas on your project.

68. Brainstorm using the x-3-5 method (where x is the number of people on your team). Use this silent brainstorming method as follows:
   • Each team member has five minutes to write down three ideas on a sheet of paper; these three ideas should be written across the top of the paper, such that other ideas can be added under each idea.
   • After the five minute brainstorming period, pass your sheet of paper to the group member next to you. Take another five minutes, and add three more ideas that build on the first three ideas. Write these "building" ideas directly under the initial idea listed

- Repeat this process as many times as you have members in your group.
- Discuss the results; see if your discussion results in more idea generation

69. A "back door" approach to brainstorming. Think about a technical problem that you are working with in your group. Brainstorm to try to find solutions to the problem. Set your ideas aside, and as a group, play the game Cranium. When you are finished, go back to the problem as a group and continue brainstorming and thinking. How many other ideas can you generate?

Chapter 5

Teaming Skills and Conflict Resolution

Individual commitment to a group effort — that is what makes a team work, a company work, a society work, a civilization work.

—Vince Lombardi

5.1 TEAMING SKILLS OVERVIEW

Teaming skills are important because engineering projects are being increasingly designed and executed in teams. Many college students are reluctant to work in teams because they have had a bad experience working in a group. Throwing people together into a group to work on a project and/or to accomplish goals will not work unless those people have learned something about how to work in groups. In this section, you will learn basic teaming skills, including working with others in a group, team dynamics, leadership skills, and conflict resolution.

Definition

"A team is a small number of people with complementary skills who are committed to a common purpose, set of performance goals, and approach for which they hold themselves mutually accountable." Katzenbach and Smith, 1993 (Harvard Business Review, 93, 111–124)

5.2 THE KEIRSEY-BATES PERSONALITY INDICATOR AND WORKING IN GROUPS

Many frameworks exist for understanding people and how they communicate and work together. One such framework is the Keirsey-Bates Personality Indicator This personality test describes the behavior of people through four indices:

- The source of personal energy: extraverts (E) versus introverts (I)
- The information-gathering function: sensors (S) versus intuitives (N)
- The decision-making function: thinkers (T) versus feelers (F)
- The lifestyle orientation function: judging (J) versus perceiving (P)

The test consists of 70 questions, each of which has two possible answers. A copy of the test and scoring procedure is included in the book by D. Keirsey and

ISTJ	ISTP	ESTP	INFP
Management	Engineer	Culinary arts	Ministry
Education	Legal secretary	Marketing	Social worker
Lawyer	Professional sports	Detective	Teaching
Engineer	Law enforcement	Auditor	Counseling
Accounting	Commercial artist	Sales/retail	Journalist
Administration	Market analyst	Entrepreneur	Artist
Dentist	Chiropractor	Insurances sales	Architect
Protection	Statistician	Paramedic	Health officer
Veterinarian	Crisis intervention	Small business manager	Social scientist
Computer analyst		Radiology technician	entertainer

ESTJ	ISFJ	INFJ	INTJ
Management	Physician	Teaching	Management
Banking	Counseling	Missionary	Architect
Engineer	Nurse	Counseling	Researcher
Career counselor	Secretary	Artist	Design
Accountant	Librarian	Marketing	Teaching
Lawyer	Office manager	Social worker	Scientist
Contractor	Inn keeper Social	Biological science	Computer analyst
Pharmacist	worker	Novelist / playwright	Engineer
Mechanic	Broker / realtor	researcher	Lawyer
credit analyst	Financial aid officer		social worker

ESFP	ESFJ	INTP	ENTJ
Social work	Social work	Management	Consulting
Selling	Physician	Ministry	Lawyer
Nursing	Counseling	Consulting	Management
Counseling	Nursing	Teaching	Social scientist
Promoter	Teaching	Physicist	Entrepreneur
Designer	Dentist	Statistician	Sales
Teacher	Sales	Historian	Academic dean
Politician	Marketing director	Sales agent	Computer analyst
Respiratory therapist	Bank employee	Pharmacist	Teaching (science)
Child care worker		Architect	Judge

ENFP	ENFJ	ISFP	ENTP
Counseling	Counseling	Radiology technician	Management
Politics	Social work	Bookkeeper	Teaching
Selling	Consulting	Legal secretary	Consulting
Teaching	Ministry	Ministry	Writer
Social work	Pharmacist	Jeweler	Scientist
Clergy	Teacher	Fashion designer	Social scientist
Advertising	Physician	Botanist	Auditor
Radiology technician	Travel agent	Physical therapist	Radiology technician
Writer	Recreational director	Mechanic	Real estate agent
Artist		Medical assistant	Engineer

Figure 5.1 Keirsey-Bates Personality Indicators.

Quote on Working On a Team

"My experience as a service-learning student reminded me of being on the crew team. When I first joined crew, I decided that I was going to be the strongest rower on the team. I expended a ton of energy to be the leader, which (to me) meant being the strongest rower, and we got out there in a race and I pulled as hard as I could. We lost because the point is not for me to pull harder than everyone else; it is for everyone to pull the same amount, which moves us efficiently through the water. By pulling harder than everyone else, I pulled us off course and we lost the race. It taught me an important thing: that I need to pull my weight, but only my weight, because one person pulling harder than everyone else can pull the entire project off course. The other important thing I realized was that it is critical that everyone pull the same amount of weight; it's the only way to keep the project on track."

M. Bates, *Please Understand* Me (pp 5–13), or at http://keirsey.com/. A person's Keirsey-Bates Type is determined from this test; the Type is a four-letter profile that describes a person's characteristics.[1] Detailed descriptions of each profile are contained in *Please Understand Me*. In this book, we will concentrate on descriptions of the individual letters and how they affect working in groups.

Note on career correlations box: Do not assume that because **engineer** was not listed among the typical occupations for your personality type, you are not cut out to be an engineer. This is not true. One of the authors of this book is an ENFX (split equally between ENFP and ENFJ). The career list is only a correlation, meaning that occupations common to the personality profiles are listed.[2] That is all it says; nothing more, nothing less.

1. The Source of Energy: Extraverts (E) and Introverts (I)

Extraverts make up approximately 75% of the U.S. population, and can be described as social butterflies. Extraverts get energy from interacting with others, enjoy interacting with large groups (e.g., in parties), and have no problem initiating conversations with people they do not know. Introverts comprise about 25% of the population, and can be described as reserved. Introverts get energy from

---

[1] Some people may have an equal number of responses for each of the indices in a given letter, for example, a person might have an equal number of introvert and extravert answers. When this happens, the letter "X" is assigned to that letter, indicating an equal preference for each set of traits. People in this category are encouraged to consult Keirsey & Bates to read the personality profiles for each type, and to choose the type that they think describes them best. Another strategy would be to take the Myers-Briggs personality indicator, which consists of approximately 135 questions instead of 70.

[2] From TYPE TALK AT WORK by Otto Lroeger and Janet M. Thuesen, © 1992 by Otto Kroeger and Janet M. Thuesen. Used by permission of Dell Publishing, a division of Random House, Inc.

The 16 Types and Their Slogans (MBTI™)

ISTJ: Doing what should be done
ISFJ: A high sense of duty
INFJ: An inspiration to others
INTJ: Everything has room for improvement
ISTP: Ready to try anything once
ISFP: Sees much but shares little
INFP: Performing noble service to aid society
INTP: A love of problem solving
ESTP: The ultimate realists
ESFP: You only go around once in life
ENFP: Giving life an extra squeeze
ENTP: One exciting challenge after another
ESTJ: Life's administrators
ESFJ: Hosts and hostesses of the world
ENFJ: Smooth talking persuaders
ENTJ: Life's natural leaders

---

doing solitary activities in quiet places (they do this to recharge) and are drained when interacting with people at parties, where they wait to be approached instead of initiating conversation. Introverts tend to have strong friendships with a few people, where extraverts have many friendships that tend to be more superficial. The following table represents typical words and phrases used to describe these differences:

Extraverts	Introverts
Sociability	Territoriality
Interaction	Concentration
External	Internal
Breadth	Depth

Words of Caution

- No one is completely one way all the time. The indices represent preferences, or what a person tends to do in a given situation. This does not mean an extravert needs no alone time, or an introvert will always want to be alone.
- The MBTI is a framework, or method, for providing perspective on yourself, others, and working in groups. It is not the only way to describe the human experience. It is presented here as a guide, and not as an absolute theory to be followed at all costs.

Extensive	Intensive
Multiplicity of relationships	Limited relationships
Expenditure of energies	Conservation of energies
Interest in external events	Interest in internal events
Gregarious	Reflective
Speak, then think	Think, then speak

2. The Information-Gathering Function: Sensors (S) and Intuitives (N)

Sensors make up approximately 75% of the population and tend to face life observantly. Sensors crave enjoyment, and are pleasure lovers and consumers; they love life as it is. Intuitives encompass 25% of the population, and face life expectantly. Intuitives crave inspiration and are inventors and promoters; they tend to be restless with life as it is. This indicator is believed to be the most important in education. Sensors learn best with hands-on experience, identify well with concepts that are practical and actual, and prefer instruction to consist of sequentially ordered facts, whereas intuitives learn best through thinking about "the big picture," identify well with theoretical concepts, and enjoy instruction that encourages imagination. In college classrooms, students are approximately equally divided into the S and N functions. However, 75% of college professors are intuitives. This difference is thought to account for a lot of the disconnect between students and professors (professors tend to teach things in a way that makes the most sense to them, which may not make sense to many of the students). One final way to sum it up is this: the sensor sees the trees, and the intuitive sees a forest. The following table describes the differences between sensors and intuitives.

Sensors	Intuitives
Experience	Hunches
Past	Future
Realistic	Speculative
Perspiration	Inspiration
Actual	Possible
Down to earth	Head in clouds
Utility	Fantasy
Fact	Fiction
Practicality	Ingenuity
Sensible	Imaginative

3. The Decision-Making Function: Thinkers (T) and Feelers (F)

People who use objective, impersonal ideas as the basis for decision making are thinkers, and people who use personal ideas and thoughts as the basis for decision making are feelers. This is the only type indicator which is not split equally between genders, as approximately 66% of men are thinkers and 66% of women are feelers (Kroeger and Thuesen, Type Talk, p 34). Thinkers value logic above sentiment, while feelers value sentiment above logic. One example to illustrate the difference between thinkers and feelers involves relationships: a T wants to understand intimacy, while an F wants to experience it. The following table represents differences between thinkers and feelers.

Thinkers	Feelers
Objective	Subjective
Principles	Values
Policy	Social values
Laws	Extenuating circumstances
Criterion	Intimacy
Firmness	Persuasion
Impersonal	Personal
Justice	Humane
Categories	Harmony
Standards	Good or bad
Critique	Appreciate
Analysis	Sympathy
Allocation	Devotion

4. The Lifestyle Orientation Function: Judgers (J) and Perceivers (P)

Judgers and perceivers are split equally in the U.S. population. This index is the most misunderstood among the four. Being a J does not mean that a person judges others, and being a P does not mean that a person perceives others. The basis for the difference between Js and Ps is how they handle situations and represents the greatest source of interpersonal tensions. A judger wants to get something done quickly and is more decisive than curious. A perceiver wants to think about a situation to make sure that all options are considered; a P is more curious than decisive. Js like deadlines, and feel stress before decisions have been made and plans have been completed; Ps feel constrained by deadlines, and feel stress after they have made decisions or completed plans. The differences in this index are contained in the table below:

Judgers	Perceivers
Settled	Pending
Decided	Gather more data
Fixed	Flexible
Plan ahead	Adapt as you go
Run one's life	Let life happen
Closure	Open options
Decision making	Treasure hunting
Planned	Open-ended
Completed	Emergent

Decisive	Tentative
Wrap it up	Something will turn up
Urgency	There's plenty of time
Deadline	What deadline?
Get show on the road	Let's wait and see

These indices should give you some ideas about how people function in life and how they might take their preferences and behaviors into a group situation. The purpose of the next section is to discuss the implications of the Keirsey-Bates Type Indicator on working in teams and how you best use these differences to have a positive experience working in groups.

Extraverts will probably not have trouble voicing their thoughts, opinions, and feelings in a group setting. They tend to thrive in activities such as brainstorming (the free flow of ideas) and will voice the first things that come to mind. Introverts tend to sit back and watch the free flow of ideas; they will think deeply about some ideas being exchanged, but may not voice their opinions unless prompted. The best case scenario for having a balanced interaction between extraverts and introverts is as follows:

- Everyone participates
- Everyone listens to each person's ideas without interrupting
- Everyone contributes to the free flow of ideas
- Ideas are thought about in depth before decision making

Extraverts should remember to include everyone in conversation.

Introverts should remember to voice their thoughts, ideas, opinions, and feelings.

In a group engineering project, sensors will concentrate on step-by-step procedures for getting things done and will concentrate on the details of the design, i.e., here's a step-by-step method for designing a car engine. Intuitives will focus on creativity and the overall process through which the design can be completed. ("I've got an idea for a completely new kind of car engine.") The best-case scenario for having a successful interaction between intuitives and sensors is as follows:

- The work has a process for completion
- The work incorporates big picture and creative ideas
- The work has a practical division
- The work uses a step-by-step method for completing each portion
- The work has sufficient detail

Sensors should remember that the process and the big picture provides a logical framework for all the details needed for a successful project.

Intuitives should remember the facts are every bit as important as the big picture and the process.

When working in groups, thinkers will ask and be interested in what you think about the design. Feelers are more interested in how you feel about the design. For example, a thinker might ask the group, "What you do think about extending this lever by two centimeters?" A feeler might pose the question as "How do you feel about extending this lever by two centimeters?" To function ideally in a team situation, groups should place equal value on how it makes decisions. That is, thoughts are as important as feelings, and vice versa.

A feeler should remember a thinker possesses deep emotions though they may not be evident.

A thinker should remember a feeler possesses logical thinking skills though they may not be verbalized.

When working in a group situation, Js will tend to make decisions about the project quickly and decisively, while Ps will want to think more about decisions and choices before making them. Create an enjoyable work environment for your project. If the environment is scheduled, structured, ordered, and planned, it will be conducive to judgers and stressful to perceivers. If the environment is flexible, spontaneous, adaptive, and responsive, it will seem like a paradise to the perceiver and a punishment to the judger. The key is to establish a working environment that contains elements of comfort for judgers and perceivers.

- Your group should have a method for making decisions.
- Your group should have a forum in which to discuss options before making decisions.
- Your group should complete the discussion and decision making without procrastinating.

Judgers need perceivers to inspire them to relax and not to make a major issue of everything.

Perceivers need judgers to help them become reasonably organized and to follow through on decisions and actions.

The basis for all successful working in groups is respect. You must respect yourself and your group members, including your community partners.

Now that you have a sense of how individuals in a group might act, let's consider teaming skills in a global sense.

5.3 TEAM DYNAMICS

The ways in which successful teams accomplish goals have been well established. The purpose of this section is to share this information at the team level. In the previous section, we talked about the characteristics of individuals in a team setting. This section will describe the characteristics of a team setting. We are concerned with two major ideas in this section: describing the features of successful teams, and describing the process through which a team develops over time.

Features of successful teams

Successful teams should have members that are familiar with the individual skills shared in the previous section and in the next 2 chapters. Members must understand themselves and others, be respectful at all times, and be willing to work toward the team mission and goals. Several other features involve the team itself. The following list describes the requisites of a successful team.

Hold relular meetings. Holding regular meetings keeps all team members on track and facilitates communication among members. The meeting should be held in the same time, day of the week, and location to ensure that everyone blocks this time out of their schedule consistently. The team leader should plan and organize the meeting in advance. The team leader is the person in the group responsible for completing the assigned team tasks. You might have one team leader throughout a project (common in industry) or you might rotate the team leader position for each meeting so all members share the project leadership.

The team leader in charge of a meeting should create an agenda, which is an outline of all activities to be discussed at the meeting. The meeting should have a set time (e.g., one hour) and should start with the reading of the minutes, which provide a written summary of the previous meeting. When all team members approve the minutes from the last meeting, the meeting proceeds.

The team leader should make sure that a recorder (note taker) is present to generate minutes for the current meeting. Ideally, the agenda and minutes from the previous meeting should be provided in written form for all team members prior to the meeting.

The team leader is in charge of ensuring that the meeting proceeds according to the agenda, and that the team does not spend too much time discussing one item. At the meeting's conclusion, each team member should articulate the tasks he or she needs to perform before the next meeting.

A Sample Agenda

ME 430: Machine Design
Team Meeting, February 4, 2004, 2:00–3:00 P.M.
Room 142 Robinson Hall

Agenda

Approval of minutes from January 27 meeting
Old business:
- Signing contracts with community partner
- Coordinating schedules with John's new job

New business:
- Initial meeting with community partner
- Finalizing group responsibilities

- Discussion of information to be gathered for design
- Preparing for first oral presentation of our project February 15

Other business?

Minutes Should Contain the Following:

- Information regarding the company or course, name of team or division, and date
- Members present
- Time the meeting was brought to order
- Approval of minutes from last meeting (note any changes to the minutes)
- Old business (discussion regarding any issues not finished during last meeting, or new information on old business)
- New business
- The time the meeting was adjourned
- Responsibilities for each team member should be clearly communicated in the minutes

Have a working knowledge of team roles. These roles can be task oriented, which pertain to the selection and execution of a team's tasks, or can be behavior oriented, which pertain to the environment in which the team functions. These roles have some overlap (behaviorally oriented team roles can become task oriented if the team identifies them as crucial to accomplishing a task).

Role	Description
Task Roles	
Team leader	Ensures that objectives and goals of the team are met effectively and efficiently.
Recorder	Writes down the team meeting discussions and distributes to all team members.
Devil's advocate	Provides the opposite point of view in team discussions (usually done on purpose to help brainstorm ideas or evaluate current ideas).
Facilitator	Summarizes group discussions, gives relationships among ideas and suggestions, provides possible directions to go based on group discussions, and elicits cooperation among members. May be a team leader.
Gatekeeper	Ensures the group gives its opinions and thoughts during the meeting.
Mediator	Ensures any differences in opinion are made explicit and reconciles these differences into a workable solution.

Behavioral Roles

Initiating	Suggesting ideas, ways of looking at a problem, ways of doing things, etc.
Seeking input	Encouraging others to voice their thoughts, ideas, and feelings. Seeking clarification on discussion.
Giving input	Stating thoughts, ideas, feelings, and opinions.
Encouraging	Providing confidence for members to speak and being understanding and welcoming of all information shared.
Evaluating	Weighing information to make group decisions and checking to ensure that the group is on track with specific and overall goals.
Relieving tension	Using humor or wisdom to dispel tension, addressing negative dynamics or feelings.

Keep in mind that the behavioral roles summarized in the table represent positive roles in a group situation. Negative behavioral roles can disrupt or dominate conversation with excessive joking around and constantly seeking attention or recognition. Methods for dealing with problem characters are discussed in section 5.5 of this chapter.

- **Share the workload and the responsibility.** Each team member must have an equal contribution to the project and must be accountable for this contribution. Because your tasks will develop as the project takes shape, successful teams tend to renegotiate responsibilities to keep them equivalent for all members. See section 5.4 for more on responsibility and accountability issues.
- **Establish a creative environment.** In a team environment, all members must be free to share their ideas, thoughts, and feelings, and to discuss, analyze, and evaluate these ideas as they relate to the design project. See section 5.5 for a more detailed discussion of creative conflict, which is a positive feature for establishing a creative environment. Group members should develop and use their creative skills.
- **Have a method for making decisions.** This matter is important for teams. Most tend to be democratic and take the majority vote for decision making. This is only one model, however, and may not work if the number of team members is even. For example, if the vote is 2-2 regarding a decision, how will the group resolve this issue? Some student teams with even numbers will ask the instructor and community partner to cast tie-breaking votes. Other models include having a team leader make decisions, or giving this person tie-breaking authority after a team vote. The decision may be left to a smaller number of team personnel if they have particular expertise with

regard to the issue. Whatever the method(s) for decision making, they must be defined and understood by all team members before the project starts.

- **Have a method for resolving conflicts and dealing with problem characters.** As stated previously, having some conflict in a group setting is productive because such conflict ensures that all ideas are shared and discussed openly. However, if a team is at an impasse, then the team must have a method for resolving its conflict. Likewise, if the team has one or more problem characters (members that disrupt the group), the team needs a method for dealing with that member. Section 5.5 is devoted to conflict resolution and dealing with the problematic behavior of group members.

Stages of Team Development

Tuckman (1965) has suggested that teams pass through several stages during their journey from the start to the end of a project. These stages are forming, storming, norming, performing, and adjourning. Forming occurs in the initial project stages when group members are getting to know one another. The team setting environment is tentative; personalities and technical information are being shared and exchanged, and some anxiety may exist because group members are not clear on what they need to accomplish and how they will accomplish it. After the initial period, storming occurs, which is characterized by conflict. Group members may experience personality conflicts and/or disagreements on how to accomplish team tasks and goals. The third stage is norming, which occurs after the disputes in storming have been resolved. Team members build trust, work together toward a common goal, and understand their individual roles and contributions. This stage is characterized by team cohesiveness. In performing, the team addresses problems and achieve goals. This stage is marked by excellent teamwork and cooperation among members, high achievement, and strong project execution in terms of decision making and problem solving. In the final stage, adjourning, the project is completed and the team may break up. This stage may be characterized by elation and sadness by team members.

Now that we've covered the basics with regard to individual and team dynamics, let's look at the management aspects of teaming skills, including leadership and conflict resolution.

5.4 LEADERSHIP SKILLS

Every person has leadership potential. You need the ability to facilitate cooperation among people and to work with people toward a common goal. According to Loeb and Kindel (1999), possessing strong leadership skills relies on five major things:

- Being a good listener
- Being a good facilitator
- Having a vision of what needs to be accomplished

- Being responsible for you and your team
- Being able to plan your project

> *Leadership should be born out of the understanding of the needs of those who would be affected by it.*
> —Marian Anderson p.133 or 134

Good Listening

Being a good listener involves active listening. This means that you are concentrating on the person and what he or she is saying with the overall objective of understanding them. People speak at about 125 words per minute, but can think at the rate of about 500 words per minute. Active listening involves using those other 375 words of capacity to concentrate on what people are saying, how they are saying it, their body language, and so on. Every ounce of your mental energy goes to listening when you are doing it well.

> *Be a good listener. Your ears will never get you in trouble.*
> —Frank Tyger

You can use several techniques to listen to another person actively. The first is to stop talking. Although this seems obvious, you can become so engaged with speaking that you forget to stop: you have two ears and one mouth; use them in proportion.

Stop what you are doing when listening to another person. Things like reading the paper, twiddling your thumbs, reading your e-mail, or answering your cell phone will distract you from listening.

Another useful technique in active listening involves reflecting or repeating what was said to you. In this way, you can ensure that you understood the main points and that you did not misinterpret what was said. For example, you might start a reflecting sentence as follows: "If I understood what you said correctly . . ." or, "You mean. . . ."

Finally, ask questions. In this way, you can clarify information and can get more information you need or want. Open-ended questions (those that require more than a yes or no answer) can get more information. Be respectful of the other person when asking questions. For example, you are more likely to understand the person with whom you are speaking and his or her motivation if you ask a question like, "How did you come to that decision?" instead of, "Why on earth did you do that?" You will have a more fruitful conversation if you convey your respect for the other person and her or his thoughts, feelings, and ideas.

Good Facilitating

According to the Merriam Webster dictionary, to facilitate means to make easier or to help bring about. As a leader, one of your main jobs (and challenges) is to create a solution or more easily address a community need. Many of the skills we have already talked about will help you to be a good facilitator. You need to be able to communicate with others, listen actively, solve problems creatively, understand team dynamics, and understand all the people with whom you are working. Facilitating means you put all these things together to reach your team's goals. Keys to remember when you are facilitating are cooperation, trust, and motivation.

Having a Vision of What Needs to Be Accomplished

To understand the concept of vision, think about the following analogy: if the project for which you are the team leader is the trees, then your vision as the team leader is the forest. A vision is an overall concept into which your project fits. One vision of service-learning is enhancing democracy and building a society in which everyone has equal access to goods and services. A service-learning project would fit into that vision in a more specific way, for example, the design and construction of a bike path in Terre Haute, Indiana (see Profile chapter for details) provided enhanced access to the community through additional transportation routes. Your vision could be an ideal, a concept, a dream, or a combination. A good leader will have the means for achieving a goal, but a greater vision into which achieving that goal will fit. You should share your vision with your team members who will hopefully accept it. Make your vision a positive thing and frame it positively. Almost everyone is interested in working to make things better.

Characteristics of Good Leaders (Stevenson and Whitmore, 2001)

Personal traits

- Manage time effectively
- Recognize the limitations of authority and expertise
- Delegate tasks effectively and fairly
- Have flexible problem-solving approaches
- Make decisions fairly and in a timely manner

Communication style

- Consult frequently with other team members about issues of concern
- Are good listeners, i.e., spend more time listening than talking
- Encourage the expression of conflicting opinions and alternative viewpoints
- Provide honest and specific feedback about individual and team performance
- Resolve conflicts between team members effectively and fairly

Motivational ability

- Keep the team focused on the tasks at hand
- Encourage team members to fulfill their personal and team goals

---

> *Credit is never diluted when shared.*

Being Responsible for You and Your Team

During the course of your project, some things will go well and others will not. A strong leader will encourage team members during good times and challenging times. As the leader, you are ultimately accountable for the team's successes and failures. Share your team's successes with everyone and publicly praise your team members for a job well done. When things are not going to plan, take responsibility in public for any shortcomings. If necessary, make adjustments and hold individual team members accountable for addressing any conflicts or issues.

> *The mark of a good leader is to know when it's time to follow.*
> —Susie Switzer

Being Able to Plan Your Project

Planning is as much art as science. Plans should be flexible to respond to the unexpected, which occur during a project. The next chapter on project management skills shows how to plan and execute a project.

5.5 CONFLICT RESOLUTION AND PROBLEM CHARACTERS

Conflict resolution skills are important for successfully working in groups. Your groups should have some conflict. Without conflict, you are not fully exercising your thoughts and sharing your ideas and views. Your group should have creative conflict, which is a happy medium between group think and chaos. Group think occurs when the group's cohesiveness is more important than the actual project at hand. Thus, people who have different ideas are reluctant to share them because it will cause some conflict in the group. A group situation is chaotic if no one agrees on anything.

Remember that groups will be most successful in a creative conflict environment in which all group members are respected. The conflict should be focused on the tasks and not on the group members' personalities. All group members should be committed to solving the conflict acceptably.

The major principle of conflict resolution is to understand before you are understood (Covey, 1989). If all group members respect one another and can clearly and confidently express their thoughts, feelings, ideas, and opinions, then resolving the conflict is easier. Below is a stepwise model for dispute resolution (from Stevenson and Whitmore, 2002):

1. Identify the problem to be resolved
   a. Describe all sides of the dispute

      b.   Listen carefully to all sides

      c.   Ensure that everyone accepts the definition of the problem

2. Generate alternative solutions
3. Evaluate alternative solutions
4. Ensure that all members accept decisions
5. Implement the solution
6. Set a target date to evaluate the solution's effectiveness

In a perfect world, problem characters do not exist. However, theory does not always translate nicely into practice, and chaos can wend its way into your group. Jalajas and Sutton (1985) have defined several problem characters in groups. Perhaps you have run across these characters and perhaps you have been one of these characters.

The bully (or the lazy bully). A person who insists on having things a certain way and will bully, cajole, badger, and even threaten other group members to get his or her way. The lazy bully plays the bully role, but does not contribute much (if any) work to the project. Often, the bully thinks that she or he can do better work without the group members and does not include other group members in assigned activities. Bullies make other group member(s) feel stupid and inadequate.

The deadbeat. A person who does not show up to meetings, does not participate in group exercises, and does not complete her or his work in a timely manner, if at all.

The martyr. A group member who goes the extra mile in terms of work or leading the group. Then he or she complains about doing all the work and publicly wishes that other group members were as responsible. "The martyr is certain he or she is getting the worst assignment, the worst chores to perform, and has the dumbest partners for group members. The martyr may complain to other group members, or to the instructor about the burden. The martyr does not want anything to change but wants others to feel guilty." (Jalajas and Sutton, 1985).

The saboteur. A person that changes the group's work without letting the group know to enhance the project's quality. Many times, these actions result in an overall decrease of the group's project quality though the saboteur did not intend this.

The whiner. A person who always complains about the project, the time commitment, the meeting times, the other group members, the project's progress, that no one else is contributing as much, and so on. "The Whiner cannot see how the project will be any good or be done on time . . . this person was [probably] snake bitten during prior group projects, and is resigned to the inevitable failure and anti-intellectualism of group endeavors." (Jajalas and Sutton, 1985).

We have all probably played these roles at one point or another. Half of the battle with problem characters is realizing you have them (or you are acting as one) in a group setting. The other half of the battle is knowing how to address these behaviors, all of which can be destructive to working in a group. The coping strategies for conflicts with problem characters are preventative and corrective (adapted from Jajalas and Sutton, 1985).

Preventative Strategies

The following strategies should prevent problem characters from creating problems.

Make the divisions of responsibilities clear and equal. At the project's outset, group members should decide who is responsible for completing the tasks, including running group meetings, the engineering design, the engineering drawings, data generation and calculations, writing up the project, and editing the final report. All group members must agree on the tasks they will perform and must agree on a timetable (see the project management chapter for more details). Having a clear and equitable distribution of tasks and responsibilities will ensure the minimization of whining, bullying, and martyrdom and will limit the saboteur from making changes. This mechanism provides a clear method for identifying deadbeats.

Do not blindly accept problems you find in your group. Every group member needs to speak up if she or he does not agree with a decision, procedure, or activity. These discussions must be conducted publicly and in a respectful manner. Your group should establish, at the project's outset, a method for dealing with conflict. Will you make decisions by voting and taking the majority vote? How will you make a decision if your group is split between or among alternatives? Under what circumstances will you approach the instructor or community partner if you are having problems in your group? Discuss these as a group and write down your rules for working in a group. You will have those rules to return to during a conflict. Although this might seem like giving the whiner creative license, if problems are introduced and discussed, it give the complaints structure and will enable group members to deal with these issues quickly.

Do not take responsibility for the happiness of others. Every group member is responsible for treating each member respectfully and for behaving ethically. However, each group member is responsible for his or her own happiness. The group should not spend energy making a whiner or martyr feel better. Conversely, group members should not worry about making suggestions for fear of bothering a bully, saboteur or deadbeat. All group members should contribute equally to the project regardless of their mood and extenuating circumstances.

Corrective Strategies

The following strategies should address problem characters and the issues they bring to the table.

Re-open discussions about responsibilities. This will probably be the case anyway, as it is often impossible to prepare for how a project will unfold at its beginning. This is an excellent strategy for addressing issues with deadbeats and for handling the whiner and martyr.

Confront the troublesome character. One group member or all other members can directly address the behaviors of a group member that need to change. Use the principles of conflict resolution from the previous section for the best results. If all else fails, talk to your instructor and/or community partner to solve these issues. You can reduce contact with the troublesome character, but only after all you have exhausted other avenues (confronting and speaking with the instructor/ community partner).

Do all editing and typing together. Everyone should be involved with the communication portion of the project because it is the best way to describe what you did. You are the person most in touch with what you did for the project, so you should be the primary communicator for this project portion. This approach stops the saboteur from making any of those last-minute changes.

This information has given you some basics for resolving conflicts and dealing with problem characters in a group setting. You can find a wealth of information on teamwork and team conflict. Use the information in this chapter as a starting point and consult additional literature if necessary. If you have an unworkable conflict, approach your instructor and/or community partner for assistance.

5.6 CONCLUSIONS

In this chapter, you have learned the basics of working in teams. The Keirsey-Bates or Myers-Briggs personality indicator is one framework for understanding your personality and how you might interact in teams with people who have different styles and ways of learning than you. Being aware of team dynamics should provide you with some insight on the process of working on successful teams. These teams interact regularly and have an organized method of meeting, a working knowledge of team roles, and a method for resolving conflicts and dealing with problem characters. Possessing leadership skills enables you to work well as an individual team member, and conflict resolution skills should provide a framework for dealing with problems that may occur with your group members or dynamics, including procrastination or laziness. In the next chapter, you will take your communication and teaming skills into principles of project management.

REFERENCES

————, ESCOP/ACOP Leadership Development Program. Athens, GA: Triangle Associates, 2002. www.triangle-associates.com

Covey, S. The Seven Habits of Highly Effective People. New York: Simon & Schuster, 1990.

Jalajas, D. and R. Sutton. Feuds in Student Groups: Coping with Whiners, Martyrs, Saboteurs, Bullies, and Deadbeats. *The Organizational Behavior Teaching Review*, 9 (4), 94–102, 1985.

Keirsey, D. and M. Bates. *Please Understand Me: Character & Temperament Types,* 5th Ed. Del Mar, CA: Prometheus Nemesis Book Company, Del Mar, CA 1984.

Kroeger, O. and J. Thuesen. *Type Talk: The 16 Personality Types That Determine How We Live, Love, and Work.* New York: Dell Publishing: New York, 1988.

Loeb, M. and S. Kindel. *Leadership for Dummies: Your Step-By-Step Guide to Building Leadership Skills.* Foster City, CA: IDG Books 1999.

Stevenson, S. and S. Whitmore. *Strategies for Engineering Communication.* New York: Wiley & Sons, Inc. 2002.

Tuckman, B. Developmental Sequence in Small Groups. *Psychology Bulletin*, 63(6): 384–399, 1965.

Yuzuriha, T. *How to Succeed as An Engineer: A Practical Guide to Enhance Your Career.* Vancouver, WA: J&K Publishing, 1998.

EXERCISES

1. Write a one to two page essay about yourself that you will share and discuss with your group members. Your essay should address the following questions:
    *   Where were you born and where did you grow up?
    *   Discuss one childhood experience that had a significant impact on your life
    *   What high school did you graduate from (name, city, state, country, year)
    *   What discipline do you plan to major in and what has motivated you to take this course?
    *   What do you plan to do with your career in the future (if you are not sure, discuss things that you're interested in)?
    *   List and discuss three to five things that you are proud of (these can be specific accomplishments, personal qualities, things you like about yourself, or anything else you think is relevant)
    *   What's your philosophy on life?

2. Work together to create a team constitution. You and your group members will adhere to the tenets described in this document for the duration of your project. This document should include
    *   a list of expected behaviors and appropriate conduct for each team member
    *   a method for providing and receiving feedback with regard to other team members
    *   a method for making decisions as a group (this is particularly important if there are an even number of people in your group)
    *   the division of work and who is responsible for what (this will probably change as your project takes shape!)
    *   a description of how conflict will be handled, should it arise

Remember that it is okay to re-negotiate any part of the constitution, just do so with everyone's knowledge and consent. Each member should pledge to follow every part of the constitution and should sign the document; all members must agree with suggested changes to this document.

3. Work together to create a team slogan.

4. Work together to create a team logo.

5. Work with your community partner(s) to create a project slogan.

6. Work together with your community partner(s) to develop a project logo.

7. Develop a system for determining how effective your team meetings are. Use this system to rate your meetings throughout the course.

8. Suppose you and your group have a huge assignment due on Monday, and you've decided to meet all day Saturday to work on your assignment with the idea that if you don't finish Saturday, your group will complete the assignment on Sunday. Now suppose that your group has agreed to meet at 9:00 A.M. on Saturday and that everyone except Bob arrives. Your group waits 20 minutes then tries unsuccessfully to reach Bob on his cell phone and by e-mail. Your group begins work, and Bob shows up at 2:00 P.M. that day, apologizes, and says he had some other business that made him late. How would you and your group address this situation?

9. Suppose your three member team is in the middle of an intense meeting and you're discussing which way you should go with a design decision. An argument erupts between two group members, one of whom is an ESFJ and the other an INTP. The ESFJ says that the INTP couldn't think his way out of a paper bag, and the INTP responds that the ESFJ wouldn't understand a true thought if it hit her over the head. How would you facilitate this discussion and ensure that the two group members resolve this conflict?

10. Suppose you're in a group of four people, three of whom are very committed to the project and one who does not seem interested or motivated. What would you do to address this situation?

11. Suppose you're in a group of four people, one of whom is intensely interested in the project to the point that s/he is spending the majority of their study time on the project and expects others to do the same. How would you work with this person on this project?

12. Suppose you're in a group with a person who acts as if s/he knows everything and is always making remarks to remind everyone how smart s/he is. One day, this team member thinks that a decision should be made one way and the other three members in the group are united in the idea that the decision should be made the other way. The "know it all" says that it is much simpler to work alone and that s/he would have a smarter design working as an individual. How would the group resolve this situation?

Chapter 6

Project Management

"Failure to plan is planning to fail."

Management courses and programs have proven this axiom true in many cases. A good plan is one of the most important attributes of successful teams and projects. Engineering projects are complex and require different tasks to be completed by different people at different times. All these tasks must come together in the end and meet specific deadlines and customer requirements. Projects that involve multiple people and steps must be organized and implemented systematically to insure success. As with the design process and problem-solving models, following systematic approaches to proper project planning will produce improved results and better solutions.

Starting a plan for your project may seem daunting or impossible, but this discipline and skill will serve you and your classmates well. Here are eight questions that can be addressed with a plan:

1. What should you and/or your team do first?
2. What should come next?
3. How many people do you need to accomplish your project?
4. What resources do you need to accomplish your project?
5. How long will it take?
6. What can you get completed by the end of the semester or quarter?
7. When will the project be finished?
8. How will we know we are done with the project?

These questions are difficult to answer at the project's beginning, and many students will make the mistake of not using a systematic approach to project planning. They will guess what they can get done and make commitments they cannot keep. Others will assume the details will solve themselves and will conclude with too many details to work out toward the end of the semester or quarter. Stories of late nights on the final project week are common and do not have to happen. Proper planning can insure you will complete your tasks and will allow your team to distribute the work load among team members so no one is overburdened. Tasks can be spread around to leverage people's expertise and abilities and to adapt to unexpected circumstances. A good plan allows resources and materials to be in place when needed to avoid delays waiting on parts or supplies.

In a classroom setting, the ramifications of missing commitments is relatively low. Once you enter the workforce, missing deadlines can result in lost customers, revenue, and people's jobs. Taking advantage of your time in class to practice project management techniques can pay large dividends later in your career.

In service-learning, project management reduces missing commitments or deadlines that can result in a loss of resources or services. Service-learning projects rely on many people and tasks before the projects are completed. For community projects, a plan allows you and your team to lay out realistic expectations and allows your community partner to plan appropriately.

At the beginning of a simpler project, the discipline of developing and managing a plan may seem like a waste of time but will serve you well over the rest of your career. Good engineering practice follows systematic processes to maximize efficiency and reduce variability and failure. Spending time to plan the project may seem as if you are losing time when you could be doing something productive, but the planning you do initially will pay off by allowing your team to progress more quickly and efficiently, which will result in a better product. This chapter highlights some of the tools that can be applied to planning and managing a project within an engineering classroom.

6.1 CREATING A PROJECT CHARTER

The first step in project planning is establishing a project charter. A project charter is a project summary. This may seem obvious, but you must define what the project will entail and how your team will know it has finished. If you have a community partner, you should share the charter document to insure that the expectations are the same for your team and customer.

The elements of a charter include the following:

1. Description—Describe and summarize what you or your team will be doing. This short summary will allow all those involved or affected by the project to understand what is needed. Include the needs and desires of the community that you are addressing.

2. Objectives—List the project objectives. Why are you doing the project? What will you or your team achieve? What issues is your team addressing that would not be addressed otherwise? What are the problems you are solving with this community project?

3. Outcomes or deliverables—What are going to be the project results? When the project is finished, what will be left behind by you and your team? Be specific. When you have achieved these outcomes, everyone should understand you have completed the project.

4. Duration—When will the project be started, and when will it meet the objectives and deliver the outcomes?

5. Community Partners—With whom are you serving on this project? Who will benefit from the project? Who will receive the project outcomes or deliverables?

6. Stakeholders—Who will be affected by your project other than your customer? Who has a vital interest in the project's success? Stakeholders are others who will need to be kept informed of the project's progress, outcomes, and results.

7. Team membership and roles—If your plan involves a team, list the team members and their roles. (Some of the roles you may want to assign are outlined later in this chapter and in the prior chapter.) Listing contact information for all of the team members makes the document more valuable and useful for those who will receive the charter document.

8. Planning information—What other information do you need for the project plan? If the project involves a design, what are the steps in the design process? Do other constraints or expectations need to be summarized before planning the project?

The project charter is a useful tool. It gives the project vision and allows all team members, community partners, and stakeholders the opportunity to comment on the vision before beginning. It helps define the roles and responsibilities of your team and others involved. It forces your team to think about the project's requirements at the start and serves as a place to summarize these results. A concise project charter becomes an excellent communication tool for your team, community partners, and stakeholders.

6.2 TASK DEFINITIONS

Once you have defined the project charter, the next step is identifying the completion tasks to achieve the objectives and outcomes. In most engineering projects, many tasks will have to be completed to finish the project. Your team might start this process by brainstorming what needs to be done for the project, but do not stop there. Many students will lay out their plans and stop with incomplete tasks. An example might look like this:

Plan
Design
Build
Deliver

For plans to be effective, they need to be detailed enough to manage. A detailed plan should allow you and your team to do the following:

1. Hold individual team members accountable for progress during the project. Do not wait until the project's conclusion.

2. Identify all needed resources, materials, funding, and people.

3. At any time, determine if your project is on schedule.

4. Manage your people and resources by shifting from one task to another as needed to complete the project.
5. Determine when you have finished.

Too general of a project plan defeats the planning purpose. The plan will not allow you to use it to your benefit A detailed plan will allow you and your team to identify who needs to be working on what task each week. Thus, each task needs to be as detailed as possible. Break larger tasks into smaller tasks whenever possible.

Effective plans need to be complete and this will require your team to take advantage of available resources to identify all the required tasks. Chances are you are not the first ones to attempt a project like this. You will have some past experience to draw upon. When I worked in a large manufacturing firm, new product plans were laid out based on what we needed to do the last time, and appropriate modifications were made for the new line. We used past experience as a guide, and your team may be able to do the same. Do you have task lists from previous semesters, quarters, or similar projects? Show your task lists to your instructors, advisors, alumni, community partners, and stakeholders for input. Gather as much data as possible to develop a comprehensive list.

Include tasks associated with other tasks. If something needs to be ordered, put in time to research for the component so you can place the order and have time for shipping. Overnight options are expensive, so initially plan on ground transportation. If you need approvals or signatures for components, incorporate those tasks. Many institutions have a process for purchasing items from outside the university (much like most companies have a purchasing department). These departments have procedures that take time and you need account for them in the plans. If you are using outside vendors for manufacturing, assembly or testing, do you need to schedule meetings before they begin work on their tasks?

To help organize the tasks, list them in an outline format. Just like an outline from an English class, similar tasks are grouped together. This process will make later steps faster and easier to complete. In the example outline, the starting and end dates are listed along with delivery expectations.

Example 6.1

Task Definition

Create a project schedule for your EPICS project.
Start date: September 10, 2004.
Due date: September 17, 2004.
Deliverable: List of milestones, a PERT chart, and a task timeline.

Outline View

1. Start: Receive assignment to create a project schedule.
2. Learn about schedules
   2.1   Attend talk on proposals, including project schedules
   2.2   Review web pages on project schedules

6.3 MILESTONES

Along with tasks, your project plan should have milestones. A milestone is a deadline for some deliverable. Deliverables may be the completion of subcomponents for your project, or they may be when all parts have been ordered and have arrived. In a design, each phase completion of the design process could be a milestone.

Milestones are useful as checks of your plan's progress. You should not wait until the final deadlines before assessing progress. Intermediate milestones serve two purposes. First, they let your team meet short-term goals and celebrate them. It can be a big morale boost for your team to hit a milestone and get some recognition. We recommend that your team celebrate short-term successes and milestones, which will help build team dynamics.

The other benefit of intermediate milestones is that you can monitor your progress to know if you are on schedule. If part of the project falls behind, you may be able to redirect people or resources from another part of the project to move that part back on schedule. When defining tasks, think of places where you could use milestones as markers or measures of your team's progress.

6.4 DEFINING TIMES

Now that you have compiled the task list, you need to determine the required task times. In full-time employment settings, tasks are measured in working days. For your project, working days are a good unit of time.

Be diligent to include the full time needed for tasks. If a component needs to be ordered, include the time it will take your institution to place the order and including shipping time. You can back order some parts. If your school's machine shop needs to make a part, how far in advance will you need to place the order, and how long will it take to start and complete? If customers or stakeholders need to test a beta software version, how long should you leave it with them before you will get your results? It may only take an hour to perform your assessment, but you may need to give them a week or two to schedule the evaluation. Student teams do not account for time lags because others will not drop what they are doing to perform the task. Give people one or two weeks and factor that into your timelines.

Working days do not always work with students' schedules. In order to plan your tasks, you will need to develop a timescale in place of working days that is acceptable for your team. Your class probably does not meet every week day, and you and your classmates have other commitments so this project is not a full-time job.

For your class, everyone has an expectation of the number of hours each person will spend each week on the project, and you can use that as a model to develop your timescale. Some of the models used by student teams include the following:

- Work Weeks: Break tasks up into weekly segments (based on the number of hours devoted to the course each week). Your team should be explicit about when the week begins and when tasks are due to check milestone progress. This gives individuals the flexibility to arrange tasks around other classes and obligations during the week as long as they meet the weekly deadlines.
- Monday and Friday: Some students prefer to split the week into two segments, the work week and weekend. This works well for teams that leave time on the weekends to do a large part of their project work. Tasks (ordering parts or communicating with outside vendors) need to occur during the week and can be assigned on Mondays with deadlines of Friday. Dedicated project work will have deadlines and milestones of Monday. This system allows your team to check on progress twice each week, but different tasks need to be planned during the week and over the weekend. Your team can pick other days of the week (e.g. Tuesday and Thursday) depending on when your team meets.
- Class periods: Some teams break up timelines by class period so that each time you meet, you can check on progress. Unfortunately, the time between classes is not uniform.

Your team can use any of a number of timescales, but your team members should be held accountable for their progress. They should not be expected to work full time at points of the project to achieve your objectives.

When assigning times to tasks, either by your team or by outside interests, use prior experience or get input on your estimates. Be conservative with your time estimates. The first time you need to do something, it will take much longer than you originally thought. Simple things like ordering a part through your college's system will take some time because you must learn the system. If you need to make a circuit board, the first time will include learning how to make it. Include time for training if needed before you complete a task. In your timelines, include researching and learning new systems, etc.

We suggested that you need to detail the tasks as much as possible; the times you assigned can serve as a check for the task detail level. If tasks span several weeks, break them into smaller tasks. If possible, break your tasks into small enough components of not more than one or two weeks. Longer times for tasks make it easier for team members to procrastinate and your team could get behind. If you wait too long, it may be hard to recover from falling behind. Short timelines make holding each other accountable and project management easier.

6.5 ORGANIZING THE TASKS

With your organized task list, the next question is task order. We will systematically optimize the project plan. The first step in this process is to determine the task relationships and sequencing. When you defined the tasks, you grouped related tasks. Now you need to relate the groups.

You and your classmates have gone through this same process as you laid out your plan of study. All your college courses have prerequisites and co-requisite classes. Some classes can be taken at any point in your four-year degree program while others must be taken early or your graduation will be delayed. You determined the classes you needed to start with and how many you needed to graduate. You used resources like printed sample plans as well as talking with other students, academic advisors, and faculty.

You will follow the same process to plan your project. Take the tasks that your team identified and prioritize what must be done first. Use your outline to link tasks together looking for prerequisites, co-requisites, etc.

PERT Charts

The US Navy developed Program Evaluation and Review Technique (PERT) in the 1950s to manage the Polaris missile project. This technique is still used in many industries as the major project tool to track and order tasks.

In a PERT chart, each task is represented by a box that contains a brief description of and duration for the task. Milestones are represented with boxes that have rounded corners. Related tasks are connected with lines. If one task must be completed before a second task can be started, they are connected with a line originating from the right edge of the first task and connected the left edge of the second task, as show in Figure 6.1. In this example, the duration is noted in terms of days, and if your team needs a component from a vendor, the task of ordering the component and shipping it have to proceed before anything else can be done. Unrelated tasks are not connected on the PERT chart.

The PERT analysis shows pathways of tasks. Some tasks have to be done in series and others can be done in parallel. These series can be laid out as the overall project plan is laid out.

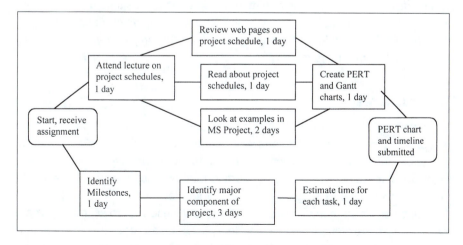

Figure 6.1 PERT Chart for Project Planning

PERT charts are a great "what if" tool during the initial planning stage. Post-It notes, 3×5 cards, chalk boards or whiteboards, or project management software can be used to capture the process flow, to find ways to reduce project completion time, and to utilize the available resources and people. What needs to be done when and by whom? By mapping out the process, a team can spread its resources and allow process tracking. The planning process using this tool can help people think of parallel tasks and what can be going on at the same time.

The sum of the times along each path gives length or duration for each path. The longest path is the critical path. The critical path will set the project length unless the task times can be reduced.

Critical Paths

The critical path is a concept from industrial engineering and project management that shows the task or a series of tasks that will pace the project. The critical path is the longest string of dependent project tasks. Tasks on the critical path will hold up project completion if they are delayed. An example of a critical path is the mathematics sequence in an engineering curriculum. If a student delays a semester of calculus class early in his or her program, it typically delays graduation for one semester. Mathematics is on the critical path for graduation in an engineering program. Delaying an English or humanities class, however, could be accommodated by rearranging other classes or taking an overload one semester. The English and calculus classes differ in that other classes have calculus as a prerequisite. It must be taken before other classes and thus, has a cascade effect on the overall study plan.

The same will be true for tasks in your project plan. Tasks that are not on the critical path may be rearranged without changing the project completion. Any delay of a critical path task will result in a project delay.

As you plan for your project, you have to know which tasks can be compressed or rearranged and which cannot. Some tasks can be accelerated by using more people while others cannot. The classic analogy is having a baby. Nine people cannot have the same baby in one month. Some tasks take time and special attention needs to be paid to tasks on the critical path, which cannot be compressed. This information will be valuable during the project if you need to rearrange tasks or team members.

Gantt Charts

While the PERT chart is for organizing tasks and placing priorities on timing and resources, it may be difficult to interpret for a project with many tasks, especially for people outside your team such as your community partner. A Gantt chart is another popular project management charting method and is easier for people to understand your team's progress relative to your plan.

A Gantt chart is a horizontal bar chart frequently used in project management in which tasks are plotted versus time. Henry L. Gantt, an American engineer and social scientist, developed the Gantt chart in 1917, and it has become one of the most common project planning tools. In a Gantt chart, each row represents a distinct task. Time is represented on the horizontal axis. Typically, dates run across the top of the chart in increments of days, weeks, months, or a time scale that you and your classmates have determined. A bar represents the time when the task is planned for with the left end representing the expected starting time for each task and the right end for the completion of each task. Tasks can be shown to run consecutively with one starting when the previous one ends. They can be shown to run in parallel or overlap. An example of the Gantt chart, created with Excel, is shown in Figure 6.2.

Notice that tasks and milestones are included on the Gantt chart. Significant milestones and reports are represented with different colors. As progress is made, the cells in the spreadsheet can be changed to a different color so that someone can easily see the progress at any time in the project. If a project is partially completed, that bar can be shaded in proportion of the work done on that task. If the task is half finished, half of that bar will be shaded. A vertical line can be drawn for the current date and progress can easily be checked based on the line. Tasks that show completion to the right of the line are ahead of schedule and those to the right of the vertical line are behind schedule.

An additional column can be added to the right of the task descriptions to show who is responsible for each task. The Gantt chart is an excellent way to see who is committed to which tasks during the project to ensure that each person has responsibilities over the entire project and no one is being asked to do too many tasks at one time.

MagRacer 2.0 Timeline (weeks)

Project Tasks	2	3	4	5	6	7	8	9	10	11	12	13	14	15	16
Bring new team members up to speed on MagRacer	■														
Solve FET prolem in demo track	■														
Concept of MagRacer2 cabinet	■														
Meet with IS people/ visit IS		■													
Finalize track/coil assembly		■	■												
AutoCAD drawings of MagRacer2 cabinet		■	■												
Finalize display concept			■												
Deliver working test track			■												
Week 4 Demo			■												
Milestone: Submit MR2 drawings to WP				■											
Complete PCB layout				■	■										
Milestone: Submit PCB layout for fabrication					■										
Final order of all circuit material					■										
Construct coils					■	■									
Construct track mounting hardware					■	■									
Construction of visual display					■	■									
Week 8 Progress Report							■								
Exected delivery of MG2 cabinet from WP (4wk)								■							
Expected delivery of PCBs (3wk)								■							
Spring Break									■						
Final assembly of MagRacer2									■	■					
Week 11 Design Review										■					
Milestone: Delivery of completed MagRacer2											■				
Troubleshoot MagRacer2												■	■		
Prep documentation for MagRacer2												■	■		
Week 16 End of Semester reports due															■

Figure 6.2 Sample Gantt Chart from an Engineering Student Team.

Many teams will use a PERT chart to arrange tasks and identify the critical path. They use this information to order the tasks and they transfer the tasks to a Gantt chart for project management. To make a presentation of your project easier, fit your Gantt chart onto one page. If you have more tasks than can fit onto one page, break the project into subprojects with their own Gantt chart, and keep one that shows the progress of each subproject.

6.6 DETAILS, DETAILS

A common mistake of many teams is to omit too many details until the end. This will often doom your plan. The final stages of a design and assembly will take much longer than you think because you had details you did not think about when making the plan. Since you most likely have not done a project similar to this, your team could not foresee many details. These details tend to pile up at the end.

Things do not go as planned. Few plans have time built in for things to go wrong but as Murphy's Law says, "anything that can go wrong will." This is true for project planning. Your plan should have space to debug or fix things.

- Are we assuming that things will fit together the first time and nothing will have to be reworked?
- Are we assuming that we have ordered all parts and that they will be the correct parts?
- Are we assuming that all materials will be shipped on time and nothing will be back ordered or late?
- Are we assuming that no parts will malfunction when installed?

A suggestion to avoid a panic or failure is to push a delivery date back a week before it is due. Your team can use this week as a buffer if things go badly. Human nature is to know you have some leeway and think that the real deadline is the one to aim for. This totally defeats the purpose. Milestones should be met and the schedule adhered to until the end of the project so that the buffer will act as the buffer if unforeseen circumstances occur in the final stages.

6.7 DELIVERY TIMING

When planning for your project delivery, allow for field experience before the end of the semester or quarter. Any product delivered to the community should be delivered with enough time for use by the community partner before the students leave for break. Your project should be in use for a long enough time when your team is still on campus in case problems surface and must be addressed. One of the mistakes we make is to place projects into the community and leave for the summer. If anything goes wrong, the community partner is left with a problem to address. Recall that the idea of service-learning is to provide real community value. Dropping off a project that develops a problem and has no one to support it can cause the community organization to expend additional time and resources to the project rather than to the need you both wanted to address.

A class of product failure modes is called infant mortality. They happen immediately or shortly after installation. Getting a project out into the community will expose these failure modes and provide opportunities for you to address these failures before you leave for break. Questions can occur after initial use. These questions can be answered easily if you are still in class. A project plan that reflects the community needs has time built into the plan for the community to begin to use the product device or system when the students are still on campus to answer questions and make repairs if needed.

6.8 PERSONNEL DISTRIBUTION

The tools that have been described can help order tasks but project management means getting the right people on the right tasks. Some models of project planning will have people identified earlier in the process based on their expertise and availability. This works when people are separated into departments with separate responsibilities and capabilities. For most student projects, we recommend assigning people after developing a draft of the plan. The people on your team will need to be assigned tasks that allow the project plan to be met. For example, one person cannot do all of the tasks in the first month. Sketching out who is the most qualified for and/or interested in each task is a great way to start. The team must look at the work distribution and make an equitable assessment. The work needs to be balanced whenever possible and must account for the team members' expertise.

When you have assigned people their tasks, add them to the Gantt charts. You can add a column next to the task description or put it on the task bar. If your timeline is detailed enough, check if each person understands what he or she is doing each week during the project. If each person does not, refine the tasks so everyone can.

6.9 MONEY AND RESOURCES

When the plan for the tasks and people is in place, you must determine the resources needed for the project. Almost all students will need to develop a project budget in their professional career, so practicing in a classroom setting is an excellent experience. This aspect, like so many in service-learning, will lay a great foundation for future work.

Setting up a budget may seem as daunting as the project plan. How can you know how much things will cost before you buy them? Though a logical question, you will be asked for budgetary estimates before you begin projects on a regular basis. In large companies, the budget request can determine if your project proceeds. If you are working for a smaller company that is bidding with other companies to provide services, your budget estimates may decide if you win the right to complete a project.

Just like estimating times for tasks, past experience is a great asset to this process. Looking back at similar projects and talking with other students, alumni, faculty, corporate representatives, or community members with similar experience can provide project funding estimates. Web searches can give quick estimates on products. You may determine boundaries for cost estimates that would result in the most expensive and least expensive costs to complete your project. These boundaries will give you a range with which to work when requesting project money.

You will also need to include item costs associated with your main costs. For example, shipping costs may be incurred for each ordered part. Will your team be charged tax on purchases? Will your group need to travel anywhere? Will your team be charged for small, expendable items like nails, screws, and resistors? If a vendor is making a part, include material costs and labor.

One team member should be responsible for managing the project budget and related financial aspects. A spreadsheet can be set up to monitor the project budget and track incurred expenses. Monitoring the financial project progress should be part of the team's regular updates in monitoring task progress.

6.10 DOCUMENT AS YOU GO

Do not procrastinate on the documentation of your project. As you assemble your project plan, you should include documentation milestones of the early parts of the project. Remember to look at the needs of the project. If you are delivering a product to a customer or to the local community, you may need user manuals or maintenance procedures. These should be drafted well before the products are delivered so that they can be reviewed. Documenting each step will make it easier if you or another class readdresses any of the completed tasks.

Another practical reason for documenting as you go along is work reduction. Reports are typically due at the end of a semester or quarter. Leaving all or most of the documentation until the end adds more work during project completion. There will inevitably be details that appear or were overlooked that you will have to deal with near the project's end. Leaving too many details or large tasks, like documentation, for the end will add unnecessary team burdens and will reduce your work quality.

In service-learning, the documentation that you leave behind is a critical component of the service you are providing. If your team compromises on the quality of this part of the project, you will reduce the community value you provide. You can avoid this by integrating writing tasks into the plan as it develops.

6.11 TEAM ROLES

In project management, designate individual team members with specific responsibilities so that they can be held accountable and will hold others accountable for completing the project. Some of the roles that are common on student teams include the following:

- *Project Leader or Monitor*—Your team is either organized with a designated leader or you might have rotating responsibilities. In either case, someone must be designated as a project leader or monitor. This person monitors and tracks the progress of the milestones and tasks according to your plan. He or she will maintain the timelines and will be the person to shift responsibilities if tasks fall behind in part of your team. During regular meetings, the timelines should be checked and reported upon; this person will be responsible for bringing this information to the meetings. A diligent project leader will increase your likelihood that you meet your goals.

- *Procurement*—If your project requires much material to be ordered from outside the university, your team may designate one person to learn the purchasing system and to track the progress of team orders.

- *Financial officer*—If your project requires purchases that are tied to a budget, designate one person as a financial officer to manage your team's expenses. Going through your estimates at the beginning will give you a roadmap but you will need to adjust it. Having one person responsible for monitoring your progress will make identifying problems faster and easier. You should identify this person early in the process and she or he can be the lead person in developing the initial budgetary estimates.

- *Liaison*—If your team has a customer outside of the class, designate one person as liaison. This person is responsible for keeping everyone informed about the project plan and progress toward meeting the plan. Most outside contacts, especially in the community, cannot track all the students and prefer one contact point. This person will share the project plan, plan progress, and any plan changes.

6.12 PROJECT MANAGEMENT SOFTWARE

The examples that have been shown for PERT and Gantt charts have been made with simple drawings and Excel spreadsheets. There are powerful project management tools that can allow you and your team to manage and track large, complex projects. One software product available to students is Microsoft's Project (http://www.microsoft.com/office/project/prodinfo). In Project, tasks can be entered on separate lines with start and finish dates. Projects can be grouped under headings as shown in Figure 6.3. Tasks can be linked by entering the preceding task's row number in the Predecessor column for that task.

A Gantt chart is generated from this entered data (see Figure 6.4). Clicking on the Gantt chart icon on the left will show a Gantt chart for the project. For this project, five main tasks are displayed.

Each project part can be broken into smaller subtasks to be managed. To view the subtasks, click on the + symbol next to the task name and an expanded view will appear as seen in Figure 6.5. This view expands the subtasks. Two of the tasks in the expanded view are shown as related, with one preceding the other. Notice that as tasks are completed, they can be shown with shading to track progress.

One of the benefits of Microsoft (MS) Project is that you can enter the data for the tasks one time and generate several other data views. A PERTstyle chart can be generated by clicking on the Network Diagram icon on the left side of the

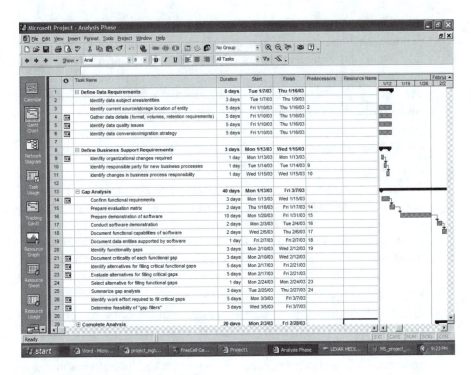

Figure 6.3 Microsoft's Project Software

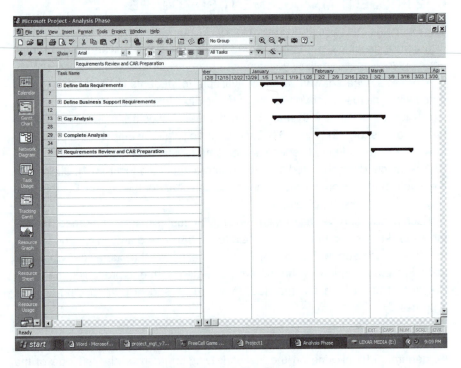

Figure 6.4 Gantt Chart with Major Project Headings

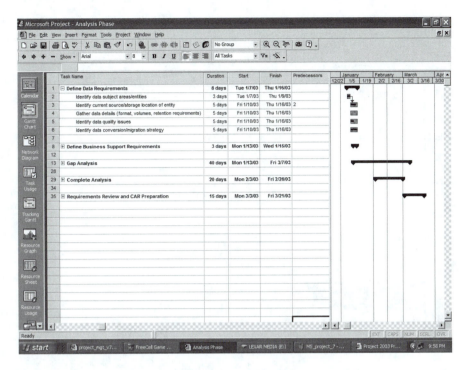

Figure 6.5 Microsoft Project Gantt Chart with Subtasks Shown

screen. This block diagram shows the same information as the PERT chart in Figure 6.6. Each task is identified and described, and is linked with related projects. This case shows two tasks related in the subcategories.

If the entire project is shown, the relationships between subtasks can be seen in Figure 6.7.

MS Project can display a calendar, which shows the projects that should be active for given days of the month. This tool can be useful if your team has designated specific days of the week for work. You can break your tasks into components that will fit into the time blocks you have arranged to do your work outside of class. A sample view of the calendar is shown in Figure 6.8.

6.13 FUNDRAISING

Sometimes in service-learning, you do not have sufficient funds to meet the identified community needs. These resources may not be available at your institution and you need to look outside the university and community for support. Several ideas exist for raising funds for a service-learning project and have been successfully used at other institutions. Before students begin raising funds for a project, they should check with three groups:

1. Their instructors
2. Their institution's development or fundraising office
3. Their community partners

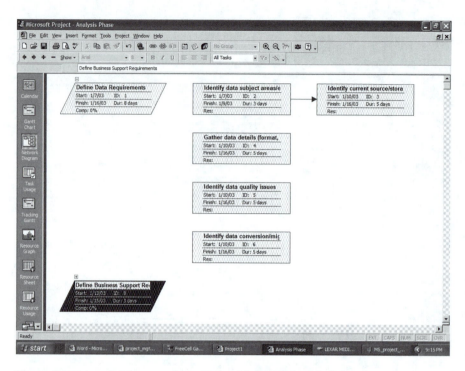

Figure 6.6 Network Diagram view of First Major Task with Subtasks

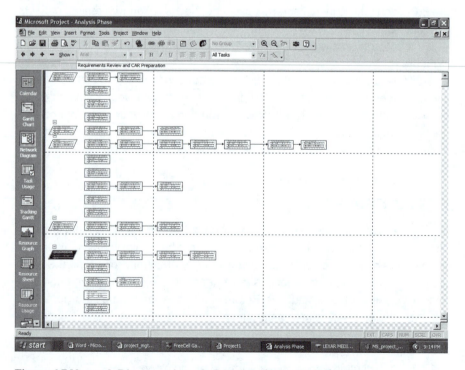

Figure 6.7 Network Diagram view of all Major Task with Subtasks

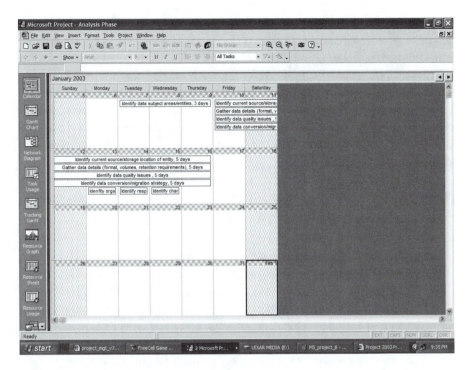

Figure 6.8 Microsoft Project Calendar View

These groups may help you raise the necessary resources for your project and will make sure you do not interfere with agreements that are already in place.

You should always consult your instructors since they will evaluate you. In some cases, completion of the project may require funds that you are not expected to provide. Your instructors have negotiated a role for you in the service-learning experience and you want to that ensure raising additional money is within your expected role.

At every institution, an office is responsible for raising money for the college or university. This office is typically called a development or advancement office. Its responsibilities are to cultivate relationships with people and organizations who are interested in donating to your institution. They coordinate these activities and your team will need to ensure that you are not approaching an organization that the development office is in discussions with. It makes your institution look bad if one part of the school is talking to a company as another school group (such as your team) shows up. Your team would not want to secure a $1,000 donation when the central office was going to receive a $100,000 donation from the same donor. If this happens, they might not get their money or your institution's president might get a check for $99,000 and a note that the extra $1,000 went to you.

The development and advancement office can help you secure funding. If it knows your project, it can add you to its list as it talks to prospective donors and funding agencies. Donors, individuals, and organizations like to fund what you do. This office can guide your plans for fundraising and give you tips to make your work easier and more productive.

The other group to coordinate with is your community partner. As with your school, your community partner has a donor network that could be confused if you said you are working "with them" on a project. In some cases, students have been given a donation the organization thought was going for its community partner. It would be inappropriate to get money donated to your project that was supposed to pay for your community partner's staff. The community partner may know of times when you should not be soliciting in your community, such as during the United Way Fundraising Campaign. The partner may have ideas for your fundraising or leads for you to follow.

After checking with your instructors, your school's office, and your community partner, you have other possibilities for raising project funds. Here are some successful ideas for finding funds:

1. *Institutional grants*—See if your school has grants for community engagement activities. Small grants may be available for similar activities. These may be grants for your professor or specifically for students.
2. *Community foundations*—Does your town or city have a community foundation that works with local organizations to supplement their work? This can be good match for engineering service-learning These local foundations require a small written proposal. Consult section 7.3.2 to get specific advice on writing proposals.
3. *Regional or national foundations*—Regional or national foundations may provide funding for organizations such as yours. These foundations require a formal proposal to fund an activity; your development or advancement office should point you to possible foundations.
4. *Service-learning organizations* such as Campus Compact (www.compact .org) have state organizations that sometimes sponsor student projects through mini-grant programs.
5. *Government grants*—Some service-learning teams collaborate with their community partners to write grants to state and federal agencies for larger projects. These may take longer than your academic semester or quarter, but you can lay the groundwork and perhaps participate in the proposal writing.
6. *Company sponsorship*—Companies and businesses in your area will probably sponsor your activity. Do not be afraid of approaching businesses not specifically aligned with your work. A business might be willing to support your activity if it finds your project worthwhile and if it gets publicity from the venture.
7. *Individual sponsorship*—a method that many organizations use to fundraise is to solicit donations from individuals for a project. They then give the donors some kind of recognition. In buildings, they might buy a brick with their name on it. If you were installing a playground, maybe their names could be written into the bricks on a walkway toward the playground or on a plaque near the playground.
8. *Fundraising events*—Many students are familiar with car washes, bake sales, fun runs, or walks. These can generate funds for projects and can be fun to implement. In some communities, local organizations like Rotary can

organize larger fundraising events to enable students to perform service-learning.

9. Another fundraising twist is to get *sponsorships for service projects.* Some church youth groups have found that people and businesses are willing to sponsor them on day-long service projects, especially when improving the local community. This idea should be transferable to service-learning teams. Students participate in a beautification or clean up project, and people sponsor them just like a walk-a-thon or other activity. The advantage of this over a bake sale is that the results of the fundraising help to meet community needs.

6.14 PUBLICITY

In your project plan, your team should plan on making a big deal about finishing your project with your community partner. Completion will be good for your school and the community partner. As with anything else involving your community partner, and instructor, you need to plan your celebration event with them. Making a big deal of project completion is a good idea and should be implemented in every service-learning project plan. Television, radio, and newspapers love to cover human interest stories and service-learning projects where students work with the community to meet a need are great stories. Your campus service-learning office or instructor has contacts with the university public relations office. We suggest that you use these contacts to secure media attention for your event. Your community partner also has local contacts and can be integrally involved in bringing media to planned events.

Do not be disappointed if a TV, radio or newspaper story does not fully capture the story, or if some of the details are incorrect. A person once told us, "If the media gets 70% of your story correct, you're doing very well." If there are egregious errors in the story, make sure you contact the media outlet that made the mistake. They will fix the mistake in future broadcasts or in written corrections. It is important to have an accurate account of the story and to insulate you, your community partner, and your university from liability.

CONCLUSION

Project management is a critical activity to ensuring the successful and timely completion of your service-learning project. In this chapter, several techniques were presented to assist you with project management, including the creation of a team charter, defining tasks, establishing milestones, defining project times, and organizing tasks. Project management tools used commonly in engineering practice, such as PERT, Critical Paths, the Gantt chart, and Project Management Software, were also presented. Project management tools should be initiated at the start of your service-learning project and revisited throughout the course of the project in order to account for any of the changes that will inevitably occur, even with the best plan possible. Work closely with your community partner and instructor throughout the project to establish tasks and milestones, and to celebrate the completion of project objectives.

REFERENCES

Brooks, Frederick P. Jr., The Mythical Man-Month, Essays on Software Engineering, Anniversary Edition, (2nd Edition) Addison Wesley, Reading, Massachusetts, 1995

Covey, S.R., The 7 Habits of Highly Effective People, Simon and Schuster Inc., New York, New York, 1989.

Fox, Terry L., and Spence, J. Wayne, Tools of the Trade: A survey of Project Management Tools, Project Management vol. 29, no. 3, pp. 20–27.

Meredith, Jack R., and Mantel, Samuel, J., Jr., Project Management, A Managerial Approach, (3rd Edition) John Wiley and Sons, New York, 1995

Modell, Martin E., A Professional's Guide to Systems Analysis, (2nd. Ed.) McGraw Hill, 1996.

Naik, B., Project Management: Scheduling and Monitoring by PERT./CPM, Advent Books, 1984.

Pyron, Tim, Using Microsoft Project 2000, Que, a Division of MacMillan Co., Indianapolis, IN, 2000.

Smith, Karl A., Project Management and Teamwork, McGraw-Hill, New York, 2000.

EXERCISES

1. Write a project charter for your project.

2. Deliver your project charter to one of your stakeholders and write a paragraph on their reaction.

3. Develop an outline for all of the project tasks.

4. Select five project tasks that you anticipate doing in the first month and estimate the time required for each task. Be prepared to present your findings, including the resources you used, to the class.

5. Develop a PERT chart for your project and present it to the class.

6. Identify the critical path for your project. List the tasks on the critical path.

7. Write a half-page essay on ways to shorten the project's critical path.

8. Create a Gantt chart for your project.

9. Write a one-page paper that compares and contrasts the benefits and limitations of a PERT chart and a Gantt Chart.

10. Contact a practicing engineer and find out what methods she or he uses for project management. Write a one-page paper on her or his experience.

11. Prepare a short oral presentation on a project management software package.

12. Write a one-page paper on the benefits and uses of Microsoft's Project software.

13. Write a half-page summary of issues or details that may occur as you finish your project that are not included in your plan.

14. Write a one-page analysis of your team's progress when you are half way through your semester or quarter.

Chapter 7

Communications

A world community can exist only with world communication, which means something more than extensive shortwave facilities scattered about the globe. It means common understanding, a common tradition, common ideas, and common ideals. —Robert M. Hutchins

7.1 COMMUNICATIONS OVERVIEW

Engineers must possess the technical skills to complete engineering analysis, evaluation, and design. Engineers must also possess strong communication and teaming skills. One of the biggest complaints of employers of entry-level engineers is lack of communication and teaming skills. Possessing these skill sets will enable you to excel in engineering. Most engineers in industry, research, and government complete design work in collaborative teams and routinely communicate their discoveries and progress to peers, managers, other engineers, and the community.

In this chapter, you will learn about oral and written communication skills. There is a section on working with community partners, who may have different perspectives and ways of communicating than you. As we get started, here are two golden rules of communication for engineers to keep in mind:

- Brevity is best.
- A shorter, simpler word is preferable to a longer, harder word.

Typically, you will be communicating with people who are making decisions concerning your work. These decision-makers have minimal time and you want to have maximal impact. While other types of communication place great emphasis on complex language and nuance (which require more words to explain), technical communication is all about getting it said and done quickly and simply.

7.2 ORAL COMMUNICATION SKILLS

In a service-learning and engineering context, you will make presentations to many audiences. The purpose of this section is to share information on planning and executing an effective oral presentation.

There are two types of presentations: formal and informal. Formal presentations involve a preset time and date and usually involve a reasonable amount of preparation. They may be made to your community partners, to expert panels, at design competitions, at the conclusion of a capstone design experience, at conferences in which engineering information is shared, or in the workplace when you communicate your information to your design team, management, the public, or funding and decision makers. For formal presentations, you will likely use a computer program such as PowerPoint; you might hand out printed copies of your slides. Formal presentations usually require formal business attire.

Informal presentations tend to be shorter and do not require as much preparation time or formal business attire. You do not usually need to prepare a Power-Point presentation either. Sometimes, you will have to make impromptu or spontaneous presentations. You might make such presentations in a business context, technical meeting, or at a meeting involving a design team.

A good presentation renders a service to your audience. A presentation is an opportunity to take the audience from where they are to where you want them to be. The best presentations will do the following:

- Give valuable information that the audience probably would not have had otherwise.
- Be in a form that the audience can put into immediate use.
- Motivate and inspire the audience to want to put the presented information into immediate use.

If You Are Nervous

Being nervous about doing a presentation is normal. In fact, the two most common fears of people living in the United States are public speaking and flying in airplanes. The following list of techniques is intended to help you combat your nervousness.

- Breathing is important; when you get nervous, your respiration rate tends to speed up and your body can go into adrenaline overdrive (a fight or flight mechanism). Controlling your breathing is one way to stay calm.
  - Take three deep breaths before you start.
  - Practice square breathing, which is inhaling seven counts, holding seven counts, exhaling seven counts, and holding seven counts.
- Visualize yourself successfully presenting your talk.
- Work with your nervousness by tailoring the talk to your strengths. Most people experience heigtened nervousness during the initial stages of speaking. Use one or more of these tips, which can be executed throughout the presentation.

- ○ **Use humor:** This makes the atmosphere less formal. Start your presentation with a joke, especially one that pertains to your presentation.
  - ○ **Use props:** It gives you something to do with your hands. A show and tell will interest the audience.
  - ○ **Use your nervous habit:** Work with that habit to your audience's benefit. If you like jingling change (coins) in your pockets, pull something visual out of your pocket to start your presentation.
  - ○ **Use trivia:** Focus your audience's attention or teach the audience something interesting that pertains to your talk.
- Have your presentation ready at least a day in advance. Being finished usually helps to cut down on your nervousness. Student Alicia Abadie says, "The more you procrastinate, the more nerve-wracking it can be."

Before the Presentation

Preparation is the key to successful oral presentations. To prepare for a presentation, you need to do the following:

- Identify your purpose and audience
- Organize the information
- Gather the information you need to present
- Create presentation material with maximal audience impact
- Practice your presentation after it is prepared

Identify Your Purpose and Audience

To give a presentation with maximum impact, know your audience:

- How many people will you be speaking to?
- How well do you know your audience? If you are speaking to a small audience with whom you are familiar, you can use their names during your talk. This focuses the attention of your audience.
- What is the background of your audience (age, professional background, personal background, etc.)? You must tailor your talk using appropriate vocabulary and information that the audience will understand and put into action.
- What is the audience expecting from you in terms of information, tone, level of formality, etc.?
- What does the audience know about your topic? You should know what they know and concentrate on the information that they do not know. The idea is to avoid being repetitive and to extend the knowledge base of your audience. If you are not sure what the audience knows, ask your contact person before your presentation, so that you can prepare accordingly.
- How long is your allotted time to speak? Speak for less than your limit to give the audience a chance to ask questions.

You need to keep the purpose of your talk in mind when you are preparing. In what capacity are you speaking? For example, are you giving a progress report on your service-learning project to your community partner or your peers? Are you presenting your final design and recommendations for your project? Focus the information in your presentation around your purpose and your audience. This will ensure that your audience is in the best position to take your information and act accordingly.

Organization

You should organize your presentation so the audience can digest the delivered information easily. The following tips will help you to organize your information.

- The key to a well-organized speech is realizing that even the most engaged audience will not pay attention all the time. Thus, you should limit your speech to three to five major points. Your talk will be successful if the audience understands and retains the information. How much your audience understands is more important than how much information you present.

Did you know that people speak 100–125 words per minute, but the human brain can handle up to 500 words per minute? This is how you can pay attention to what is going on when someone is speaking while your mind is on something else.

- **Have a one-page summary.** For a presentation longer than five minutes, an oral one-page summary at the beginning of the talk is useful. This lets the audience know what is coming and in what order, and will help your audience to follow your presentation.
- **Use the power of repetition.**
  - Repeat your main ideas; the audience will remember only three to five of the ideas you present
  - Repeating key points makes it easier for the audience to stay with you
  - Repeat your main message at least three times, in three different ways
  - Remember an adage from an accomplished speaker: "Tell them what you're going to tell them, tell them, then tell them what you told them."
- **Provide a written supplement if appropriate.** A written supplement helps people to focus on what you are saying instead of writing it down. This is a security thing; if people already have the information in front of them, they are more likely to listen and focus on your presentation. The more ways in which you present your message, the more likely the audience is going to remember it.

In terms of organizing the information itself, a sample outline of a presentation could be as follows:

- **Introduction:** Who you are and why you did this.
- **Need:** Why your engineering design needed?
- **Solution:** You have the design that addresses the need, and here it is. Include major design features and why you did what you did (explain how your design specifically addressed the needs).
- **Bottom line:** What are the benefits? How much it will cost?
- **Conclusion:** Re-state the main ideas and benefits.

Gather the Information You Need to Present

Although this point seems self-explanatory, remember these few tips when gathering information for an oral presentation:

- The information you include in your presentation should pertain to three to five main points you plan to share with the audience. This information will support your main points and will help with the organization of your presentation.
- Make use of graphics, pictures, and photographs because they communicate a wealth of information in a concise way
- Make sure that you do not include too much or too little information in your presentation. You should have approximately one slide for every minute that you speak. Some speakers can include more slides, but you should not exceed one slide per 30 seconds. Thus, if your presentation is ten minutes long, you should not have more than 20 slides.

Create Presentation Material with Maximal Audience Impact

Your impact can be visual (what people see), auditory (what people hear), or kinematic (what people do; hands-on experience). Remember, keep it simple. Your audience will stay with you if you use accessible language and the audience will retain information better if you provide information in more than one of the ways mentioned above.

The following tips will assist you in maximizing the visual impact of your talk.

- Present one central idea per slide.
- Be as brief as possible; make two clear, understandable slides rather than one cluttered slide with too much information.
- Font size (the size of your type) is important. Use at least 18-point font size for overheads. You can use smaller font size for slides but not much smaller (12-point, the size of the printed words in this book, is too small for slides).

- Slides do not need to be complete and self-explanatory; the speaker can add details (handouts are helpful here).
- Orally identify or locate colors to help listeners who are color blind (10% of all males are color blind).
- Use high contrast colors (white and blue, yellow and navy, etc.) with slides or overheads; this helps people with color blindness.
- The more you must use a pointer, the worse the slide; keep it simple.
- If you have many numbers in a table, use multiple slides with the empha-sized number circled or highlighted. If you are discussing only five numbers, why show more than five on a slide?
- Do not use all capital letters because they are difficult to read. Use capital letters sparingly for emphasis of an important point.
- Use graphs or charts instead of tables. Most people can comprehend graphs and charts more easily than tables.

The following tips will assist you in maximizing the auditory impact of your presentation.

- **Be an enthusiastic speaker**
  - Be enthusiastic about your message and your audience; everyone en-joys listening to speakers who care about their subject.
  - You do not have to be a cheerleader. Show with your voice, eyes, and body language what you are saying is important and meaningful.
  - Another adage: "There are no boring topics, only boring presentations."
- **Master your subject.** You need to be able to concentrate on reaching the audience, which means you should make eye contact with the audience and concentrate on "reading" your audience (are they engaged, bored, etc., and what can you do to get and keep their attention?). This takes energy. You should know your material well enough so that you appear confident.
- **Never read or memorize your presentation.** Reading reduces eye con-tact and memorization makes your talk appear canned and boring.
- **Use pauses to your advantage.** When you make an important point or when you have presented something complicated, give the audience time to think about and digest your point. You can build pauses into your presen-tation to slow down the pace if you tend to speak more quickly when doing public talks.

Using **Kinematic Methods** will engage your audience. The methods can be di-rect, where your audience does something, or indirect, where they watch as you do something hands-on. Make use of the following tips for kinematic methods:

- If you are demonstrating something, make sure that your audience can see the entire demonstration from their viewpoints. Make sure that you point out the major concepts or ideas.
- If you have the audience do something, especially if it involves multiple steps, make sure that the entire audience is with you as you step through the process. You can ask, "has everyone completed this step?" before pro-ceeding to the next one.

Practicing Your Presentation

Practice your presentation out loud because it will give you insight into your technique. First, most presentations tend to be scheduled, and you do not want your presentation to go longer than its allotted time. Long winded speakers will often alienate their audiences or will lose their attention. Most people tend to finish their presentations ahead of time because they speak more quickly when nervous. If you practice your presentation, you will know how long it takes to complete. If you are nervous, practice will enable you to build several places into your presentation in which you can check yourself and slow down if necessary. Second, the more you practice, the more familiar you become with the material that you are presenting. This familiarity can be important if your information is technical. Showing the audience you are familiar and comfortable with the presented information will help them (and you) gain confidence in your subject. Most likely, you will explain the concepts better as you understand them more fully.

Now that we have talked about everything you can do before a presentation to maximize its effectiveness, let's think about the presentation itself.

Getting Started

The first 15 to 30 seconds of a presentation are critical; establish eye contact and rapport, especially if you are going to turn down the lights for slides or PowerPoint. You can establish a connection with the audience in several ways:

- You can start by saying, "Good morning (or afternoon or evening), my name is [name], and I am going to discuss [subject.]"
- You can establish the level of formality. For example, you can tell the audience that it is okay to ask questions at any time.
- You can establish your tone with humor (telling a joke), or by asking a trivia question with a small reward (e.g., a piece of candy) for the winner.
- Interacting with the audience is an excellent way to establish good rapport. After you introduce yourself and the subject of your talk, you may involve the audience by asking a general question. Those interested can raise their hands or interact with an answer. This information could be useful to you (you can learn something about the audience for a better presentation) and can provide you with a good lead into the rest of your talk.

During your presentation, monitor your audience. Do they look engaged, confused, or bored? If they look engaged, do not change anything that you are doing. If your audience is confused, you could ask them a question, or say, "I know that this information is difficult and some of you look confused. Can I clear up anything for you?" If your audience appears bored, you might re-engage your audience with another trivia question or by asking the audience to become active.

The conclusion of your talk is important. You need to let your audience know that you have finished, e.g., "This concludes my presentation. Do you have any questions?"

Presentation Hardware

- Know how the equipment (PowerPoint, overhead projector, etc.) works beforehand. For overhead projectors, if you can read the overhead when you place it on the projector, the audience can read it. You may have to focus the image, but your overhead will not be backward or upside down.
- Ensure the proper video projection system is available and that the computer and system are compatible. You can bring your own just in case.

7.3 WRITTEN COMMUNICATION SKILLS

In your engineering travels, you will volunteer or be called upon to communicate your ideas, designs, findings, and concepts in writing. Many technical writing books contain detailed information about this. In fact, many of you will take an entire course in technical writing, during which time you will get experience writing technical papers, reports, cover letters, executive memos, engineering design notebooks, proposals, etc. This section of the chapter is intended to provide conceptual information with respect to the writing you will encounter in engineering, including reports, proposals, memorandums (memos for short), résumés, and cover letters. These next sections include brief descriptions on how to best craft these writing pieces. For more detailed information, consult a resource like S. Stevenson and S. Whitmore, *Strategies for Engineering Communication.*

7.3.1 Reports

A report is a technical communication that contains detailed information about a project in an organized way. One easy way to think about the main parts of a report is to consider that each can have an ABC format:

- **A**bstract gives a summary of the main points
- **B**ody supplies the supporting details
- **C**onclusion gives readers what they need to act

An **Abstract** summarizes a document's main points. It always includes a clear purpose statement for the document and the most important points for decision makers. It is a "capsule version" of the document and should answer the readers' typical questions, e.g., how does this document concern me? What is the bottom line?

The body is the middle section(s) of the document that should provide the following details:

A Couple of Common Grammatical Errors to Avoid

Its and it's: "Its" (without an apostrophe) is used to denote possession. For example: The dog chased its tail. "It's" is a contraction that means "it is." For example, It's sunny outside. If you are not sure which to use, simply insert the words "it is" in place of "it's." If the sentence makes sense, keep "it's." If not, use "its."

Affect and effect: "Affect" is a verb meaning to influence, e.g., Her leadership positively affected the situation. "Effect" is a noun meaning result, e.g., One effect of securing the contract was the hiring of more student workers. The tricky part is that effect can be used as a verb meaning to bring about, e.g., He effected considerable change when he became manager.

- The project background (if this is a service-learning report, you should include information on the history of the community and community agency, and a description of how you came together to work on the project.)
- Field, lab, office, or other work upon which the document is based
- Details of any conclusions and recommendations or proposals that make up the document

In the **body**, you provide detailed support for the points put forth in the abstract. You should do the following:

- Separate fact from opinion (what you know versus what you think or recommend)
- Adopt a format with structure by using headings and subheadings to help the reader follow the document
- Use graphics whenever possible (e.g., photographs, drawings, and tables or charts with data)

The **conclusion** brings readers (decision-makers) back to one or more central points detailed in the body. It should answer the following questions:

- What major points have you made?
- What problem have you tried to solve?
- What should the reader do next?
- What will you do next?
- What single idea do you want to leave with the reader?

The following example is an excerpted technical report from a team of engineering seniors.

POLYDIMETHYLSILOXANE (PDMS) SPIN-COATING SYSTEM FOR MICROSTRUCTURE FABRICATION

Conceptual Design Report
Prepared by:

Stuart Feilden
Chrissy Guidry
Lee Miller
Scott Noel
Wesley Plaisance

Submitted to:
Dr. Marybeth Lima, Associate Professor
December 12, 2003

TABLE OF CONTENTS

The title page should always contain the title of your report, the names of the people who worked on the project and/or wrote the report, the date, and information that specifies to whom the report is directed.

The table of contents contains all major headings and subheadings in the report. This report has figures and tables built into the text. Other reports may have separate sections for a list of figures and a list of tables. You should follow the format specified by your professor, community partner, or the organization to whom you are reporting. If no format is specified, choose a tentative format and ask the group if the format is acceptable before submitting the report; this could save you and/or your team a lot of work!

ABSTRACT

This report details the conceptual design of an automated spin-coating system specifically used for microstructure fabrication. Polydimethylsiloxane (PDMS) is the polymer used exclusively in this particular system. The purpose of this project was to design and construct a more economical spin-coating device used specifically for PDMS microstructure fabrication. This design will help to make BioMEMS and microstructure research economically feasible for small-scale research laboratories. After conducting a patent search on spin-coating devices, we determined that no patents existed for a PDMS-specific spin-coating device for our applications. We conducted research on several areas of interest, including electric motors, circuitry, electronics, PDMS properties, spin-coating and its governing physics, microstructure fabrication and microstructure applications. Our initial designs were conceived, discussed, and thoroughly analyzed to select and consolidate the most feasible ideas and concepts. An AutoCAD rendering of this conceptual design enabled us to visualize the design and make necessary adjustments. Appropriate calculations were conducted to select integral components of the design, for example, motor specifications were based on calculated torque and speed values. The major components of the spin coating system are a motor, chuck, basic stamp, user interface, catch basin, and casing. The final design presented in this report was engineered to fit pre-established criteria for reliability, precision, cost, and ease of use. Next semester, a prototype will be built and thoroughly tested for precision, accuracy, reliability, and repeatability.

This abstract provides information on the device being designed and details the design process followed to arrive at a conceptual design. The authors used this section to talk about the design process and to introduce the major components of their design. The last sentence indicates that a future report will contain information on the detailed design of the device, and building and testing information for this device.

Notice that this report is written in active voice (the abstract reads "We conducted . . ." and ". . . we determined . . ." instead of "research was conducted" or "it was determined"). Writing in passive voice used to be the preferred method of written technical communication, but active voice is becoming increasingly common. We suggest writing in active voice whenever possible because it is more concise and easy to interpret.

INTRODUCTION

The body of this report is divided into two major sections, introduction/ background information and presentation of the design components. Introductory and background information are presented in several subsections including introductory information on the design, a review of existing technology in this area, background information necessary for understanding the spinning process and the components necessary for the design. This information is organized in order from the general to the specific, an approach that facilities easy understanding for the reader. An excerpt of the body is contained below.

Problem Definition

The current spin coating devices used in microstructure fabrication are not cost effective for bench-scale research laboratories. Currently, introductory, bench scale spin-coating machines cost at least $3000 and additional features add dramatically to the cost of such devices. Our goal is to design and construct a spin coating machine for the fabrication of polydimethylsiloxane (PDMS) microstructures for $1000 or less.

Need for a PDMS Spin Coating Device

Spin coating devices are used extensively in the microlithography manufacturing of integrated circuits. In the biotechnology arena, PDMS, a biocompatible polymer, is spun onto prefabricated wafers that contain master molds of an intricate system of microchannels. These microchannels form the base architecture for microelectromechanical systems (MEMS), which are becoming extensively used in biotechnology research and industry. The integration of MEMS and biology (BioMEMS) is an exciting area of rapidly advancing discovery, allowing many assays and sensors to be improved in sensitivity and speed for biotechnology applications. The creation of PDMS films of precise, uniform thickness is necessary for many BioMEMS related efforts, such as fabricating stacked layers of microchannels, wells, and valves to form a lab-on-a-chip device, or embedding enzymes in thin films for use in biosensors. An economical, automated PDMS-specific spin-coating device has not been constructed for small-scale use, which results in a need for investigators who wish to conduct research at this scale. An economically-feasible system will expedite the advancement of micro-scaled research by enabling a larger number of laboratories to become involved and by increasing the number of devices that can be used for research purposes.

Purpose of our Proposed System

We will design and build a more economical spin-coating device for small-scale research facilities. In the spring of 2004, we will produce the corresponding protocol to fabricate microstructures with PDMS.

Benefits

- Decreased Cost of Spin-Coating Device
- Increased availability of Spin-Coating Technology
- Easy Method to Fabricate Microstructures
- Accuracy, Precision, and Reliability

GENERAL BACKGROUND

The Process of Spin-Coating

Spin-coating is a technique that is used in a wide variety of fields. The fabrication of micro-environments is a specific use of spin-coating in the biotechnology arena. The process of spin-coating involves the deposition of a polymer onto a thin silicon wafer (similar in shape to a compact disc). This wafer is then spun at varying speeds and times to uniformly coat the wafer with the polymer. During the spinning process, certain engineering processes must be accounted for, including fluid flow and evaporative effects.

CONCEPTUALIZATION AND SELECTION OF FINAL DESIGN COMPONENTS

This section depicts the components contained in the final conceptual design of our spinning device. The overall device is sketched in the figures below, and the individual components that comprise the design are described.

The previous two sentences provide the "big picture" in terms of what is contained in this section, and provides the reader with a framework for understanding what is coming next. Such information facilitates the readability of a report, especially if the report contains a lot of information.

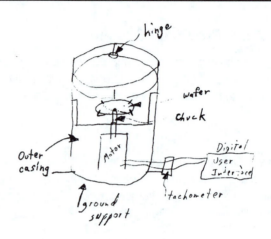

Figure 4 Prelimanary Design Sketch

Chuck

A rigid and lightweight material was needed to minimize the motor torque required. Aluminum was selected for its high strength relative to its weight. Although aluminum is more expensive than steel, a relatively small amount of aluminum is required for the chuck. The chuck is dimensioned in the figure below. The mass is 120 grams (0.263 pounds) and the moment of inertia is 0.60 lb-in2 (0.004167 lb-ft2). These values were used to select and size an electric motor using calculations contained in Appendix I. The final chuck design is shown in the figure below.

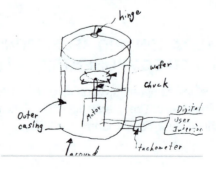

Figure 5 Final Chuck Design

Table 2   Cost Analysis

PROPOSED BUDGET	
PARTS WITH COST ANALYSIS	
Precision DC Electric Motor with	
• Optical Tachometer	$ 500
• Variable speed control	
PVC pipe-Body Housing	$ 50
Aluminum Chuck Fabrication and Materials	$ 125
Wafer supply	$ 75
Polydimethylsiloxane (PDMS)	$ 100
User Interface (electronics)	$ 100
Basic Stamp / Electronics (simple computer chip)	$ 75
AC/DC Converters (2)	$ 2 × 25
Testing Expenses and Supplies	$ 400
• Prefabricated wafers (microstructure mold)	
• Profilometer evaluation of PDMS height (micrometer scale)	
• Center for Advanced Microstructures and Devices	
Total	**$ 1075 for fabrication**
	$ 400 for testing

CONCLUSION

We used the engineering methods discussed in class and in our book (Dieter, 2000) to create a conceptual design of an automated spin coating system specific for PDMS. This project was initiated in response to a need for economical, bench-scale system for fabrication of BioMEMs and biosensors. The components of our design include a motor, chuck, basic stamp, user interface, catch basin, and casing. Our goal was to fabricate this device for $1000 or less. Our conceptual design exceeds this budget by $75. Though we did not reach this design goal, the cost of such a device was reduced to approximately one-third of current devices on the market. Next semester, we will build and test our device for precision, accuracy, reliability, and repeatability. We believe that the spin coating system presented in this report addresses an important need by providing an economical alternative to existing spin coating systems.

The conclusion reiterates the major concepts presented in the report, and addresses the questions that should be answered in a conclusion (see description of report conclusion for details).

REFERENCES CITED

There is no current standard for reference style in technical writing! Many nontechnical writing publications use APA (American Psychological Association) style, but this reference style is not widely practiced in engineering. Use the style suggested by your professor or community partner. The excerpted references above are representative of the type of reference style that you will see in technical publications.

References should include the authors of the publication, the year of publication, the title of the publication, and further descriptive information that will enable you (sometimes with the help of a librarian) to locate the publication.

Web sites should include the author and title of the site, in addition to when the site was accessed. This information is critical should the web address change or be deleted. The extra information may enable others to still find the site if the web address listed is incorrect.

> Birnie, D.P. 2004. *Coating Quality and Spin Coating.* Department of Materials Science and Engineering, University of Arizona. http://www.mse.arizona.edu.

Book titles should be italicized.

> Dieter, G. 2000. *Engineering Design: A Materials and Processing Approach,* 3rd Ed. New York: McGraw-Hill.

The titles of journal articles can be italicized to set off the title from the rest of the reference. The title of the journal, the journal volume (and volume number in parentheses if provided) and the page numbers are provided in that order after author, date, and title information.

> Charati, S. and S. Stern. 1998. *Diffusion of Gases in Silicone Polymers: Molecular Dynamics Simulations.* Macromolecules. 31: 5529–5535

> ## APPENDIX I
>
> ## Initial Motor Calculations
>
> $$\alpha = \frac{\omega}{t} \quad T = I\alpha$$
>
> *Symbols*
>
> α = Angular Acceleration $\left(\dfrac{\text{rad}}{\text{sec}^2} \right)$

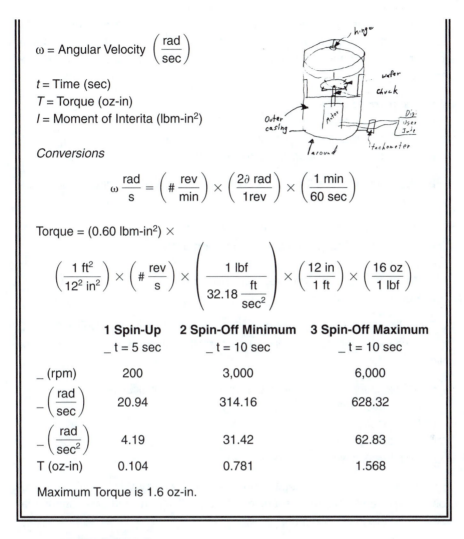

ω = Angular Velocity $\left(\dfrac{\text{rad}}{\text{sec}}\right)$

t = Time (sec)
T = Torque (oz-in)
I = Moment of Interita (lbm-in²)

Conversions

$$\omega\,\frac{\text{rad}}{\text{s}} = \left(\#\,\frac{\text{rev}}{\text{min}}\right) \times \left(\frac{2\partial\ \text{rad}}{1\,\text{rev}}\right) \times \left(\frac{1\ \text{min}}{60\ \text{sec}}\right)$$

Torque = (0.60 lbm-in²) ×

$$\left(\frac{1\ \text{ft}^2}{12^2\ \text{in}^2}\right) \times \left(\#\,\frac{\text{rev}}{\text{s}}\right) \times \left(\frac{1\ \text{lbf}}{32.18\ \dfrac{\text{ft}}{\text{sec}^2}}\right) \times \left(\frac{12\ \text{in}}{1\ \text{ft}}\right) \times \left(\frac{16\ \text{oz}}{1\ \text{lbf}}\right)$$

	1 Spin-Up _ t = 5 sec	**2 Spin-Off Minimum** _ t = 10 sec	**3 Spin-Off Maximum** _ t = 10 sec
_ (rpm)	200	3,000	6,000
$-\left(\dfrac{\text{rad}}{\text{sec}}\right)$	20.94	314.16	628.32
$-\left(\dfrac{\text{rad}}{\text{sec}^2}\right)$	4.19	31.42	62.83
T (oz-in)	0.104	0.781	1.568

Maximum Torque is 1.6 oz-in.

7.3.2 PROPOSALS

Written proposals are documents that address a need and usually describe a need or problem, define a solution, and request funding or other resources to solve the problem. Proposals can be solicited (when an organization asks for proposals) or unsolicited (when you send in a proposal and ask for funding without waiting for the organization to ask). Solicited proposals involve a Request For Proposal (RFP) with the following guidelines:

- What the proposal should cover
- What sections it should have
- When it should be submitted
- To whom it should be sent
- How it will be evaluated with respect to other proposals

For proposals, you follow the ABC format for report writing but you concentrate on addressing a need.

A: The **Abstract** gives the summary or big picture for those who will make decisions about your proposal. The abstract usually includes some kind of hook or grabber, which will entice the audience to read further. The abstract will include the following:

- The purpose of the proposal
- The reader's main need
- The main features you offer and related benefits
- An overview of proposal sections to follow

B: The **Body** provides the details about your proposal. Your discussion should answer the following questions:

- What do you want to solve and why?
- What are the technical details of your approach?
- Who will do the work and with what?
- When will it be done and how long will it take?
- How much will it cost?

Typical sections in the body portion of the report will be given to you in the RFP, or else you will have to develop them yourself, making sure you address the following:

- A description of the problem or project and its significance
- A proposed solution or approach
- Personnel
- Schedule
- Cost breakdown of funds requested

Give special attention to establishing need in the Body. Why should your proposal be chosen? What makes it unique? How will your design or recommendations contribute to the community?

C: The **Conclusion** makes your proposal's main benefit explicit and will make the next step clear. This section gives you the opportunity to control the reader's final impression. Be sure to:

- Emphasize a main benefit or feature of your proposal
- Restate your interest in doing the work
- Indicate what should happen next

In the next section, you will see a sample report completed by students in engineering courses that worked on a service-learning project. An evaluation of this sample is included.

> Did you know that one of the major jobs of professors is to write proposals in order to get grant money to conduct research projects?

For Reports and Proposals

Make strong use of appendices for added, detailed information that would take up too much space in the report or proposal itself.

Commonly Used Proposal Lingo

RFP or **rfp**: request for proposal

PI: principal investigator: the person responsible for the administration of the project

co-PI: the persons responsible for the administration of the project. If there are two or more people primarily in charge or with significant duties for a project, then they are co-PIs.

Proposal: the document that you prepare to request funds for a project

Grant: the money that you receive if you've written a successful project

Contract: Most granting agencies require you to sign a contract—a legally binding agreement that ensures that you will complete the objectives of the project using the money provided by the agency.

Program Officer: The primary contact person at the agency that is conducting the RFP. Any questions that you might have about your project would be addressed to the program officer. These people can often give you extra information that may not be contained in the RFP!

Proposal reviewer: A person who reads the proposal and critically reviews it. Reviewers check to make sure that the science and engineering are sound, the project is important, the objectives are measurable, the proposed plan of work is excellent, the proposal is well written, and the budget is reasonable.

Resubmission: Grant proposals are hard to get! Usually there are many more potential projects to fund than money to go around. Many federal granting agencies fund only about 10% of the projects submitted! This means that some excellent ideas and projects will not receive funding. If your project is not funded, look at the comments from proposal reviewers (these are usually included with a letter telling you that you didn't receive funding). If you do a good job addressing these comments and re-submit your proposal during the next funding cycle, your chances for funding on this resubmission are much better!

EXAMPE PROPOSAL

The following successful proposal was written by two biological engineering students in response to an RFP from the LSU College of Agriculture (engineering students were encouraged to apply). The actual RFP is also included for your reference.

COLLEGE OF AGRICULTURE
LOUISIANA STATE UNIVERSITY

Undergraduate Research Grants for 2001

The College of Agriculture offers competitive grants for research by undergraduate students in the college. The purpose of these grants is to encourage research by students as a part of the educational process.

Research can be in any area of study in the College of Agriculture. Multidisciplinary projects are encouraged. All research must be under the direction of a College of Agriculture faculty member. Each grant will be limited to a maximum of $2,500. Projects must be completed by December 31, 2001. Grant funds will be administered in the Department and may be used for supplies, equipment, operating services, and travel. Funds may not be used for salaries or wages. Any unexpended funds remaining at the completion of the project must be returned to the College. Students may receive academic credit under appropriate research or special topic courses.

Proposals must include the following:

Title
Principal Investigator(s), Department(s)
Faculty Supervisor(s)
Objectives
Procedures/Methodology
Beginning Date (1/1/04) and Ending Date: (no later than 12/31/04)
Proposed Budget (with narrative)
Approvals: P.I.(s), Faculty Supervisor(s), Departmental Head(s) or School
    Director(s)

Proposals will be evaluated and ranked by a faculty committee. Meritorious proposals will be funded. Awards will be announced at the beginning of the Spring 2001 semester.

Full reports of results, including proposed presentations and publications and possible patents must be submitted within 30 days of the completion of the research (ending date of grant). A complete financial accounting is to be submitted with the final report.

VITAMIN A DEGRADATION KINETICS DURING CONVENTIONAL AND OHMIC HEATING

Co-PIs: Julianne Forman and Jennifer Holtan

Department of Biological & Agricultural Engineering

Faculty Advisor: Dr. Marybeth Lima

Project Narrative

Vitamin A degradation in tomato juice during electrical and conventional (non-electrical, hot water) heating will be studied to determine if the presence of an electric field alters the rate of vitamin degradation. The experiments will be performed using an ohmic heating apparatus, identical heating histories, and statistical procedures. Ohmic heating involves passing an alternating current through a food sample; the food generates internal heat due to its inherent resistance. This study seeks to quantify the breakdown of fat-soluble vitamin A in tomato juice as a result of conventional and ohmic heating. The FDA has not yet approved ohmic heating for commercial use in the U.S. However, research in ohmic heating is receiving more attention for its applications and improvements in food quality and food processing costs. Studies in ohmic heating serve to aid in finding more applications of the ohmic heating process and how it enhances biological properties. As a result, the FDA can establish qualitative and quantitative characterizations of ohmic heating and approve applications of this technology. This study is significant for the potential use of ohmic heating as a sterilization option and the importance of the effect an electric field will have on vitamin degradation. A prior study on water-soluble vitamins has been done (Lima *et al.*1999), however fat-soluble vitamin degradation kinetics during ohmic heating have never been studied.

Objectives

Degradation kinetic parameters (the order of the reaction, the reaction rate constant and the activation energy) of vitamin A in tomato juice will be determined. A previous degradation study involving vitamin C (water-soluble) in orange juice was performed and found Vitamin C to be unaffected by an electric field strength 18.2 V/cm within the temperature range of 65–95°C. (Lima *et al.*, 1999). The objectives of this study are (1) to determine the effect of the presence of an electric field on the rate of vitamin A degradation in tomato juice and (2) to determine the kinetic parameters involved under conventional and ohmic conditions.

Procedure/Methodology

50 mL samples of tomato juice will be used in both conventional and ohmic heating using the same time-temperature combination for each case. We will test four different temperatures: (1) 65°C, (2) 75°C, (3) 85°C, and (4) 95°C. All samples will be heated for one hour. For each treatment, 0.5 mL samples will be taken at 0, 15, 30, 45, and 60 minutes and each time-temperature combination will be repeated three times. All statistical analyses and kinetic parameter determinations will be performed according to the methodology in Lima *et al.* (1999).

Samples will be withdrawn using a pipette and then immediately stored in ice and out of direct light. The samples will then be analyzed using High-Performance Liquid Chromatography (HPLC). The vitamin A concentration will be determined using standard methods (Helrich, K., 1990).

Beginning Date (1/1/01) Ending Date (12/31/01)

Activity	Jan–March	April–June	July–Sept	Oct–Dec
Purchase/receive materials	xxxxxx			
Begin kinetics experiments	xxx	xxxxxxxxx		
Present work at ASAE meeting			x	
Finish kinetics experiments			xxxxxxx	xxx
Disseminate information			x	xxxxxxx

Proposed Budget

Glass tee (for the ohmic heater)	150
Teflon covered thermocouples	200
(for measuring temperatures during experiments)	
Materials/supplies/solvents	150
(tomato juice, pipettes, pipette tips, epp tubes for storing samples)	
HPLC Column for vitamin A analysis	600
Partial travel expenses for presenting	1,336

this work at the 2001 ASAE meeting, Sacramento, CA.

(airfare ($450 each (2) + 80/day for hotel + $29 day/person for meals; registration sponsored by the Biological Engineering Student Organization)

Total:	$2,436

Dr. Marybeth Lima's departmental funding and related grants will cover any expenses exceeding the proposed budget.

REFERENCES

Helrich, K., ed. 1990. AOAC Official Methods of Analysis, 15th, p.717. AOAC Inc. Arlington, VA.

Lima, M., Heskitt, B., Burianek, L., Nokes, S., Sastry, S. 1999. *Ascorbic Acid Degradation Kinetics During Conventional and Ohmic Heating.* Journal of Food Processing Preservation 23: 421–434.

This proposal was funded for the full $2,436. The proposal reviewers had the following comments concerning this proposal:

Proposal Analysis

- Reader has to wait too long to learn why one would even heat tomato juice (sterilization). What were the results of ohmic heating on water soluble vitamins?

- Literature review seems too brief.
- Budget seems high for work described (especially for travel).
- Looks good.

Notice that the student-written proposal follows the same headings in the same order as those presented in the RFP. Instructions in an RFP should be followed exactly. **Many proposals are not considered if they have even one small preparation error!**

The authors do a good job of describing the project specifically in the proposal narrative. They could have included more general information to provide a better context that the project specifics would fit into. For example, the authors could have mentioned that food processing is an essential part of guaranteeing a safe, nutritious food supply, and that the overall goal of this research was to provide more information on a relatively new food processing method. This information would allow engineers to design appropriate food processing equipment.

The project timeline is unconventional because the research is being presented at a conference before it is completed. Although it is better to present research when it is fully finished, the students were constrained by the time available to complete the project and expend the funds. The premier meeting in their discipline was held in July, and this was the only July in which they had funding to attend the meeting.

Other Proposal Writing Tips

Graphics

Remember the adage "a picture is worth 1000 words"? Because proposals involve concise writing, it is often useful to include diagrams, flow charts, pictures or other graphics to illustrate parts of your proposed project that would take many words to explain. One successful proposal writer said, "Always put a graphic on page two of your proposal. It breaks up the monotony for proposal reviewers!"

Objectives

Organizations that grant money are very interested in project objectives. One of the most important things that they look for is this: are the objectives measurable? That is, at the completion of the project, can they see that the money they put into the project has had a measurable positive impact?

Budget

Remember that funds that are not spent by the end of the grant are sent back to the granting agency, UNLESS you can get an extension on the time needed to spend the money. These so-called no cost extensions are commonly granted.

For example, if you are writing a proposal to receive money to complete a service-learning project, which objective do you think is better:

- To improve the community
- To improve the community through the construction of a bike path
- To improve the community through the construction of a bike path that connects the east and west ends of town

One other thing to think about is the type of objectives in your proposal. There are two types: formative and summative.

- Formative objectives are those that you measure/monitor during the project period.
- Summative objectives are those that are evaluated at the end of the project.

Good proposal objectives (especially those for long term projects, meaning longer than one year) include both types of objectives!

Service-Learning Success Story

Engineering students in a technical writing class worked with a community partner to write proposals to the Baton Rouge Area Foundation. These proposals were written to fund a playground designed in another service-learning course. The Baton Rouge Area Foundation awarded $50,000 to the community partner to fund the playground, which was built by student volunteers from both classes!

7.3.3 Memorandums (See Sample Memo on Next Page)

A memorandum, or memo for short, is a brief technical communication intended to share information with decision makers. You write a technical communication when you need to document your work in writing. Typical examples include memos to go into a personnel file (congratulations or job improvement details) or those to go into technical files (i.e., engineering projects you are working on).

Memos contain introductory information that summarizes the memo's purpose. The memo's conclusion restates the main points and contains any recommendations. The example memo below includes a critique so you can better learn the appropriate approach to drafting memos.

7.3.4 Résumés

A résumé is one of the most important documents you will ever create. It sells you and your qualifications. There are two types of résumés: skills résumés and experience résumés. A skills résumé is for people who have not yet completed significant work experience. The skills résumé highlights the skills and talents to benefit the potential employer, even if the applicant has little or no technical work

SAMPLE MEMO

March 19, 2005

To: Josephine Smith, Senior, Mechanical Engineering

From: Leslie Moore, Co-chair of the Volunteer Recruitment Committee

Re: Instructions for playground volunteers

The beginning of this memo is standard in terms of its format, and contains the date, the name of the person to whom correspondence is directed, the person who sent the correspondence, and a subject line describing the purpose of the memo. The subject line is indicated by the abbreviation "Re," which stands for the word "regarding." The person sending the memo often signs or initials the "From" line.

Thank you for dedicating part of your day this Thursday, March 25, to the construction of the playground at Roosevelt Elementary School! The following paragraphs contain all the information that you will need to have a successful experience. Please contact me at lmoore@lsu.edu or 208 8858 if you have any further questions.

Contact information is listed toward the top of the memo in case there are any questions that volunteers might have.

The Roosevelt Elementary School campus is located at 2500 Brightside Drive. From the LSU campus, you would go to Nicholson Drive and turn left (heading south/east, toward Tigerland). Go about 1.3 miles and turn right onto Brightside Drive. After you've turned on Brightside, go about a half mile and the school is on the right hand side of the road. Signs will be posted that will direct you to the construction site and appropriate parking.

   Please plan to be at the site by 7:30 A.M. Free breakfast and lunch will be provided, in addition to water, soda, and snacks at all times. Things that you might bring to make your day easier include suntan lotion (expected weather for tomorrow is partly cloudy, high 79°, low 58°) and garden gloves. There will be a volunteer check-in table at the entrance to the site, where you will sign in and fill out a volunteer waiver form. You will be assigned to a work team of 10–15 people which will include a team leader. You will be working with this team during the entire construction day (I realize that many students are unable to stay for the entire construction day; this is okay, just do what you can while you're on site).

   Your work day will begin at 8:00, and your team will break for lunch at about noon. Construction should be completed at approximately 2:00 in the afternoon with a board cutting ceremony (in lieu of a traditional ribbon cutting) to commemorate the successful construction of the playground. All volunteers will have the opportunity to participate in the ceremony, so please stay for this event.

Three distinct pieces of information are included in this memo: how to get to the playground site, when and what to do upon arrival, and what will happen throughout the day. Each of these ideas is included in a separate paragraph to facilitate easy understanding for the reader.

Thank you once again for your commitment and interest, and please contact me if you have any further questions!

The conclusion of the memo reiterates appreciation for the volunteer and encourages the volunteer to contact the author of the memo if there are any questions.

experience. Experience résumés highlight prior work experience related to the job for which a person is applying. In general, most engineering students in the first two years of study and those who graduate without technical work experience will use a skills résumé; engineering students with co-op or internship experience in an engineering context would use an experience résumé.

The following sample and bulleted explanation is intended to assist you with more detailed information on crafting a résumé. A sample evaluation form is included, so you can evaluate your own résumé.

A few important things to remember about résumés:

- A résumé should be crafted for a specific position or job. This shows the employer that you care about the position. Your résumé's objective section should reflect some specificity as a result.
- You may need to change your résumé for "scannable format," if you apply for jobs with larger engineering companies. These companies use a computer to scan each résumé submitted to them for keywords. If so, you should consult your career services office or look at the company's recruitment information to determine these keywords and use them on your résumé. The scanner will target you and your résumé as a potential employee more quickly.
- If possible, keep your résumé to one page. Many employers frown upon résumés longer than one page.
- The format of a résumé is important. Your information should be arranged to be visually pleasing and readable. Use the following strategies in terms of format:
  - List dates in reverse chronological order (starting with your most recent information)
  - Use at least 11-point font size (preferably 12) and traditional, legible font types, such as Times New Roman
  - Use one-inch margins around the page
  - Headings such as Education, Work History, Skills, Honors and Activities, etc., should be in bold, can be in capital letters, and should be the only information on that line of the page
  - Your résumé should be printed using a high-quality laser printer on excellent bond paper (at least 40-pound ivory-colored or off-white paper)

Remember that skills are learned through paid experience, and also through:

- Volunteer experiences: civic, community, or political campaign work
- Social experiences: college organization responsibilities
- Academic experiences: course work, class projects, and honorary or pre-professional organizations related to your curriculum
- Service-learning experiences: highlight these as work-related and academic experience.

Julianne Marie Forman
jf777@lsu.com

Local Address:
500 Campus Street, Baton Rouge, LA 70808
(225) 123-4567

Permanent Address:
100 Main Street, Baton Rouge, LA 70808
(225) 555-1212

Objective	To obtain admission to the masters program in Biological Engineering at the University of Arkansas

Education	**Louisiana State University**, Baton Rouge, LA
	  Bachelor of Science in Biological Engineering, December 2002
	  Cum GPA: 3.97 GPA in Major: 4.00
	Louisiana Tech University, Ruston, LA, 1998–2000

Related Courses	Bioprocess Design, Transport Phenomena, Biomechanics, Mechanical Design, Engineering Properties of Biological Materials, Technical Writing
Computer Skills	• Proficient in Microsoft Office 2000, AutoCAD 2000, FemLAB • Familiar with Microsoft FrontPage, MathCAD, 3D Studio Max, Nastran, SuperPro
Research Experience	*Virginia Tech Bioprocessing Engineering Internship*, Summer 2001 • National Science Foundation Research for Undergraduates Program • Conducted research on electronic-nose created correlations using TBAR analysis *Undergraduate Student Worker*, Biological and Agricultural Engineering Dept., 2000–2002 • Investigated the design of animal habitats from a biological engineering perspective • Researched Vitamin A degradation during ohmic heating *LSU PLUS (Program of Learning thrU Service) Participation*, 2000–2002 • Designed and constructed playgrounds and a bird sanctuary for local elementary schools
Professional Achievements	• Forman, Julianne M., Claude, L., Albright, A., Lima, M. 2001. The Design of Enriched Animal Habitats from a Biological Engineering Perspective. *Transactions of the ASAE* 44(5):1363–1371. • Received Undergraduate Research Grant ($2,436) for project entitled *Vitamin A Degradation Kinetics During Conventional and Ohmic Heating* from the LSU College of Agriculture • Presented research on ohmic heating at the Institute of Biological Engineering Meeting in Sacramento, CA, 2001 • Received Bank One Award for Outstanding Presentation at the Teaching in Higher Education (THE) Forum, LSU campus, 2002, panel on service-learning (invited speaker)
Academic Achievements	• NSF Graduate Research Fellowship 2002 • LSU College of Engineering Scholarship • Engineer in Training (Oct. 2002) • ASAE Robert E. Stewart Engineering Humanities Award • Outstanding Sophomore, LSU College of Engineering • Wiley D. Poole Scholarship • Harold T. Barr Scholarship
Activities	• Tau Beta Pi • Golden Key National Honor Society • Phi Kappa Phi National Honor Society • Society of Women Engineers Member • Vice-President of Biological Engineering Student Organization • Biomedical Engineering Society • Gamma Sigma Delta
Hobbies	Working out, traveling, reading

Checklist for Self-Evaluation of Your Résumé

Information
- Objective is clearly stated.
- Clearly convey how your education, experience, activities, and honors support the objective.
- Experience, education, and/or skills segments are effective.
- All activities, honors, and other data are appropriate for the employment and the reader.

Organization
- Name and key headings stand out.
- Information within each heading is ordered from most to least important.
- Experience segment is arranged to highlight your strengths and career objective.

Style
- Language is simple, direct, and precise.
- Noun phrases are consistently used for headings.
- Strong verb phrases or clauses are consistently used to describe experience, skills, and activities.
- Parallel structure is used effectively.
- Have no errors in grammar, punctuation, or spelling (no typos whatsoever).*

---

* (The above information was provided by Deborah Normand, Instructor of English at Louisiana State University.)

7.3.5 Cover Letters

You should always send a cover letter with your résumé. This document introduces you to the potential employer in a more conversational manner. The following information will assist you in creating a strong cover letter.

A good cover letter:

- Identifies the position for which you are applying
- Explains why you should be considered for the position
- Highlights specific aspects of your accomplishments, especially those that are noteworthy and make you stand out with respect to other applicants
- Provides detailed information not in your résumé
- Should not exceed one page

Here is a list of recommended action verbs you may want to use in your résumé, categorized by topic:

Human Relations
worked with
volunteered
interacted
sponsored
taught
served
counseled
directed
helped
assisted
trained
guided

Research and Design
researched
analyzed
solved
discovered
investigated
experimented
tested
verified
devised
evaluated
observed
assessed
designed
created

Communications
drafted
designed
composed
published
presented
edited
revised
prepared
taught
instructed
addressed
interpreted
lectured
conducted
published

Management
managed
rated
evaluated
devised
planned
organized
coordinated
contracted
maintained
established
negotiated
controlled
purchased
saved
scheduled
sold
verified
produced
improved

The above information was provided by Deborah Normand, Instructor of English at Louisiana State University, who adapted from documentation entitled "Résumé Writing" from the LSU Career Planning and Placement Center.

Cover letters contain:

- Your contact information (address and phone number) and the date
- The full name and contact information of the person at the company/school to whom you must address the letter
- A formal greeting (Dear Dr. Jekyll or Mr. Hyde)
- An opening paragraph that should contain an explanation of how you heard about the position and should specifically identify the position itself. For example:
  - As you suggested during last week's career fair at <Your University>, I have enclosed a copy of my résumé for your consideration.
  - I am submitting my résumé in response to the position description for a consulting engineer in the want ads section of <Your local paper> on June 21, 2004).
  You can also state your interest in the position, and briefly highlight your experience and/or education that make you well suited to the position.
- The central section of the letter will contain one or more paragraphs in which you describe and draw attention to relevant aspects of your education or experience. You can also indicate your knowledge of and enthusiasm regarding the potential employer. Try to expand on things especially of interest to the company/school, and/or things that are important but that you couldn't detail in your résumé.
- The concluding paragraph should refer to the résumé for further details, and politely but confidently ask for an interview. Include your contact information (phone and e-mail). Thank the reader for their consideration.
- Include a formal closing, and make sure you sign the letter

The sample cover letter included on next page contains further information on writing a successful letter.

7.4 COMMUNICATION WITH COMMUNITY PARTNERS

What Is a Community Partner?

A community partner could be a non-profit agency, a school, a group of people in the community, or one person in the community. Sometimes your community partner might be a combination of the above or a coalition of groups. The community partner usually has a need that you can address through your service-learning project, or the community partner might be working on a community issue, and through this work you will work on this community issue. The community partner has expertise, resources, and knowledge to share with you, and you have expertise, resources, and knowledge to share with the community partner.

Some people use the term client to describe their community partners. We prefer the term community partner to client because community partner promotes an equal exchange among partners and students, while client implies that the engineering student provides a service that the client does not return. Engineering

July 17, 2005

Ms. Michele Broderick
Department of Human Resources
Pfizer Discovery Technology Center
620 Memorial Drive
Cambridge, MA 02139-4815

Dear Ms. Broderick:

I am applying for the assistant bioprocess engineer position at Pfizer as advertised on your website. I expect to graduate summa cum laude in August 2005 from Louisiana State University with a Bachelor of Science in Biological Engineering. My independent research and internship experience have prepared me to meet the qualifications for this position.

Presently, I am working on an independent research project with an undergraduate research grant that I received from the College of Agriculture Undergraduate Student Grants Program ($2,500). By studying the effects of ohmic heating on vitamin A degradation, I am expanding my knowledge of kinetics, software, and equipment widely used in bioprocess research, such as HPLC (high performance liquid chromatograph). I conducted bioprocess engineering research through a National Science Foundation Research experience for Undergraduates (NSF-REU) Internship at Virginia Tech. Working in a team of four, I gained research skills in using an electronic nose, analytical skills through data collection and interpretation, and interpersonal communication skills important to working effectively in a team.

My analytical skills will enable me to understand new technologies being used in separation processes, such as the purification of therapeutic products at Pfizer. The new Discovery Technology Center of Pfizer is unique with its integration of genetics, biological sciences, engineering, and informatics. As one of the world's largest and most respected pharmaceutical enterprises, your exclusive program would fulfill my desires to continue exploring and discovering drug development processes.

A career in bioprocess engineering at Pfizer will provide me with excellent opportunities in biotechnology, as well as a strong basis of chemical design and drug development. Please contact me to schedule an interview any weekday after 3:00 P.M. at (225) 123-4567.

Sincerely,

Julianne Forman

Enclosure: Résumé
Julianne M. Forman
100 Main Street, Baton Rouge, LA 70808
E-mail: julianne@lsu.edu (225) 555-1212

professionals work with clients in a business sense, where there is money exchanged for service. In service-learning, engineers work with community partners in a democratic sense, where there are services exchanged for the common good of people in the community.

We included a separate section on communication with community partners. Even if you understand oral and written communication skills, these fundamentals are not enough to interact with a community partner. We decided to include this section to show you how to put together your communication skills and interpersonal skills to address and enjoy the challenges and opportunities inherent in working with community partners and community issues.

The first thing to keep in mind is that your service-learning experience should possess four to five essential characteristics to be successful:

Shared mission. You, your peers, professor, and community partner should have a similar mission for the project's outcomes. For example, if you are working with an agency that rebuilds community parks, your goal should be to rebuild community parks. This means you should be familiar with the community partner's mission. Even if you have a shared mission, each stakeholder in the process will have different goals. This is okay, but everyone needs to be committed to the basic mission of the project.

Reciprocal benefits. Though your mission is the same, your benefits will be different. The community partner will benefit from your service (this could be a specific task, such as building something or preparing a design or report). You will benefit by the education provided by the community partner (learning from community members, from hands-on experience, etc.). You must both receive benefits from the project, and these benefits should be as equal as possible. The education you receive from the project completion will probably outweigh the benefits provided to the community and community partner.

Clear communication. You must understand the mission, vision, goals, and expectations of your community partner and your professor for the project's success. The community partner and the professor must understand your project and student goals to provide you with the optimal service-learning experience. Communicating your needs, challenges, and progress throughout the service-learning project will make the project run more efficiently and be successful.

Shared resources and rewards. You and your community partner will bring resources to the table in the form of brainpower, history, people power, and possibly finance and/or infrastructure. Recognize the resources you have and work together to use these resources to address community needs. You should share in addressing the challenges and celebrating your service-learning project's success.

Sustained commitment (if applicable). This will depend on the project you work on and is often up to your professor and the community partner. Your project may not require long-term commitment. You may present lectures on math and science to high school students, and the project ends when the school year is complete.[1] On the other hand, construction of community infrastructure (parks, buildings, playgrounds, etc.) or devices for community members should include plans for maintenance and what should be done with the structure at the end of its useful life. These plans must be shared with the community partner.

The key concept to keep in mind is that if you are working with a project involving the physical construction of a device or structure, you must complete a lifecycle design. This design contains specific details regarding the device construction, a plan on how to maintain it throughout its useful life, and how the device will be re-used, recycled, or remediated for minimal environmental impact at the end of its useful life. (Consult chapters 2 and 3 for more information on this topic.)

The aforementioned characteristics sketch out the big picture in terms of communicating and working with community partners. The following section will give you more specific tips with regard to your interaction.

1.   *Know as much as possible about the community partner and the community you are working with before you visit.* Having knowledge the community's history and culture is critical for understanding the community and for working with the community partner to create appropriate solutions or recommendations to meet community needs. You should know what the community thinks of the organization that you are working with and the school that you attend.

2.   *Go with a plan.* When you interact with a community partner, you must do more than show up and say "What do I do?" You should have an agenda or a plan when you visit the community, including the activities you need to complete, how long it will take to complete each activity, and an ordered activities list. A detailed list of questions to support these activities is also useful. This will make your visit efficient for you and your community partner.

3.   *Take meticulous notes.* You need an accurate record of everything that you learned and observed, so you will not have to return to the community to obtain the same information again. Include written reflection on what was said and done. How will this impact your service-learning project?

4.   *Be respectful* of the community and community members at all times
     •   When having conversations, allow others to finish what they are saying before you say something

---

[1] Although this project may not be long term for you, the professor and community partner may have a long term partnership that involves high school and college students working together to improve their understanding of math.

- Use your manners; greet people appropriately
- Assume that every person in the community is an expert, not necessarily a technical expert, but an expert on problem solving, the community, and its people
- Be aware of your body language (look interested, make eye contact, listen actively, sit or stand up straight)
- Observe; do not stare
- Remember that this is a learning experience for you, not charity work for the community

5. *Keep open communication lines*
   - Do not be afraid to relate to anyone, but remember that personal questions are off limits
   - Explain, discuss, and converse in casual language (it may be difficult for others to understand "tech speak" or slang)
   - Communicate your findings to your community partner
   - If you do offend someone, tell them that you are sorry and understand why you offended the person(s), rather than getting defensive or angry.
   - Ask questions if something is not clear to you initially

Community Partner Quote

"I like students to be honest. Many students that come to this community are afraid. I know they are afraid, and I know why they are afraid. I like it when students speak their fear because when it is out in the open, we can talk about it. I can talk about stereotypical media images and how they generate fear. I can talk about how students need to lock their doors and be safety conscious, but these are things you do everywhere. I like to talk about the crime statistics in this neighborhood; most are surprised to learn that the crime rates are higher in the area of the city in which they are living.

Another thing that students think initially is "Oh, we're here to help the poor people." It is not about that. The students are here to learn, not to help. When students learn about the community's pride and history, the interstate that was put through the middle of this neighborhood, and school desegregation, they realize that they are not here to help poor people. They are here to learn about the community's history and how that integrates into this nation's history. They are here to address community needs by joining their talents and the community's talents to work to make our city a better place to live."

Judy Bethly, formerly with the Community-University Partnership,
now Executive Director, Volunteers in Public Schools.

Community Partner Quote

"Many people in this community see white skin first, while many of the students that come here see black skin first. What everyone needs to remember is that only humanity exists. Everyone is the same; we have cultural differences, but those are

things we can take pride in. I hope that our differences can enhance our lives, and not divide us because we are looking at skin color and not seeing anything else."
Shelley Jourdan, Community-University Partnership

Questions Frequently Asked by Students in Service-Learning

I am having difficulty getting in contact my community partner. What should I do?

Here you need to strike a balance between the good old college try and being overwhelming. Community partners are busy; collect the contact information for your community partner and the best times and means to reach that person(s). Contact your community partner in the way in which he or she asks, and make contact well in advance of any deadline you may have, so you are not pressed for time. Give your community partner at least 48 hours (during the business week) to get back to you. If you get no response, contact him or her again. You can contact your community partner in many ways, including by phone, e-mail, post, and with a personal visit. You must respect the time constraints on your community partner, and at the same time, follow up so that you can get the information that you need.

I need more information on the project. How can I get it?

Service-learning projects can be a change of pace from other courses you have taken because the information you need to address a community issue may not be readily available from your professor or from a trip to the Internet or the library. You will have become proactive with service-learning projects. You will have to visit the community partner/agency and community on your own or in your group. You may have to return to collect physical or geographical measurements, get perspectives or community members' testimonials, study the sun's movement, study the distribution of people, plan your project's execution, etc. Make a list of the information you must collect and how to collect it. Contact the community partner to ensure the day and time of your visit is convenient and share your goals for going that day. The community partner may assist you in this regard. Make sure you take complete notes while on site so you do not forget anything. Collect all the information you can from alternate sources so you do not overburden your community member with providing information that you can get from other sources.

I am getting different answers to the same questions. To whom do I listen?

This can be one of the most frustrating experiences as an engineering student. Once you master the basics of engineering, getting answers can be the most rewarding as it delves into the art of engineering. Students tend to make two mistakes in this regard. 1) They listen only to the "expert" and do whatever that person suggests, and 2) their design most reflects the ideas of the last person with whom they spoke.

Remember that one of the most important tasks of the design process involves research and gathering data. Talking to community partners and other experts is a critical part of this process, but remember that you need to collect technical data that will help you make design decisions. It is critical to collect a wealth of information from multiple sources; it is only at this point that you weigh all the information and make a decision accordingly. Often times, technical information will provide you with the general knowledge and range of options you have to complete a design; you can successfully make specific decisions by working closely with the community partner.

The following example illustrates how information from speakers influenced the final design: Students collected technical information on surfacing a playground from multiple sources, and correctly came to the conclusion that sand was an acceptable means for surfacing a playground. The engineering students decided not to use sand on the playground after speaking with the teachers at the school with whom they were designing this playground, because the teachers said that the students would often take sand and throw it at one another, and that this was a long-standing cause of behavioral issues on the current playground. Thus, the students chose a safe, technically sound surfacing material for the playground that could not be thrown.

In another case, students designing a zoo exhibit for a large cat listened to an expert who suggested that the bottom of the exhibit consist of concrete because it was easier to maintain than grass, dirt, or other bottom surfaces. This student group specified concrete in their design without collecting other data or speaking with other experts. These students did not realize that the research and general consensus of experts was to use surfaces besides concrete[2] because they stopped gathering information after collecting one expert testimonial.

Getting everyone to agree on everything is almost impossible. Using a democratic approach in decision making can be helpful. For example, holding several community meetings to discuss the location of the construction of infrastructure coming to consensus may be a good way in which to make final community recommendations.

This community is much different than the one I grew up in. I am not sure that I am comfortable here.

Human nature is such that we are drawn to people similar to ourselves. We are comfortable with people who think as we do, process information as we do, and

---

[2] Concrete is hard and causes pad abrasions and arthritis in large cats

have the same cultural norms regarding work, play, and personal values. The world consists of different people with different interests, values, and cultures. Your ability to succeed with a service-learning project is dependent on how successfully you work with people of diverse backgrounds.

The tips for working with community partners (see above) should give you a solid start for working with others who differ from you. You should be prepared to question your assumptions, to question others' assumptions, and to have your assumptions questioned by others. Open communication will enable people with differences to explore these differences in an effort to understand them and to use those differences to improve the project. Approach everyone with an open mind. Our first impulse upon experiencing a difference is to rely on stereotypes to explain the situation. In effect, this enables us to perpetuate our own (and many times erroneous) assumptions, and to ignore examining the cultural and social values of someone different. Be aware of your own stereotypes, and think beyond these to come together to achieve a goal.

Stevenson and Whitmore (2002) sum up this sentiment nicely: "In this context, the interpersonal skills engineers need most to meet the demands of twenty-first century engineering are an appreciation and respect for diversity, an eagerness to share ideas with people from different backgrounds, and a willingness to seek solutions in conjunction with people who know little, if anything, of the technical side of a project."

Quick Tips for Working with Community Partners

- Find out as much as possible about your community partner, agency, and the people being serving before you get there
- Listen carefully (see listening skills in section 5.4)
- Be respectful of the community partner's feelings, thoughts, and time
- Use respectful language
- Think before you speak
- Ask for clarification if you are not sure about something
- Understand your duties and execute these tasks in a qualified and timely manner
- Follow up
- Be professional at all times

Quote: A Good Service-Learning Experience

"I learned about the importance of perspective in engineering. I had to think like a child to design the best playground. I had to think like a parent to design a safe playground. I had to think as a member of the community to design a playground that reflected the unique aspects of the community. I had to think like a politician to sell the playground to potential funders."

An Example of a Poor Service-Learning Experience

The first service-learning student in my classroom was supposed to assist me in teaching math to my second graders. Instead, the student picked up on the exuberance of my students and began playing karate with some of my students during class time. My students were excited about having a college student in the classroom and were doing their best to show off. I expected the service-learning student to respect me and the other students in the class by calming the other students down and acting as a role model in terms of good classroom behavior. The service-learning student made it more difficult for me to run my math class.

7.5 CONCLUSION

In this chapter, you learned about oral and written communication skills and tips for interacting with your community partner. Keep an open mind and think about what you are communicating and how you want to communicate it before you initiate a formal communication.

EXCERCISES

1. Interview one of your professors or a practicing engineer to learn more about speaking skills. You might ask them some or all of the following questions:
   - Do you ever get nervous before doing a public speaking engagement? If so, what do you do to relax? What advice do you have for me to relax if I get nervous?
   - How do you prepare for an oral presentation?
   - Do you employ any methods for engaging the audience at the beginning of a talk?
   - How do you keep your audience interested throughout your talk?
   - Do you have any advice for me as a public speaker?

2. Go to a public speaking engagement at your university with a speaker of regional or national prominence. Critique this person's speaking style with respect to the guidelines for oral presentations presented in this chapter. What did the speaker do particularly well? What could s/he have improved upon? What things did the speaker do that you would like to integrate into your own speaking repertoire?

3. Write a report on your service-learning project. Your report should follow ABC format and should include the following information:
   - Background: give information on community partner, for example, history, service to the community, mission of the organization, etc.
   - Explain specifically why there is a need for your project
   - Discuss your design process (which considerations were paramount and why?)

- Describe the design that you came up with and discuss it specifically (why is it the way it is?)
- Include a maintenance plan for the entity that you designed (what needs to be done to successfully maintain the device or system, how often should these activities be completed, and who will complete these activities?)
- Discuss costs for the design.
- Dimensioned drawings of your design and all pertinent calculations you made with regard to the design should be included in the Appendix

4. Choose an organization that you are interested in working with for a specific purpose, for example, a community project, summer internship, co-op, or future employer. Write a résumé and cover letter to this organization.

5. Interview an experienced community partner. Ask this person the following questions:
   - Describe your experiences working with students in a service-learning context.
   - What are the most rewarding and most challenging aspects of working with students on service-learning project?
   - What do you expect of students during this process?
   - What information do you share with students in order to get the maximum benefit from working together?
   - Do you have any advice for me in terms of working with community partners?

Chapter 8

Engineering Standards and Liability Issues

Agnes Allen's Law: Almost anything is easier to get into than out of.
—Paul Dickson

8.1 OVERVIEW

We included a separate chapter on standards and liability because both are important to the engineering design process. "A standard is a common language that promotes the flow of goods between buyer and seller and protects the general welfare." (ASTM.org) Standards are important in engineering design for many reasons. Standards can achieve the following:

- Provide interchangeability between similarly functional products and systems manufactured by two or more organizations, thus improving compatibility, safety, and performance for users
- Reduce the variety of components required to serve an industry, thus improving availability and economy
- Improve personal safety during equipment operation and products and materials use
- Establish products, materials, or systems performance criteria
- Provide a common basis for testing, analyzing, describing, or informing regarding the products, methods, materials, or systems performance and characteristics
- Develop a sound basis for codes, education, and legislation, and to promote practice uniformity
- Provide a technical basis for international standardization
- Increase the efficiency of engineering effort in design, development, and production (ASAE, 2000)

Liability is a comprehensive legal term that describes the condition of being subject to or potentially subject to a legal obligation (Torres and Sinton, 2000). Because engineering involves the design and construction of devices, products, processes and systems used by people, the chance exists that someone can be injured. Thus, engineers must approach all designs with special attention to safety issues during the design process and after the design has been adopted for public use.

All engineers must be aware of the liability risks inherent in their designs, and they need to minimize this liability by paying scrupulous attention to standards. These standards often define the safety issues and how to proceed in a way that will minimize the chances of someone getting hurt. Service-learning projects present unique issues involving liability.

In this chapter, we will discuss the ways in which engineering standards and liability issues have an impact on the design process. We will illustrate these points using the design of a playground. A playground is designed almost entirely around standards and is an excellent example how liability issues have an impact on engineering design and service-learning in engineering.

Did You Know?

Approximately 200,000 children visit hospitals and emergency rooms each year due to playground injuries, making them the number one cause of pediatric hospital visits.

8.2 THE USE OF STANDARDS IN ENGINEERING DESIGN

Standardization is an old concept. Cylindrical stones were used as weight measures in Egypt circa 7000 B.C. English nobility used the length of their body parts to establish standards; in 1120, King Henry defined the "ell" as the length of his forearm. The city of Boston made brick size standard in 1689, stating that it was a crime to manufacture bricks in any other size than $9'' \times 4'' \times 4''$ (nist.org).

Eli Whitney (1765–1825), an inventor and mechanical engineer, is referred to as "the Father of Standardization" because he brought the concept of mass production to the United States. The federal government awarded Whitney a $134,000 contract in 1798 to manufacture 10,000 identical muskets. Though his idea of a uniformity system was initially met with resistance, Whitney proved that standardized parts with the same dimensions (or specifications) could be used interchangeably in any musket. This concept became the basis for mass production, an important part of the Industrial Revolution. (http://technology.ksc.nasa.gov/ETEAM/whitney. html, http://www.invent.org/hall_of_fame/152.html)

Widespread development and implementation of engineering standards has come about in the past century. The devastating Baltimore fire of 1904 highlighted the desperate need for standardization. Though fire trucks from as far as New York City came to assist with the blaze, any truck outside of the city of Baltimore was useless to fight the fire because their hoses would not fit the fire hydrants in the city. The Baltimore fire destroyed more than 1,500 buildings over approximately 70 city blocks and ruined all power and communications systems in the city. City leaders had addressed this issue when a large fire in Fall River, Massachusetts, in 1928 was controlled because the standardization of hydrants and hoses enabled fire trucks from 20 neighboring towns to help quell the fire.

Mass transit spoke to the need for standards. In 1927, a national code for colors was created by the American Association of State Highway Officials, the National Safety Council, and the National Bureau of Standards (now the National Institute of Standards and Technology, NIST). Prior to this, green on traffic signs meant stop in some states, and go in others. The railroads' standard track gage is used by the United States, Canada, the United Kingdom, and much of Europe to enable railroad cars to travel on a standard size track.

World War Two was the driving force for thinking about the establishment of international standards. Supplies and facilities of the Allied Forces were not standard, and the resulting incompatibilities involving tools, parts, and equipment made the war effort more difficult.

Several organizations exist for the development, maintenance, and dissemination of standards. The American Society for Testing Materials (ASTM) was founded in 1898. ASTM is "a not-for-profit organization that provides a forum for the development and publication of voluntary consensus standards for materials, products, systems, and services." (astm.org) These standards are published in the Annual Book of ASTM Standards. ASTM has members from more than 100 countries that serve on committees in charge of developing and disseminating standards on many subjects, such as consumer products, biotechnology, forensic science, and physical and mechanical testing.

The American National Standards Institute (ANSI) was formed in 1916 when the American Institute of Electrical Engineers (now the Institute of Electrical and Electronics Engineers, Inc. or IEEE), the American Society of Mechanical Engineers (ASME), the American Society of Civil Engineers (ASCE), the American Institute of Mining and Metallurgical Engineers (AIMME), and ASTM established a national organization to coordinate the development of industrial and engineering standards and to provide a clearinghouse for the standards developed by each member society.

The International Organization for Standardization (ISO) was founded in 1947 to provide individual countries membership in an international forum for standards development. The mission of the ISO is to encourage the standardization development and related activities in the world to facilitate international exchanges of goods and services and to provide governments with a technical base for safety, health, and environmental legislation (http://www.iso.org). ISO is perhaps best known for its 9000 and 14000 standards; these refer to groups of standards involving quality management and environmental management respectively.

Using engineering standards in the design process is important. Following the most up to date standards will not insulate you from lawsuits, but will ensure you hold public safety paramount and represents the best that you can accomplish from a technical and ethical engineering standpoint.

To locate standards of interest to the device, process, product, or system you are designing, you should consult the publications of the above standards organizations. These organizations have standards on specific subjects indexed online. If you cannot locate a standard from the major standards organizations (ISO, ANSI, ASTM, or NIST), then consult your major professional society for standards in your engineering discipline:

- ASAE: the Society for Engineering in Agricultural, Food, and Biological Systems, *http://www.asae.org*
- American Society of Civil Engineers (ASCE) *http://www.asce.org*
- American Society of Mechanical Engineers (ASME) *http://www.asme.org*
- Institute of Electrical and Electronics Engineers (IEEE) *http://www.ieee.org*
- Institute of Industrial Engineers (IIEE) *http//www.iienet.org*
- The Engineering Society for Advancing Mobility in Land Sea Air and Space (SAE) *http://www.sae.org*
- Websites for The Biomedical Engineering Society (BMES.org) and the American Institute of Chemical Engineers (AIChE.org) do not contain standards information.

8.3 CASE STUDY: THE USE OF ENGINEERING STANDARDS IN THE DESIGN OF A PLAYGROUND

Playground design standards have been developed by the ASTM in its Standard Consumer Safety Performance Specification for Playground Equipment for Public Use, and by the Consumer Product Safety Commission, which publishes the Handbook for Public Playground Safety. This case study does not include all the information and detail needed to design a playground. It does provide sufficient information to explain the process of using standards to design portions of a playground.

The Case

You have been asked to design a playground at a public school for kindergarten through fifth grade children. The site has been surveyed and the land is level and has no drainage problems. The area available for the playground is rectangular, and is 120 feet long by 160 feet wide. A few trees are in this area, shown in Figure 8.1. You have interviewed the school children and have found that they want swings, slides, and something to climb on. The parents, teachers, and administrators have stated that they need to see the children at all times and that they need a comfortable place to sit while watching the children play. Design a playground to meet the children's, teachers', and administrators' needs using the standards and recommendations set forth by the CPSC.

Solution

The overall approach to designing this playground involves using the engineering method described in Chapter 3. Standards use in the design process would come under the steps entitled Specification, development/planning, Conceptual design and Detailed design. Generating a preliminary design is highlighted in this case study though background information on playgrounds is included.

Initial Design Approach

First, think about the playground design from multiple perspectives. These perspectives will provide you with information to design your playground. Sometimes, the information that you get may be conflicting in nature; use your judgment and experience to resolve these conflicts. For this case study, playground design is considered from three perspectives: community needs and desires, environment, and democracy. A look at these perspectives yields the following:

I. Community Needs And Desires

A. Children

They want swings, slides, and something to climb on.

Design Implication

Include swings, slides, and climbers

B. Parents, Teachers, And Administrators

They need a place to sit and need to see children at all times.

Design Implication

Place equipment at locations that adults can see the children (no cluttered sight lines) and place benches or other supporting structures (gazebo, table, etc.) at these locations, or possibly near heavily used playground locations.

II. Environmental

Playground should be designed and constructed with minimal environmental impact.

Design Implications

- Minimize cutting down trees by placing equipment sufficiently far away from trees; do not drill into the root systems of trees.
- Provide protection from environmental elements using shade or places that people can escape inclement weather.
- Play equipment should be environmentally safe (pressure treated wood created prior to Dec. 2003 contains arsenic).
- Equipment should be fabricated with minimal environmental impact and should be re-used or recycled at the end of its useful life.

III. Democratic

The playground reflects democratic society and values.

Design Implications

- Should be accessible to everyone. The Americans with Disabilities Act of 1990 (ADA) influences playground design. This law requires equal access and accommodation of public places to people with disabilities.

- Should reflect the unique aspects of the school and surrounding community, e.g., emphasizing the school colors or organizing the playground around a theme that reflects community. The theme could be the school mascot, historical figures, future initiatives, subjects of importance, or artwork contributed by children or local artists.
- Should provide for the development of the whole child, including physical, social, emotional, and creative needs. These needs change as each child gets older and more developed (consult the stages of childhood development for more information). The playground should include a range of physical challenges through play equipment, devices for motor skill development and for educational development, quiet places for reflection and discussion, and open space for imaginative games.

An Initial Look At Your Design

After thinking about these perspectives, you have information that you can begin to assemble into a usable design.

You also need more specific information that's going to tell you where to put this equipment, its dimensions, its materials, and so on. Standards now enter the design picture. Playground standards are based primarily on safety. In playground design, you need to look at the safety of each piece of play equipment and the layout of the entire playground (all the play equipment together). The standards

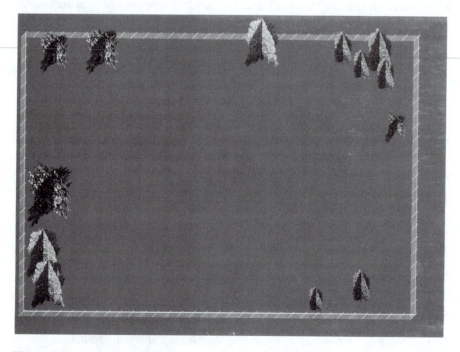

Figure 8.1 Area for playground   *(AutoCad drawings by Stuart Feilden)*

and graphics are excerpted here from the CPSC Handbook for Public Playground Safety:

A Use Zone

This is the surface under and around a piece of equipment onto which a child falling from or exiting from the equipment would be expected to land (CPSC). The surface is a shock absorbing material, such as wood mulch, sand, crushed tire, rubber, or certain stones. Placing the surface material throughout the use zone is referred to as surfacing.

I. Community Needs

A. Equipment

Climbers (Figure 8.2). Many specific requirements pertain to climbers. Some include the following:

- Climbers should not have bars or other structural components in the interior onto which a child may fall from a height greater than 18 inches.
- Climbing equipment should allow children to descend as easily as they ascend.
- Free standing arch climbers are not recommended for pre-school age children.
- The use zone of climbers should extend a minimum of six feet in all directions from the perimeter (outer edge) of the equipment.

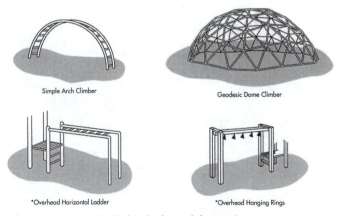

Simple Arch Climber

Geodesic Dome Climber

*Overhead Horizontal Ladder

*Overhead Hanging Rings

*Note: This design shows how upper body equipment is typically integrated with multi-use equipment

Figure 8.2 Typical Climbing Equipment

Swings[1]

- Minimum dimensions for swings are shown in (Figure 8.3).
- No more than two swings per bay of the supporting structure (a bay is the space in between two swing supports).
- Swing seats should be for single children.
- Lightweight rubber or plastic swing seats are preferred.
- The use zone for a swing is shown in (Figure 8.4).

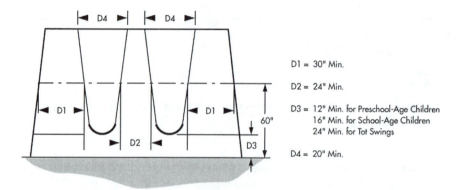

D1 = 30" Min.

D2 = 24" Min.

D3 = 12" Min. for Preschool-Age Children
16" Min. for School-Age Children
24" Min. for Tot Swings

D4 = 20" Min.

Figure 8.3 Minimum Clearances for Single-Axis Swings

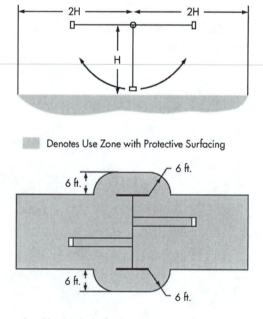

Denotes Use Zone with Protective Surfacing

Figure 8.4 Use Zone for Single-Axis Swings

---

[1] Here we are talking about single axis swings, which move forward and backward. There are different standards for multi-axis swings, such as a tire swing.

Slides

- May provide a straight, wavy, or spiral descent either by means of a tube or an open slide chute.
- All slides should be provided with a platform with sufficient length to facilitate the transition from standing to sitting at the top of the inclined sliding surface. This platform should have a minimum area of 22" × 22".
- The average incline of a slide chute should be no more than 30 degrees, and should never exceed a maximum of 50 degrees.
- The use zone of a slide is shown in (Figure 8.5).

B. Equipment Layout

- Active, physical activities should be separate from more passive or quiet activities.
- Popular, heavy-use pieces of equipment or activities should be dispersed to avoid crowding in any one area.
- Moving equipment (swings, merry-go-rounds) should be located toward a corner, side or edge of the play area.
- Use zones for moving equipment should not overlap the use zone of other equipment.

II. Environmental

Playground standards do not apply to this area, but the following additional information is helpful in this regard:

- The root system of a tree is generally considered to extend to the leaf canopy. The implication is that if you place benches under a tree, place them

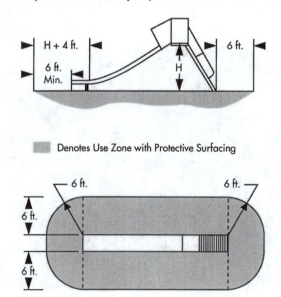

Figure 8.5 Use Zone for Slides

further out from the canopy so that one can benefit from shade and you can minimize root system damage.

- Coated metal holds up longer than wood and does not heat up tremendously in the sun.

III. Democratic Considerations

The ADA says that portions of each playground must be accessible and that the number of play activities available on ground (wheelchair) level must equal the number of activities on an elevated level. Other nonstandards-based considerations are helpful for the design:

- Choose school colors (e.g., green and yellow).
- Include a gazebo for people to sit together and to escape the sun.
- Include an open area for running around (grass).
- Include educational panels and simple games in the playground.
- Include a model for imaginative play, which can reflect the community. For example, if space exploration is an important subject at the school, choose a model spaceship large enough to accommodate several children at once.

Now that you have the information from the initial look at your design and the standards that pertain to this initial look, you can put the two concepts together into a preliminary playground design. Consult the graphic below to see how these aspects of information fit in to our playground design (Figure 8.6).

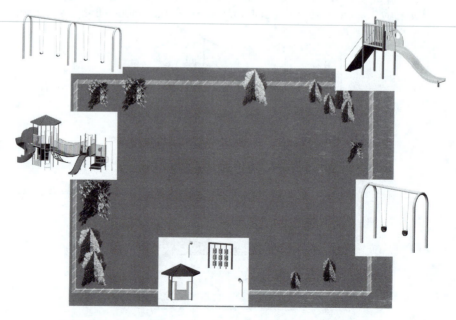

Figure 8.6 Playground design elements not yet placed in the land area.

Keep in mind that this is one preliminary design. Many changes could (and should) be made to the design based on community partner input, further design refinement, and full consideration of all aspects of playground design. See Figure 8.7 where the play elements are placed in the available area according to equipment layout specifications in I.B.

8.4 LIABILITY IN ENGINEERING DESIGN

Liability issues in engineering are becoming increasingly important (Dieter, 2000). The purpose of this section is to give you some idea of this complexity. Entire books and careers are based on engineering and the law. You should consult appropriate references if you need more information on liability.

If you are found liable in an engineering context, then you or your company are obligated to pay damages that stemmed from some legal wrongdoing. Two major ways a person or company can be found liable are:

- **Breaking A Contract:** You fail to perform all parts of the contract that you signed:
  - You do not produce a design, drawing, or product (a "deliverable") you promised.
  - You do not produce that deliverable on the date you promised.
  - You do not produce the deliverable in the way that the contract stated you would (dimensions, color, etc., could be incorrect).

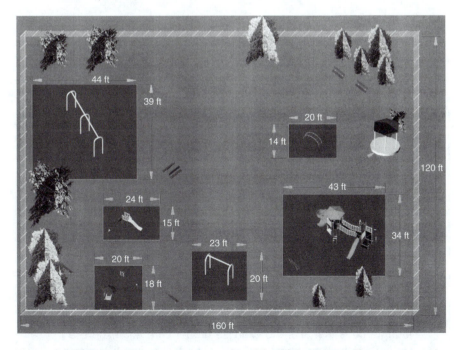

Figure 8.7 Playground design elements placed in the land area. Use zones are also shown in two dimensions to facilitate easy reading of dimensions.

AutoCAD drawings by Stuart Feilden

Useful Note About Design

Engineering design can be deductive or inductive. Deductive design is analogous to being a detective: you start with the situation and manipulate the design. With inductive design, you start with the design and manipulate the situation. Think about the size and shape of a playground. If you are given a fenced-in area and told that this is where the playground will be, you will start with that situation, and manipulate your design to fit inside the fenced area (deductive). If you are given an open area and asked to design a playground, you will start with the play elements, and the final size and shape of the playground will be determined by your design (inductive).

- **Committing Fraud Or Negligence** (known as torts, or civil wrongs, that usually involve monetary settlements rather than jail time):
  - You include a part on a device that is not up to code or standard.
  - You make a miscalculation and your device or system fails.
  - You compete with other companies for a contract to construct a building, and you use different (cheaper) building materials than those specified in the contract.
  - You bill someone for more engineering service time than you actually performed.

The engineering code of ethics (chapter 2) contains specific information on how to avoid liability in an engineering context. Remember that even if you follow all engineering ethical laws, you can still be involved in a lawsuit.

Definitions

A **Contract** is a promise that you will do (or not do) something. These promises must be enforceable by law. In other words, you can have a contract to produce a detailed drawing of a product by a certain date, but you cannot have a contract to sneeze every day at 3:00 P.M. When you do engineering work, you are usually involved in a contract, whether it be with the company that you are working for or your company (with you as an employee) doing work for another company, the government, an individual, or the non-profit sector.

Fraud is an intentional, deceitful action to deprive another person/company of his or her raise or to cause injury in some way.

Negligence is the failure to exercise proper care and expertise in accordance with the standards of the profession that result in damage to property or people.

(all definitions from Dieter, 2000)

> **Useful References For Liability And Engineering Information**
>
> Dieter, G. *Engineering Design: A Materials and Processing Approach,* 3rd
>   Ed. New York: McGraw-Hill Series in Mechanical Engineering, 2000.
> Hunziker, J. and T. Jones, Eds. *Product Liability and Innovation: Managing
>   Risk in an Uncertain Environment.* National Academy of Engineering.
>   National Academies Press, 1994.

Service-learning adds a layer of complexity to liability issues. In addition to the liabilities inherent in engineering design and the construction of devices, systems, processes, or structures for public use, other critical issues exist:

- What if you are hurt while constructing your project, traveling to the community partner site, or performing any activity affiliated with the service-learning project?
- What if the community partner, agency, or community member is hurt directly or indirectly by your actions or lack of actions (e.g., you reveal confidential information, a community partner is hurt during the construction process, you injure a child while working on the project, or you fail to report a violent incident)?

Though these issues seldom come up in a service-learning situation, they are tangible concerns. The case study below will illustrate how to address these concerns.

8.5 LIABILITY CASE STUDY

To see how the principles of liability are taken into consideration in engineering design, we will look at the playground designed in section 8.3. from a liability standpoint. Think about two major aspects: the playground design (design, construction, and maintenance), and the service-learning process.

Liability In Playground Design

All components of the playground, individually and together, have been designed according to the latest versions of the CPSC Handbook for Public Playground Safety, the ASTM Standard Consumer Safety Performance Specification for Playground Equipment for Public Use, and the ADA. This minimizes liability in the design process because you have followed the newest laws and recommendations regarding playground design to the letter.

In addition, your design should be checked by a certified playground safety inspector (CPSI), certified by exam through the National Recreation and Park Association's National Playground Safety Institute (see *http://www.nrpa.org* for more information). This will ensure that all design parts are safe. For most designs you create, engineering work must be done by or in close conjunction with a Profes-

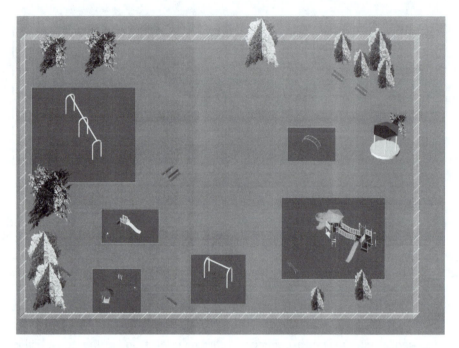

Figure 8.8 Playground layout.   *AutoCAD drawings by Stuart Feilden*

sional Engineer (see Chapter 2 for more information), who will seal the work and deem it safe for public construction and use. The professional engineer (and in our case, the CPSI) becomes responsible for this design.

A new set of liability issues arises for the playground construction designs. These involve the components of the playground and the construction process. Pre-fabricated pieces of equipment are used to construct the playground because the liability involving the individual playground components is carried by the manufacturer. Although this may decrease the creative license of the design, it minimizes the liability an engineer can incur.

Another liability risk involves the playground assembly. If the prefabricated play equipment is manufactured correctly but installed incorrectly, then the installers can be liable in the case of injury. To minimize construction liability, employ a playground company with certified playground inspectors to supervise the construction process, or have that play company install the equipment. If volunteers or community members assist in the playground construction, they should be made aware of all construction risks, trained to use dangerous equipment, and have health insurance in case of injury. They should be aware of any safety protocols during the construction process (see the next section for more details).

Liability is possible after the playground is constructed. Children can get hurt while playing on the playground even if it was designed and constructed properly. Additionally, injuries can occur if the playground is not maintained properly; no playground design is complete without a maintenance plan, which should specify tasks to be performed to keep the playground as safe as possible. A maintenance checklist supplied by the CPSC is contained in Figure 8.9. The community or group in charge of the playground after it is constructed should be given the maintenance

APPENDIX A
Suggested General Maintenance Checklist

The following checklist may be used to determine the condition of a playground. Numbers in parenthesis refer to sections in the handbook that discuss these issues. Place a check mark next to each of the following items that apply.

Surfacing (4)
___ The equipment has adequate protective surfacing under and around it and the surfacing materials have not deteriorated.

___ Loose-fill surfacing materials have no foreign objects or debris.

___ Loose-fill surfacing materials are not compacted and do not have reduced depth in heavy use areas such as under swings or at slide exits.

General Hazards
___ There are no sharp points, corners or edges on the equipment (9.1).

___ There are no missing or damaged protective caps or plugs (9.1).

___ There are no hazardous protrusions and projections (9.2).

___ There are no potential clothing entanglement hazards, such as open S-hooks or protruding bolts (8.2, and 9.4).

___ There are no pinch, crush, and shearing points or exposed moving parts (9.5).

___ There are no trip hazards, such as exposed footings on anchoring devices and rocks, roots, or any other environmental obstacles in the play area (9.7).

Deterioration of the Equipment (7.2)
___ The equipment has no rust, rot, cracks or splinters, especially where it comes in contact with the ground.

___ There are no broken or missing components on the equipment (e.g., handrails, guardrails, protective barriers, steps or rungs on ladders) and there are no damaged fences, benches, or signs on the playground.

___ All equipment is securely anchored.

Security of Hardware (7.2)
___ There are no loose fastening devices or worn connections, such as S-hooks.

___ Moving components, such as swing hangers or merry-go-round bearings, are not worn.

Drainage (6.1)
___ The entire play area has satisfactory drainage, especially in heavy use areas such as under swings and at slide exits.

Leaded Paint (8.1)
___ The leaded paint used on the playground equipment has not deteriorated as noted by peeling, cracking, chipping or chalking.

___ There are no ares of visible leaded paint chips or accumulation of lead dust.

General Upkeep of Playgrounds (7.2)
___ The entire playground is free from miscellaneous debris or litter such as tree branches, soda cans, bottles, glass, etc.

___ There are no missing trash receptacles.

___ Trash receptacles are not full.

NOTES:

Figure 8.9 Sample Checklist

plan and should know how to follow it. Additional standards in the CPSC regarding specific safety warnings for parents or supervising adults should be displayed prominently. The playground in this case study was built for kindergarten to fifth grade students; these students are defined as school-age children by virtue of their ages (5–12). Pre-school age children (defined as ages 2–5) should not be allowed to play on any part of this playground without direct adult supervision because the playground was not built for them. Even with adult supervision, pre-school age children should not play on swings designed for school-age children, vertical sliding poles, long spiral slides (with more than one turn), and free-standing arch climbers (this information in included in the standards section of the CPSC, not reprinted here). In addition, children wearing hood or neck drawstrings should remove them if they plan to use the slides on the playground.

Warning signs describing potential hazards should be posted prominently if the playground is a public playground. If the playground is not public, then the group that the playground was designed for should be made aware of these issues. This group is responsible for addressing safety issues after the construction process is complete.

The Service-Learning Process In Playground Design

In terms of the service-learning portion of the case study, we will assume that the service-learning project involved the following steps:

- Engineering students worked with elementary school students, parents, teachers, and community members to create a school playground design. The final design was agreed upon by all and was checked by a CPSI.
- Engineering students, parents, teachers, and community members constructed the playground under the supervision of a playground company. At least one CPSI was on site during the entire construction process. Volunteers with the most construction experience were chosen to be group leaders; only these people used dangerous tools and only after the playground company provided safety instruction.
- Liability regarding the playground was determined as follows:
    - The CPSI was liable for design flaws that he or she did not detect in the final design proposed as a result of the service-learning project.
    - The playground manufacturer was liable for all pre-fabricated play components supplied for playground construction.
    - The play company that supervised the construction process was liable for all issues regarding the installation of the playground.
    - The school's grounds crew was responsible for all maintenance after the playground was constructed.
    - The school (and school board) was liable for playground injuries after the construction process was complete, provided that the injuries were not caused by a design flaw or installation.

We have discussed the technical issues involving liability in the engineering design process. A service-learning project brings a new dimension to liability issues, namely, that in working directly with a community partner, you could potentially commit acts that make you liable or have acts committed upon you which make others liable. The purpose of this section is to describe how to minimize liability in engineering projects that have a service-learning component.

To minimize liability, when you work with your community partner you should follow instructions set forth in your service-learning partnership agreement if you have one. See below for a sample agreement, or service-learning contract.

Sample Contract

This contract is completed by student and community partner supervisor and returned to instructor; all parties should have a copy of this agreement.

Service-Learning Partnership Agreement
Please *print clearly* for permanent service-learning records.

Course/ Faculty Partner Information
Course name _____ Instructor _____
Abbreviation _____ Number ___ Section _____ Semester: F Sp Sum Yr: _____

Student Partner Information
Name _____ ID (SS #) _____
College/Major _____ Gender (circle) M F Yr: 1 2 3 4 grad 6 7
Local street address _____ Perm. street address _____
City/State/Zip _____ City/State/Zip _____
Local Phone _____ Perm. phone (____) _____
E-mail _____

Community Partner Information
Organization Name _____ Site _____
Volunteer Coordinator _____ Immediate Supervisor _____
Mailing Address _____ Site address _____
City/State/Zip _____ E-mail _____
Phone (____) _____ Fax _____

Student Partner/Community Partner Agreement
Initial and/or review points of agreement, sign, and date below.

1. I will maintain consistent communication with my service site.
2. I understand the organization's mission.
3. I have communicated my skills, talents, interests, and course requirements to the organization through an interview, résumé, or narrative.
4. If a problem arises, I will discuss it with my supervisor.
5. I will schedule an appointment with my supervisor to discuss the evaluation of my service.

Student signature _____ *Date* _____

1. I have discussed the learning goals in my course plan with my immediate supervisor. (List number of hours_____, project description, requirements, and/or goals you will achieve). I will maintain consistent communication with the student.
2. I have provided information about the mission of our organization.

3. I am aware of the student's skills, interests, and course requirements and will seek to utilize those appropriate to meet the need of our organization.
4. If a problem arises, I will discuss it with the student.
5. I have informed the student of our holiday schedule and closures for this semester.
6. I understand the student's course learning goals and requirements and am prepared to provide opportunities for achieving them as the student serves to meet the goals of our organization.

Supervisor signature(s) _____ *Date* _____
*Call or e-mail [contact name and information] with any questions. (reprinted with permission from the LSU Service-Learning Faculty Handbook)

Know the contact information for your community partner and anyone you may need to contact in an emergency (police, fire, ambulance, etc.), or have this information recorded in a place that you can always access. Be aware of all potential dangers for your project. For example, see the sample informed consent form prepared by the community partner and instructor.

Informed-Consent Form

My work as a service-learning student with (community partner or agency) is entered into willingly, as a component of my academic coursework in (course name, number, course term, and year). I understand that completing service-learning work in conjunction with (community partner or agency) involves potential risks including the following:

*   Travel in remote, rural areas where access to telephones or human assistance may be limited or nonexistent
*   Travel in remote, rural areas where residents may be suspicious of my presence
*   Travel in remote areas where there may be open, unmarked well sites
*   Travel in rural areas where there may be contact with poisonous plants, insects, or animals (snakes, scorpions, etc.)
*   Probable exposure to contaminated water
*   Probable exposure to toxic materials used to clean wells
*   Use of equipment that has the potential to harm me

I am consenting to enter into this service-learning project aware of these potential risks. I assume responsibility for my welfare and agree to consider the precautionary measures recommended by (instructor of course and/or community partner), including the following:

*   Traveling with at least one other classmate and with a cell phone if at all possible
*   Traveling with documentation to prove my identity, and to demonstrate the project and community partner with whom I am working

- Training to ensure I am familiar with the safety issues involved in unmarked well sites; poisonous plants, insects, or animals; and working with equipment, contaminated water, and toxic materials.
- I have a copy of the emergency management protocol with me at all times.

Student signature _____ *Date* _____

(reprinted in part from the LSU 2003 Faculty Partner Handbook)

Other tips

- Work with more than one person in "open door" settings at all times.
- Be respectful of community partners and members at all times (see Chapter 7.4 for details).
- Make sure that you receive proper instruction regarding any safety issues involved in the service-learning project. For example, make sure that you are properly trained with regard to the use of power tools before using them, etc.
- Know what to do in case of an emergency. See the sample emergency management protocols below for more details.

Sample Emergency Management Protocol For Students

Bodily Injury Or Harassment During A Service-Learning Project

In the event that the service-learning student or a person with whom he or she is working is injured bodily or is harassed in some way, the student should do the following:

- Remain as calm as possible
- Call for help
  - His or her immediate supervisor should be prepared to assist in such a situation according to community partner protocols.
  - In the event that the supervisor is not present, then other staff should be able to assist in such a situation according to agency protocols.

The community partner supervisor or staff should follow any emergency management protocols generated by the agency. If no existing agency protocols exist, the supervisor or agency should do the following (in addition to agency protocols):

- Assess the situation and tend to the injured/harassed person
- Make sure the area around the person is safe and secure
- Avoid moving the injured person(s), particularly in the case of back, neck, or other serious injuries
- Send a messenger to get help. The messenger should do the following:
  - Call 911 (or the designated emergency number) and give the location of the emergency, the number of injured, and the type of attention needed
  - Call the faculty member and the service-learning program director at [contact information]
  - Contact the university's risk management office at [contact information]

- Designate an assistant, for example, another staff member, to do the following:
  - ○ Take charge of securing the surrounding environment to ensure no further emergencies exist
  - ○ Assist the agency supervisor or staff member
- Direct emergency personnel to the injured party when they arrive and give a verbal account of what occurred
- Document everything. Fill out agency, police, and/or other pertinent parties' incident forms and be sure to get witnesses' names, addresses, and phone numbers

In an emergency situation, only the community partner and/or the service-learning program director or their designee may make statements to the media. Others should respond to the media by saying, "I really do not have the information you need. It would be best to talk to the agency supervisor or service-learning director."

Here is a second sample protocol when a service-learning student is responsible for a liable act:

In the event that a service-learning student threatens or engages in physical/sexual assault, the community partner supervisor should[2] do the following:

- Contact the faculty partner
- Escort the student away from the location of the event, ask the student to leave the agency, and/or if necessary, have the student removed by law enforcement officers

The faculty partner, upon being notified of the situation, should do the following:

- Document everything. Fill out agency, police, and/or other pertinent parties' incident forms and be sure to get witnesses' names, addresses, and phone numbers
- Immediately contact the student to schedule an appointment for discussing the event
- Forbid the student to return to the agency until further notice
- Immediately contact the service-learning program director to adequately and appropriately handle the emergency
- Not respond to the media except to say, "I really do not have the information you need. It would be best to talk to the service-learning director." Only the community partner administrator or the service-learning director or their designees may make statements to the media.

---

[2] If you witness another student engaging in such behavior, try to address the behavior directly and contact the community partner supervisor immediately.

As a service-learning student, if you follow the list of tips provided above, you will minimize your chances of being held liable for your activities, or having things happen to you that could make others liable.

What Your Professor and/or Community Partner Should Do to Address Liability Issues

All service-learning projects should have a risk management plan, which is a process to identify any threats, control losses, reduce the severity of losses should they occur, safeguard against unauthorized use of funds, protect against injury, and take appropriate action to ensure legal compliance (Torres and Sinton, 2000). A risk management plan has three steps: identify all risks in the program, evaluate and prioritize these risks, and manage these risks (take steps to minimize risk). Your professor and/or community partner should have an emergency management protocol to specify the activities that you must follow in case of an emergency.

8.6 CONCLUSIONS

Issues involving engineering standards and liability are important in engineering and engineering design, especially regarding public works. Whenever you are designing in an engineering context, ensure you follow the latest standards and recommendations regarding your device, system, product, or process. Full consideration of liability issues involving your design is necessary and will probably result in a final engineering design modification. Strictly adhering to technical and ethical standards and minimizing liability will not insulate you from lawsuits, but will minimize your chances of being found liable for your work.

REFERENCES

ASAE. 2000. ASAE Standards, Engineering Practices, and Data. St. Joesph, MI: ASAE Press, 2000.

Dieter, G. *Engineering Design: A Materials and Processing Approach.* 3rd Ed., New York: McGraw-Hill, 2000.

Torres, J., Eds. *Establishing and Sustaining An Office of Community Service.* Liability and Risk Management. Providence, RI: Campus Compact, 2000.

EXERCISES

1. Locate the an engineering standards publication based on the discipline in which you are interested, for example, ASME Standards, ASAE Standards, ASHRAE Standards, ASTM Standards, or SAE Standards. Answer the following questions:
   - How is the standards book organized? Why do you suppose it is organized in this way?

Choose one standard within the publication and carefully read the entire standard.

- Based on what you read, do you believe that you could successfully design the device, process or system you read about? Why or why not?
- What knowledge have you gained in your education thus far that you can use in the design of the device or process outlined in the standard? What other courses might you need to fully understand the information presented in the standard?

2. Research the organization(s) that publish standards for use in your engineering discipline of interest. Write a short report on how standards are created and published for this organization(s).

3. Go to the Consumer Product Safety Commission web site (http://www.cpsc.gov). See if you can locate standards information on specific products, for example, baby rattles, playground equipment, or fire safety. Print a copy of one of these documents, and submit with the answers to the following questions:

- What historical context led up to the development of these guidelines or requirements
- What liability issues are involved in this product?
- How would the information in this publication impact the engineering design of this product?

4. Write a short report about an engineering disaster. Include information on what led up to the disaster, what caused the disaster, and what could have been done differently to avoid the disaster. Did liability issues play a role in this disaster? How?

5. Brainstorm all potential liability issues involved in your service-learning project. Use the results to create an informed consent statement.

Chapter 9

Profiles of Service-Learning Projects

The significant problems we have cannot be solved at the same level of thinking with which we created them.

—Albert Einstein

This chapter contains a collection of profiles of engineering service-learning projects to serve as successful examples of problems engineering undergraduates and their community partners addressed. They illustrate the diversity of engineering service-learning projects and show that community-based projects can be integrated into any engineering discipline(s).

This survey of engineering projects is not complete; to represent the breadth of engineering service-learning possibilities, we would need an entire book. In the next chapter, we have given leads to other organizations and programs with example projects. This information will provide additional ideas and potential resources for your own work.

These examples come from schools on semesters and quarters. They include first-year students to seniors in capstone design courses along with some graduate courses. One example shows a high school program started by service-learning alumni.

The table below summarizes the projects highlighted in this chapter.

Project	Institution	Majors	Year
9.1 Interactive Displays for a Children's Museum	Purdue University	EE, ME, AAE, IE, CHE, Comp. E, Vis. Des., Engl., Edu., Comm.	Fr.–Sr.
9.2 Terre Haute Bike Trail	Rose-Hulman Institute of Technology	Civil Engineering	Sr. (Fr.)
9.3 Girl Scout Climbing Wall	University of Dayton	Mech. and Aero. Engineering, Health and Sports Sciences	Jr.
9.4 Clean up of Environmental Hazards	Ohio State University	Food, Agricultural and Biological Engineering	Sr.
9.5 Environmental Impact of Chemical Processes	North Carolina State University	Chemical Engineering	Sr.
9.6 Hands On Atlanta's Project Development Process	Georgia Tech	Industrial and Systems Engineering	Sr.

Project	*Institution*	*Majors*	*Year*
9.7 Spanish in Action	Butler University	Computer Science and Software Engineering	Fr.–Sr.
9.8 Taking Engineering to the 6th Grade	University of San Diego	Engineering	Fr.
9.9 Trinity Mission Outlet Store	Purdue University	Engineering	Fr.
9.10 Software Applets for Learning	Iowa State University	Computer Engineering	Sr.
9.11 Adaptive Agricultural Machinery	Pennsylvania State University	Mechanical and Agricultural Engineering	Sr.
9.12 Children's Clinic at Wabash Center	Purdue University	EE, Comp E, ME, IE, Child Dev., Psych, Nursing	Fr.–Sr.
9.13 Design and Construction of Playgrounds	Louisiana State University	Biological and Agricultural Engineering	Fr.
9.14 Constructed Wetlands	Purdue University	CE, ME, ABE, EE, Forestry, NRES, Bio., Env. Sci., Chem..	Fr.–Sr.
9.15 Light Manufacturing for Adults with Disabilities	Purdue University	Industrial, Mechanical, Electrical Engineering	Fr.–Sr.
9.16 Habitat for Humanity, Lafayette, Indiana	Purdue University	Electrical, Computer, Mechanical, Industrial Engineering	Fr.–Sr.
9.17 Habitat for Humanity International	Notre Dame, Wisconsin and Purdue University	EE, ME, Comp. E., IE, C.S., Management, Marketing	Fr.–Sr.
9.18 Dynamics of a Playground	U. Mass Lowell	Mechanical Engineering	So.
9.19 Partnerships with Villages in Peru	U. Mass Lowell	Mechanical and Solar Engineering	Sr. & Grad.
9.20 Low Cost Communication Satellite	Taylor University	Physics (Astronautical and Electrical Engineering)	Sr.
9.21 BNL High School	Bedford North Lawrence High School	High School Physics	H.S. Jr. & Sr.
9.22 Student Profile	Louisiana State University	Biological Engineering	Sr.

9.1 INTERACTIVE DISPLAYS IN A CHILDREN'S MUSEUM

Course Description

Engineering Projects in Community Service (EPICS) at Purdue University is a multidisciplinary and vertically integrated (freshmen through seniors) engineering service-learning program. In 2004, it had 30 teams with about 300 students per semester working with local community partners. A typical EPICS team has 12 to 20 students. EPICS programs exist on several campuses across the country http://epicsnational.ecn.purdue.edu.

Project Description

The EPICS team has worked with the director, staff and board of the Imagination Station to develop several interactive exhibits. These examples illustrate different types of displays and content that they illustrate.

- Electromagnetism: In 2000, a seven-foot-long interactive display was developed that challenges children to move a car equipped with a permanent magnet down a track by activating a series of electromagnetic coils distributed along the track using buttons on the side of the display. The display is designed for the children to see the electromagnetic coils and signage explains how current flowing through the coils creates the magnetic forces.

  The Mag Racer was popular with the museum visitors but after two years of use, parts needed to be replaced. As the team looked at how to maintain

Figure 9.1 Children playing with the original Mag Racer at the Imagination Station

Figure 9.2 Redesigned Mag Racer museum display

the project, they came to the conclusion that they should redesign the display to make it more robust and easier to maintain while making it more engaging and professional looking. The new display used a new a partner with EPICS, the Indiana Women's Prison, that has a wood working shop for offenders to learn vocational skills. The engineering students designed a new cabinet for the Mag Racer and the prison's shop built it. The result was a professional-looking display that was delivered in the spring of 2003.

- Material Properties: Another project engaged students from chemical, electrical and mechanical engineering, under the direction of a chemical engineer from Eli Lilly Co., to design and deploy a display that illustrated density and fluid properties. The Mixer contained water and oil dyed yellow and blue respectively. The children pushed buttons to mix the liquids to make a green mixture and then could see them settle back out.

- Aerodynamics: A third project engaged mechanical and aerospace students to design an interactive wind tunnel with an interactive test section that let children see an airfoil suspended by the lift force when the wind tunnel was turned on. Additional test sections will be added to let the museum staff conduct lessons and allow the children to create their own shapes to test.

Community Partners

The Imagination Station is a hands-on, interactive children's science and space museum located in Lafayette, Indiana. Its mission is to provide a place for children

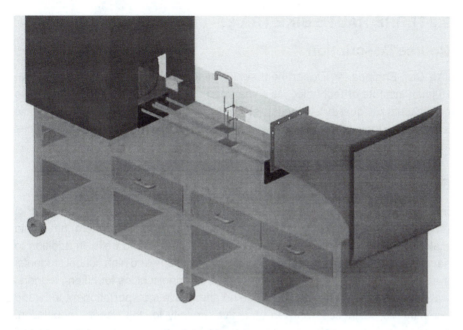

Figure 9.3 CAD Drawing of the Wind Tunnel

and their families to explore the worlds of science, engineering, and technology through interactive displays, activities, and workshops. The museum opened in 1996 through the efforts of a volunteer community organization.

Student Profile

Freshman through seniors participate from 20 departments across Purdue University's campus. These projects involved students from electrical engineering, computer sciences, civil engineering, mechanical engineering, industrial engineering, aeronautical engineering, materials sciences, chemical engineering, visual design, communication, and child development.

Advice for Students

Understand the context for your project. Spend time in the environment where your project will be used. In our case, spending time at the museum with the kids showed the team the children did not always use the displays as we had intended and so we improved the designs. Children are hard on the displays and effective designs have to be durable. From the design's beginning, your team should consider the project's maintenance and support. In the circuits, design check points to verify voltages and/or current levels and include these in a maintenance manual. Signage instructs the children how to operate the displays and teaches the older children and/or parents about the science and engineering principles. Do not leave the signage until the end; integrate it into the design process.

9.2 TERRE HAUTE BIKE TRAIL

Course Description

The Civil Engineering Department senior design and synthesis class at Rose-Hulman Institute of Technology is a year-long experience (six credit hours for two credit hours per quarter). In the fall, students select from a list of potential projects according to their interests. The civil engineering faculty reviews their preferences and forms teams of three to five students per project.

Project Description

In the early 1990s, the West Central Indiana Economic Development District (WCIEDD) developed a master plan for the Terre Haute trail system that would make use of some of the defunct railroad lines, i.e., rails to trails. In addition to serving as a transportation network for the city's college and high school students, the new trail system would provide recreational opportunities for bikers, joggers, walkers, and hikers. The trail was to be an alternative transportation route for the community's businesses and an attractive amenity for the general population. However, to sell the vision and take the plan beyond the concept stage, the trail system had to be designed and the trail's cost ascertained.

Community Partners

The primary community partner was the WCIEDD, a private, nonprofit corporation funded largely by federal, state, and local governmental agencies. Its services include programs to assist the elderly, highway and transit planning, economic development, and manufacturing technology assistance. WCIEDD's executive director submitted the project, but the key contact was the agency's transportation planner. A secondary community partner was the Terre Haute City Engineer. The city engineer's office works closely with WCIEDD on all transportation projects and economic development plans. The mayor of Terre Haute was involved, but the key contacts were the city engineer and his assistant. The engineer's office supplied general information on right-of-way, mapping, city codes and standards, and general planning and design guidelines.

Student Profile

Seniors in civil engineering worked in teams of three to five students per team. In addition, several freshman design teams worked on trail concepts and smaller issues during that same span of years. Other senior design teams worked on various park designs and rehabilitations that would become a part of the park and trail system.

Challenges and Successes

In the summer of 2002, the City of Terre Haute completed Phase I of the Terre Haute trail system. This 5.5-mile spur connects Rose-Hulman on the east side of the city with Indiana State University in the city's center. The community citizens embraced the trail. Traffic along the trail has steadily increased, and the city has received few citizen or editorial complaints. This was somewhat unexpected since some people raised objections before the trail was built.

One of the biggest challenges faced by the first team of students in 1994 was the mayor's opposition to the trail. The mayor voiced his objection to the trail early and often. His biggest concern was the required city maintenance in addition to police protection. The final project presentation was made in the mayor's office. He had not softened to the idea, which left the students feeling discouraged.

By the time the second student team worked on the trail, a new mayor had taken office. Unlike his predecessor, he was a runner and a strong supporter of the trail system. He appropriated trail funding but lost his reelection bid prior to the construction commencement. The next mayor campaigned against the trail, but she saw it gain public support. After it was built and the community embraced it, she embraced it, too. In fact, the Rose-Hulman contribution was hardly mentioned in the ribbon-cutting ceremony as the politicians moved in to take credit.

Conclusions and Recommendations

The Civil Engineering Department of the Rose-Hulman Institute of Technology has developed a successful senior design and synthesis class focused on client-based projects, many of which are service-learning projects. Student learning is enhanced by some key class elements:

- The year-long time frame allows for idea and design maturation, lost time due to conflicts, and solid relationship building among team members and the client.
- Intermediate deliverables (proposal, progress report, and final report) are critical to keeping students on schedule and obtaining continuous client feedback.
- Student attendance at stakeholder meetings is vital to service-learning projects.
- Presentations to clients and other stakeholders enhance student learning.

In conclusion, the City of Terre Haute is the proud owner of the first leg of a new trail system thanks to the sustained effort of Rose-Hulman Institute of Technology civil engineering students. These students have long since graduated, but the faculty has enjoyed seeing and spreading the fruits of its labor. More importantly, its efforts have resulted in a significant community contribution. Use of the trail has exceeded expectations, and community support for the remainder of the trail system is strong. Completion of the system will require community and grant funding, which takes time. Our alumni who worked on the trail will be reminded during their campus visits that the trail that connects their alma mater to the center of the city resulted from their efforts. We are convinced that service-learning projects not only make better engineers, they make better citizens.

9.3 THE GIRL SCOUT CLIMBING WALL MULTIDISCIPLINARY SERVICE-LEARNING PROJECT

Contributed by Margaret F. Pinnell, Ph. D., Corinne Daprano, Ph.D., Gabrielle Williamson, University of Dayton

Course Descriptions

The Girl Scout Wall (GS Wall) project was implemented in two classes at the University of Dayton (UD): a Mechanical and Aerospace Engineering (MAE) course, and a Health and Sports Science (HSS) course, and Sport Facility Management. The MAE course, Introduction to Materials, is a three-semester hour, third year required where students learn about the basic structure and properties of materials as well as the principles of material selection. The Sport Facility Management course is a three-semester hour, required HSS course where students are introduced to the processes of planning, constructing, equipping, maintaining, and managing sport facilities.

Project Description

The service-learning coordinator at UD and representatives from the Girl Scouts of Buckeye Trails Council (GSBTC) identified the need for the repair or replacement of a climbing wall at Camp Whip-Poor-Will that had been shut down for the past several years. This climbing wall was a major component of a challenge course which was designed to enhance the participants' self-esteem and confidence, encourage team building and cooperation, and improve physical fitness and skill.

To provide the students with a real world experience, the project was created with GSBTC as the client, the HSS class as the contractor, and the MAE class as the subcontractor. MAE student teams comprised a company owner (CEO), principal investigator (PI), and engineers. HSS teams consisted of a facility owner, project captain, and building committee members. The project began with a field trip to Camp Whip-Poor-Will. After the visit, the HSS student teams prepared Requests For Proposals (RFPs). The MAE student teams responded to an RFP selected by the HSS instructor in the form of team design proposal presentations. Once they had a final wall design, the HSS students designed sponsorship proposals to present to potential sponsors.

The GS Wall project culminated with the HSS and MAE students going to Camp Whip-Poor-Will to tear down the existing wall. Students were treated to a cookout where the service-learning coordinator facilitated a reflection session. Additional opportunities for structured reflection were facilitated by the individual instructors during class time. Construction of the wall took place the following semester by MAE student volunteers and is shown in Figures 9.4 and 9.5.

Community Partner

The GSBTC serves approximately 17,500 girls between the ages of five through seventeen and 4,500 adults in eight counties in southwest Ohio, and includes

Figure 9.4 Student Assembling the Climbing Wall

urban, suburban, and rural communities. GSBTC owns operates five camps in five counties totaling more than 700 acres. Camp Whip-Poor-Will is one of the largest facilities

Student Profile

UD is a small, Catholic, residential university in Dayton, Ohio. Approximately 60 students participated in the GS Wall project. About half of these students were third year MAE students and the other half were HSS students. A majority of the MAE and HSS students had some prior work experience through co-op, internships, or part-time jobs.

Challenges and Successes

The MAE students found some project aspects favorable, such as getting hands-on experience, having the opportunity to apply their engineering knowledge to a

Figure 9.5 Finishing Climbing Wall

real situation, and having the freedom to be creative in generating a practical and safe design. The students enjoyed the responsibility of managing the project and that this project was done for a good cause. They enjoyed working on a team, getting to know their teammates, developing leadership skills, and developing teamwork skills. A few students indicated that what they enjoyed most was tearing down the wall. Several of the students indicated they liked having the opportunity to work with people from other majors. The MAE students did not like the lack of organization and communication among the GSBTC, HSS, MAE classes, and the service-learning coordinator. Several students felt the project was too time consuming, and they did not like that most of their research and design had to be completed within the semester's first half. Some students felt that the design constraints did not allow enough creativity. Many students expressed disappointment in postponing wall construction until the spring semester.

The HSS students felt project participation helped them understand the various phases of facility planning and the complexity of working with facility designers and engineers, but they felt intimidated by the MAE students' technical knowledge and became frustrated by their inability to communicate safety and programming concerns regarding the climbing wall to the MAE students. The HSS students felt they gained valuable experience that will help them in their careers and be included on their résumés.

Both instructors felt that the students' frustration provided them with a greater understanding of the pitfalls when working as a professional. Many of the complications, deadlines, communication problems, and delays in this project occur in the real world.

Advice for Students

For students undertaking a collaborative service-learning project with students from another major, do not procrastinate. Student teams should meet as soon as possible to develop a list of objectives and action items and then delegate specific duties and due dates to team members. Ask many questions: All service-learning projects are different and involve a real client. Therefore, the course instructor cannot plan for every project aspect or problem. However, the course instructor should be willing to provide guidance, find answers, and help solve project problems. Communicate with teammates, instructor, students from the other course, and the client. Be responsive to questions and concerns of teammates and students from the other course. Many times the work of one student cannot begin without input from another student.

9.4 CLEANUP OF ENVIRONMENTAL HAZARDS

Contributed by: Ann D. Christy, Ph.D., P.E., Department of Food, Agricultural, and Biological Engineering, The Ohio State University

Course Description

Design and Modeling of Biological Systems (FABE 625): a required senior-level biological engineering course in the Food, Agricultural, and Biological Engineering.

Project Description

The project was an environmental site investigation at an abandoned Superfund site, the Uniontown Industrial Excess Landfill (IEL) in Stark County, Ohio. The purpose was to assist the township and to provide a real world design experience for the students. Students received base documents including government agency references (e.g., US EPA, US Geological Survey, and Ohio Department of Natural Resources), environmental engineering consultant materials, legal papers from previous lawsuits, and in-class tutorials covering the fundamental soil and geologic sciences needed to understand the site's setting. Student team projects included designing an *in situ* landfill bioreactor remediation system, assessing air pollution effects (from direct off-gassing, bioremediation metabolic by-products, and incomplete combustion by-products from the site's gas flare), designing three vegetation scenarios for site phytoremediation, designing a bioremediation system for the peat bogs and wetlands directly down gradient from IEL, and analyzing a web page created by the potentially responsible parties. Team-to-team interactions were important because some projects built on information from other projects.

Community Partner

Lake Township trustees (representing the citizens of Uniontown and Lake Township, Ohio) and Bennett and Williams Environmental Consultants Inc.

Student Profile

Senior undergraduates and a few graduate students in the Food, Agricultural, and Biological Engineering program.

Community Needs Addressed Through Project

The community had been in conflict for more than thirty years over its local toxic waste dump, the Uniontown Industrial Excess Landfill (IEL). Known hazardous materials were placed in this unlined, unprotected landfill even as area citizens and health departments wanted to shut it down for over a decade. Complaints continued about uncontrolled fires, increased cancer deaths, and controversies over the illegal creation of direct connections between on-site liquid waste lagoons and a neighboring agricultural drainage ditch.

In 1978, the landfill closed, and the owners declared bankruptcy and fled the country. The EPA designated it a Superfund cleanup site in 1984. From 1985 to 1991, several emergency actions were taken including extending a water supply line from a neighboring community to provide water so residents would not have to drink from their own contaminated wells. A technical assistance grant provided the community with funds to hire an environmental consulting firm to explain the technical information coming from the EPA via a series of public meetings and to act as an advocate in deliberations with the EPA. However, no real progress was made on cleaning the site for almost twenty years. Several nagging unaddressed technical problems continued for which the community wanted answers. By the mid 1990s, the technical assistance grant had run out, and the community could no longer afford to pay the environmental consultants' fees.

In 1999, the service-learning project began. Student teams provided short-term consulting expertise. Their annual visits attracted local media attention, which kept the issue alive and the community energized. Finally, in 2003, a cooperative cleanup agreement was signed by those companies which had sent waste to the landfill. County residents suggested that the students' presence and site work was instrumental in reaching this final compromise agreement among the polluters, the community, and the EPA.

Figure 9.6 Analyzing Water Test Data

Figure 9.7 Students Meeting with Trustees

Challenges and Successes

The challenges and successes are best summarized in the words of the students who participated in this project:

> "We learned about dealing with society and how it views scientific and engineering solutions, especially when society does not fully understand."
>
> "Having a real world example . . . has taught me a lot about the importance of doing what is right as an engineer and how important it is to please the customer or whomever [the project] affects."
>
> "I realized how engineers must be able to cope with the politics of any project."
>
> "The group learned a valuable lesson regarding the limited influence engineering sometimes has on society at the expense of the welfare of that society."
>
> "The most effective path in the formation of practical solutions . . . is for communities to become educated about the issues, to organize within their communities, and to link up with other communities with similar problems."

Advice for Students

Start early and do a little bit each week. Read as much background material as you can to familiarize yourself with the community and the problem's history.

When working with community partners, develop a set of questions prior to meeting with them. The biggest challenge is defining the project or translating the client's concerns into an engineering problem. Developing a workable engineering solution to an environmental problem is half of the battle. You must address the problem's social, political, legal, and economic aspects, or you will never implement the best engineering solution.

9.5 ENVIRONMENTAL IMPACT OF CHEMICAL PROCESSES

Instructors: Dr. Steven Peretti and Dr. Lisa Bullard, Chemical Engineering, North Carolina State University.

Course Description

Chemical Engineering Senior Capstone Design Course at North Carolina State University

Project Description

The instructors and the Southeast Chatham Citizens Advisory Council (SCCAC) developed the following project descriptions:

Spring 2002—The air quality in Moncure, North Carolina, is a problem that has concerned its local residents. Moncure is a small town (population ~ 630) in Chatham County, approximately 23 miles from Durham. As a low-income, rural community close to a major urban center, Moncure provides an amenable site for industry, and has become the site for plants from several area industries. Though federal and state regulations govern emissions and other pollution from individual factories, this oversight neglects the cumulative effect of chemical emissions from several companies to a particular area. The Moncure community industries release over four million pounds of emissions and create approximately 46 million pounds of total waste each year. The students determined the cumulative effect of the air emissions and if these amounts are harmful. To study this problem, the students must analyze the pollution control equipment these industries are using and what the Industry Best Practices are for these processes. The project outcome is to assist and educate the community residents and the industries on what types of pollutants they are being exposed to and what they can do to improve the situation.

Spring 2003—After the project's conclusion, the SCCAC was enthusiastic about the team's findings and wanted to have another student group continue the project in Spring 2003. After evaluating the content of the Spring 2002 project, the instructors wanted to redirect the focus of the project to increase the technical content. Based on the previous team's results, the instructors focused on two top air pollutants, ethylene glycol and formaldehyde, identified as being much higher in Moncure, NC, than in similar plants nationwide. The student teams would focus on how to reduce these emissions.

One of last year's design groups studying concluded that the emissions for Chatham County are among the highest on the East Coast. Two of the large emission sources were identified for analysis. This project involved analysis of the processes across the chemical industry to understand the sources of emissions and potential process configurations to reduce emissions. Students benchmark similar processes by leading market producers and contacted equipment vendors to understand the impact of equipment design on emissions. Students interacted with Moncure community leaders to understand concerns about emissions and provide input on benchmarking results.

Community Partners

The Southeast Chatham Citizens Advisory Council (SCCAC) is a group of citizens who meet monthly to discuss environmental, political, and economic issues affecting them. In particular, SCCAC was concerned about Moncure, NC, a small town with a large chemical industry concentration. Many citizens had complained about strong odors, particularly near the manufacturing plants in the area.

Student Profile

Chemical Engineering Seniors.

Community Needs Addressed Through Project

Identification of air pollutants in a small community with a large concentration of chemical industries. Recommendations for improvements for air quality of the local community.

Conclusions and Recommendations

In our experience, the environmental arena is a good chemical engineering fit vis-à-vis senior design projects. Problems of this nature require knowledge of environmental regulations, emission calculations, economics, and process changes in the spirit of green engineering. Though the line between service and advocacy can often blur to the detriment of the prudent exercise of technical judgment, you can strike a balance and incorporate the technical and service components into an appropriate, engaging project.

Students are motivated to work on projects they perceive to have societal benefits, either directly in terms of service or indirectly through the utility of the products generated by their designs. Service-learning projects offer these students the opportunity to bridge the academic-community gap meaningfully and productively.

The community of Moncure is better off because of its interaction with chemical engineering students from NC State. Citizens are more aware of the emissions in their local area and how local companies compare with their counterparts throughout the country. As a result of this information, citizens have become more proactive in working with industry and state regulatory agencies to ask for increased monitoring.

Some stumbling blocks exist to implementing service-learning in chemical engineering. Including sufficient technical considerations to make it meet CHE design criteria remains a challenge. You must identify a partner who doesn't have preconceived notions of the desired outcomes. Having partnerships in place, in the local community and industry can make the project more meaningful for the partners and the students. [Bullard, Clayton and Peretti, 2004]

9.6 HANDS ON ATLANTA: IMPROVEMENTS TO THE DESIGN OF HANDS ON ATLANTA'S PROJECT DEVELOPMENT PROCESS

Prof. Faiz Al-Khayyal, Industrial and Systems Engineering, Georgia Tech

Course Description

Engineering Projects in Community Service (EPICS) can be taken as an option for the Industrial and Systems Engineering (ISyE) Senior Capstone Design Course. EPICS programs exist on several campuses across the country http://epicsnational.ecn.purdue.edu.

Project Description

Hands On Atlanta (HOA) has three major project type classifications: Ongoing projects, Group Projects, and Special Events. Each project type has a different development process resulting in redundancy and poor resource allocation for each project. The EPICS team identified four major problem areas: allocation of resources, project development redundancy, volunteer recruitment and retention, and extra planning time. The team's project focused on defining a solution to the problems affecting the development process.

Community Partners

HOA is a non-profit organization assisting individuals, families and corporate and community groups to volunteer their services in the metro Atlanta area. HOA is headquartered in Atlanta and is an affiliate of CityCares, which is an international urban community service organization that includes over 40 "Cares" and "Hands On" organizations across the United States and United Kingdom.

HOA was founded in 1989 by a small group of friends and has since grown into Atlanta's premier volunteer organization. Since its founding, HOA's yearly budget has increased from $50,000 in 1989 to over $5.1 million. The HOA volunteer staff has grown, increasing from ten volunteers in 1989 to over two million in 2002. There are over 25,000 volunteers working with HOA each year. These volunteers work daily to improve the community and help schools, parks, senior citizen homes, food banks, pet shelters, and low-income neighborhoods to meet their critical needs.

Student Profile

Seniors in Industrial and Systems Engineering

Community Needs Addressed Through Project

With over 25,000 volunteers working with HOA each year, efficiently placing the volunteers is time and resource intensive. By improving the efficiency of the organization, HOA can use its resources to continue to look at new community needs and programs.

Challenges and Successes

After a thorough observation of HOA's project development process, the students defined the problem areas and recommended alternatives to address the problems. Some of the project deliverables included the following:

a) Creating new forms for processing community service partnership service agreements
b) Recommending improvements in the utilization of human resources, including staff and volunteer training, handbook creation and utilization, shared methodologies and technologies, automated phone menu, and resource database system creation
c) Developing a standard Master Process Flow template and charts

Implementation of the students' project results will improve HOA's project, resource and membership structure. By shifting some of the paid staff work to volunteers, efficiency in project development will improve. HOA will use a process evaluation template, with best practices, for the creation of future projects. A flow chart and computer technology will reduce project development time and facilitate the resource allocation and volunteer management processes.

Thanks to the partnership of the nationally based EPICS Program and Microsoft Corporation, a generous software gift was donated to HOA. Microsoft's University Relations (Microsoft Research) is a national sponsor of the EPICS program. This software, Microsoft Project 2000, allows the organization to implement the system, which the senior design students designed, to improve its special events planning.

9.7 SPANISH IN ACTION (SIA) PROJECT

Instructor: Prof. Panos Linos, Computer Science, Butler University

Course Description

Engineering Projects in Community Service (EPICS) is offered at Butler University through three Computer Science and Software Engineering (CSSE) courses named CSSE 283, CSSE 383, and CSSE 483 for students of the second, third and fourth years respectively. Second-semester freshmen students can also take CSSE 283. Students receive elective credit for EPICS in Computer Science and can use EPICS as a Computer Science-Software Engineering Elective in the Software Engineering undergraduate degree program. EPICS programs exist on several campuses across the country http://epicsnational.ecn.purdue.edu.

Project Description

The first EPICS project at Butler University began in the fall of 2001 and was named Spanish In Action (SIA). Today, SIA entails a web-based suite of educational software for teaching the Spanish language to middle school students. It includes an interactive game called QuickDrop (QD), which allows sixth grade students to practice their Spanish vocabulary. In addition, SIA provides a teaching aid for preparing and conducting exams, tracking students' progress, and generating various statistics for students' past performance.

The implementation of the QD game was divided into two parts: the front-end, web-based graphical user interface (GUI) and the support for the database back-end. The front-end was implemented using *Macromedia Flash 5.0* and the *ActionScript* language, which are part of a commercial drawing and animation package. For the back-end, we used the *mySQL* relational database, and we used the HTML and PHP languages for the web-based part.

The user interface of the QD game consists of four visual elements: a flying object such as an airplane, moving clouds, a dropping package, and a moving train. While playing the QD game, the user can choose and navigate the flying object above a selected background landscape. As the train runs across the screen, various Spanish words display on each of its wagons as shown in Figure 1. Simultaneously, an English word appears on the screen's top left-hand corner. The game's goal is to drop the package from the flying object so that it lands on and matches the train's corresponding Spanish equivalent. The game becomes more challenging as bigger storm clouds move at different speeds and in various directions between the flying object and the train. If the package, when dropped, goes through a regular cloud, a parachute will open and the package will be slowed down. On the other hand, if the package falls through a storm cloud, it begins flaming and its descent is speeding up. When the package lands on the correct word, points are added to the player's score; however, points are deducted for wrong responses. The entire game is composed of ten attempts per level up to five levels.

Community Partner

Crispus Attucks Middle School (CAMS), located in Indianapolis, Indiana, is part of the Indianapolis Public School district. CAMS teaches 6th, 7th, and 8th grades and is home to 900 students. Named after a great Revolutionary War hero, the school is rich in history. In 1927, the school, known as Crispus Attucks High School, became the Indianapolis school for African-Americans and remained so for a long time. It was converted into a middle school in the mid-1980s. A museum tracing the history of CAMS and African-American culture resides in the building. The Crispus Attucks Center, on campus, has a mission to act as the catalyst of knowledge, scholarship, and resources for the teaching, learning, and under- standing of the diverse population groups in the Indianapolis Public Schools, the city, the state, and the nation.

Student Profile

Second-semester Freshmen, Sophomores, Juniors and Seniors in Computer Sci- ence and Software Engineering.

Community Needs Addressed Through Project

Improving the educational experience for middle schools students, specifically, helping middle school students learn Spanish.

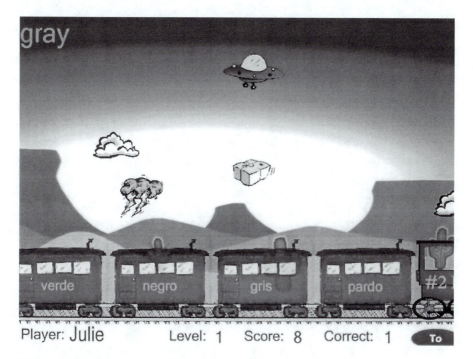

Figure 9.8 The User Interface Of Quickdrop (QD)

Challenges and Successes

The SQA team has been testing the QD game at various stages of its development. During this effort, a prototype implementation of QD was given to more than forty middle school students for playing and practicing their Spanish vocabulary in the classroom. After that, the students were asked to fill out a questionnaire, providing input about the features and usefulness of the game. About 76% of the students indicated that the QD game helped them learn their Spanish vocabulary, and they would be willing to play it at their home.

SIA is an example of a thriving EPICS project at Butler University. It has grown since the fall of 2001 to include an online game and a Web Administration System. The team hopes SIA can grow to include a collection of games, teaching tools, and subjects, creating an educational suite, and prolonging the project's life. Our customer has expanded to include several more Spanish teachers and students, spanning sixth through eighth grade in the middle schools. This expansion creates a challenge for the team members because the system must be flexible enough to accommodate their needs. SIA's long-term goal is to provide all teachers with a useful product, which will enable them to teach more effectively, while involving computers in the students' lives.

9.8 TAKING ENGINEERING TO THE 6TH GRADE

Instructor: Susan Lord, Electrical Engineering, University of San Diego (USD)

Course Description

This course is an introduction to the field of engineering and involves the exploration of problem solving using the engineering design process in lecture and laboratory projects. All engineering students take this course in the first semester of the first year.

Project Description

First-year engineering students developed hands-on and fun activities on basic science, technology, and engineering principles for middle school classrooms.

Community Partners

The USD Office for Community Service-Learning staff and the instructor identified middle school, specifically sixth grade, as a good age for a partner. Middle schools need to keep students interested in math and science and motivated to go to college, become technically literate, and pursue technical careers. First-year engineering students should feel comfortable they have more knowledge than sixth graders. We chose a school with an economically disadvantaged and ethnically diverse student body that is within a few miles of USD. Many of these students may not know anyone who has gone to college, so the USD students can serve as role models for college as well as engineering. Once we chose a school, we found two teachers who agreed to work with us on this project.

Student Profile

First semester engineering students.

Community Needs Addressed Through Project

Middle schools need to keep students interested in science and motivated to go to college, become technically literate, and pursue technical careers. First-year engineering students need to learn what engineering is, why it is useful to society, and communication and teamwork skills.

Conclusions, Recommendations, and Advice for Students

We were nervous before the first presentation. However, we left the classroom with a great feeling amidst sixth graders chanting for specific USD students to come back next time. The sixth graders impressed us with their knowledge and one provided a better definition of engineering than the freshmen had given. We learned several valuable lessons the hard way: Do not give candy until the end, let the students into the hallway, or visit a classroom with a substitute teacher. One group asked the sixth graders what they remembered from two previous groups' visits and were excited that students remembered the main ideas of friction and bridge building (Lord, 1999).

9.9 TRINITY MISSION OUTLET STORE

Instructor: William Oakes, Purdue University

Course Description

The service-learning project is used as a substitute for the first of two traditional projects in the first engineering course, Introduction to Engineering Problem Solving and Computer Tools taken by all first-year engineering students at Purdue University. Students were divided into formal teams of three or four students for the course, and they used these teams for the service-learning projects. The project spanned the first half of the semester and accounted for 15% of the course grade.

Student Profile

First-year engineering students from Purdue University

Project Description

Two teams were assigned to Trinity Mission Outlet Store. Trinity Mission Outlet store frequently receives donated computers, various computer components, and electrical appliances. The challenges were to help the staff of the Outlet Store determine which appliances and computers were useable and could be sold in the store.

The first team worked to match the computers and subsequent components. The team tagged the computer and components such that if the computer and components were separated and/or misplaced, the tags would instruct a person on how to match the computer and its components. The team determined if the computer would work and the capacity of each computer. If the computer did not work, the team tried to repair the computer. The team color coded the components to specific computers and detailed the operating system, available memory and the programs installed on the hard drive. These details were compiled in a booklet. (Three copies were made: one attached in some fashion to the computer, one given to the store manager, and one given to the Executive Director of Trinity Mission.)

The team developed a manual of procedures that would instruct staff and residents and volunteers on recognizing compatible computers and computer components as they were received through the donations. The manual contained a decision tree helping staff, residents, and volunteers to assemble a computer with compatible components. (Example: if you have a printer cable with pins versus a USB printer cable). The final part of the project was for the team to hold a training class at the store to teach staff, residents, and volunteers all of the above.

The second team assigned to Trinity Mission Outlet store examined small appliances/machines to determine if they were in working order. If they were not in working order, the team tried to repair the appliance. After appliance repair, the team created a manual (one copy for the store manager and one copy to the Executive Director) that included step-by-step instructions, photographs, and diagrams for the repair of each type/brand of appliance/machine. At the completion of the project, the team presented a training session to the staff, residents and volunteers on repairing and troubleshooting appliances.

Community Partners

Trinity Mission is an Evangelical Christian Ministry that provides housing for homeless people and rehabilitation for substance abuse victims.

Community Needs Addressed Through Project

Assist Trinity Mission's Outlet Store staff in assembling working computers and appliances for resale in the local community. Residents of Trinity Mission work in the Outlet Store, so the training materials assist the residents in gaining job skills for employment after they leave Trinity's programs.

Challenges and Successes

One of the challenges for these projects was that the first semester students did not know how to assemble working computer systems, especially older and less familiar systems. They were unfamiliar with how common electrical appliances worked and how to fix them. They were initially hesitant to "jump in" and get things to work.

After this hesitation, the students produced excellent results that allowed the outlet store's staff to increase its productivity. The manuals included pictures of components. Other students checked the copyrights for photos from the web. Some useful websites were copyrighted. The web site owners allowed the students to use the information in their training manuals as long as their site was credited and they received a copy of the finished manuals.

9.10 SOFTWARE APPLETS FOR LEARNING

Contributed by Prof. Dan Berleant, Electrical and Computer Engineering, Iowa State University

Course Description

The project has been done by senior design students. Senior design is a two-term sequence. Independent study students would also be eligible. These students build on a foundation created by students in my Java programming course. One of the homework assignments has been to build an applet that any child (with disabilities or not) can use, helps them learn in some way (e.g., arithmetic, letter recognition, object recognition), and entertains them. Students in the EPICS program choose good ones to expand, polish, and perfect in consultation with a client. EPICS programs exist on several campuses across the country http://epicsnational.ecn.purdue.edu.

Project Description

An applet is a Java program that runs in the browser window when someone uses a Web browser like Internet Explorer to access a URL. Applets typically take advantage of the graphics and user interface capabilities of the Java language. Applets developed for this project should have large buttons so people with low motor skills can manipulate a computer mouse to get the cursor over them relatively easily. The applet should be usable for people with short attention spans and little computer experience. The applet should be a fun way to move users toward basic educational goals.

Community Partners

We have worked with Sawyer Elementary School in Ames, Iowa and with an elementary school in Utah through a teacher with a web site at www.mrhall.org.

Student Profile

Senior-level computer engineering students. Computer science students could do this project.

Community Needs Addressed Through Project

An applet can potentially be run over the Web and, therefore, be available to anyone anywhere. Although it might be developed for a particular client, the potential exists for it to be used by others on the Web.

Challenges and Successes

The difference between writing any software and writing quality software for use is something students are often not used to. Typical software that students write

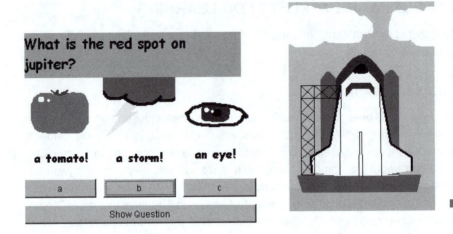

Mission Accomplished!

> **Figure. Students answer multiple choice questions about astronomy. Each correct answer adds another piece to the space ship launch scene. When the scene is complete, then "Mission Accomplished!"**

Figure 9.9 Example Applet for Learning

for class assignments is not of deployable quality. Getting students over this mind-set is a challenge that helps them in careers.

Conclusions, Recommendations, and Advice for Students

Any student who can program in Java can write an applet. This type of project is quite accessible to students. However, identifying clients, working with them, and producing a quality product can be challenging.

9.11 ADAPTIVE AGRICULTURAL MACHINERY

Course Description

Capstone senior design course at Penn State can be taken as a multidisciplinary design team approach through a centralized clearinghouse called the Learning Factory. Students select their senior projects through this clearinghouse. Engineering Projects in Community Service, EPICS, host projects for not-for-profit clients through the Learning Factory. EPICS programs exist on several campuses across the country http://epicsnational.ecn.purdue.edu.

Project Description

The student team developed a modified braking system to allow a driver to operate a tractor with limited use of his or her legs. The brake system was modified to operate using a hand control that regulated a pneumatic actuation system. An air compressor supplied pressurized air to actuators that deployed the brakes. Valves allowed the pressure to the actuators to be varied, which gave the operator intermittent control over the brakes. A hand-held control system allowed the driver to regulate the valves and the brakes. The control mechanism was to be held in one hand but allowed the driver to activate the right and left brakes separately using two fingers, one for the left and one for the right brakes.

A second accommodation was made to the tractor's hitch to reduce the need to dismount and remount the tractor. A remotely activated three-point hitch system was designed and powered by a twelve-volt battery. Electric actuators allowed the hitch to be operated remotely by hand from the tractor's cab.

Community Partners

AgrAbility for Pennsylvanians is a not-for-profit organization that provides direct services to farmers and farm family members who continue in agricultural production despite an injury or on-going health condition. Examples of disabilities include amputation, stroke, hearing impairment, spinal cord injury, back injury, and arthritis.

AgrAbility services include the following:

- Conduct an on-site farm visit to discuss the tasks the person with the disability finds difficult.
- Provide information on appropriate assistive technology, equipment, or modification that can enable the person to do the task independently and safely.
- Link farm families with potential funding sources as well as state and county services.
- Provide peer and caregiver information
- Conduct disability awareness activities for farm safety day camps, 4-H leaders, and other groups.

- Provide educational presentations for agricultural and health care professionals.

Student Profile

Seniors from across engineering participating in their capstone design course. This project involves mechanical engineering students.

Community Needs Addressed Through Project

This team worked with AgrAbility whose mission is to enable farmers with disabilities continue to farm. The specific need addressed by the team was to modify a tractor to accommodate drivers with limited or no mobility in their legs.

9.12 CHILDREN'S CLINIC AT WABASH CENTER

Course Description

Engineering Projects in Community Service (EPICS) at Purdue University is a multidisciplinary and vertically integrated (freshmen through seniors) engineering service-learning program. In 2004, it had 30 teams with about 300 students per semester working with local community partners. A typical EPICS team has 12 to 20 students. EPICS programs exist on several campuses across the country http://epicsnational.ecn.purdue.edu.

Project Description

The EPICS Wabash Center Children's Clinic (WCECE) teams began in 1995 with a goal of bringing technology to bear on therapy and play activities. The clinicians asked the EPICS teams to develop play environments that would achieve several objectives:

- Provide a rich set of multi-sensory experiences the child with disabilities could control
- Allow the child with disabilities to interact with the play environment using modalities consistent with the child's abilities
- Provide experience with cause and effect relationships
- Allow children with disabilities and their peers to play together in a cooperative way with the child with disabilities in control of some of the play aspects
- Be easily stored in the clinic's limited space

Although some commercial products are aimed at children with disabilities, they can be expensive. The clinicians found that these products were too simple to engage children for long, and few encouraged interactive play.
The EPICS teams have tackled and delivered several projects to the clinic:

- Custom software with a large input keyboard to allow children to animate faces
- Animated story books using multimedia software
- Animations of songs and nursery rhymes that incorporate images and voices of the clinic children
- A custom interface and set of interchangeable handles for a toy record player to allow children to activate the record player using motions that do not depend on fine motor skills.
- A toy phone with large buttons and cushioned handset.
- Dump truck city, which is an electrically controlled dump truck able to travel forward and backward on a circular track and controlled by a panel of large buttons.
- A posture sensor prototype that interfaces a hat-mounted posture monitoring device with electronic toys. The toy is activated as long as the child main-

tains an upright posture. The purpose of the system is to build muscle strength in children with cerebral palsy by encouraging good posture.

- Three rooms of a custom multi-sensory electromechanical doll house.

The doll house provides an example that has integrated electrical engineering design, computer interfacing and programming, and mechanical design. The first system, a kitchen, included an electronically controlled refrigerator door, lights, and kitchen sounds that a child selectively activated with a large, easy-to-use wired or wireless touchpad. The second-generation system, a bathroom, included an electronically controlled toilet lid, a swimming/singing rubber duck, lights, and sounds, and added a simple speech recognition interface. The third system, a bedroom, included a ceiling-mounted rotating mobile, a cupboard with two electromechanical doors that opened, a phone, radio sounds, lights, and (at the request of the clinicians) a vibrating bed so the children could feel the motion. In addition to the touchpad and speech interfaces, the design included a custom finger sensor interface that activated the bedroom devices when a child successfully inserted a finger into a hole that detected the insertion with infrared emitters and sensors. This interface encouraged children to develop their fine motor skills and practice pointing motions. The rooms were used as a part of therapy sessions in which the clinician placed the touchpad to encourage specific motions in cooperative play involving children with disabilities and their peers.

Figure 9.10 Student demonstrating to a child how to operate the mechanized pieces of the dollhouse room

Community Partners

The Wabash Center Children's Clinic provides early intervention programs for children with disabilities or developmental delays. Many of the young children have cerebral palsy. The clinic works with the children and their families to provide therapies and treatments that enhance opportunities for learning and acquisition of skills.

Student Profile

Freshman through seniors participate from 20 departments across Purdue University's campus, including electrical engineering, computer sciences, mechanical engineering, industrial engineering, child development, nursing, psychology, and audiology.

Advice for Students

Understanding the context for your project is important. Spend time in the environment where your project will be used, e.g., in a children's clinic. Talk regularly with the product users and keep them engaged in the design process. Adding students from outside of engineering adds a great deal to the design team and improves the final products.

9.13 DESIGN AND CONSTRUCTION OF PLAYGROUNDS

Course description

Biological Engineering 1252: Biology in Engineering is a freshman level design course. The course objectives are for students to learn about engineering, biological engineering, design and themselves; to determine if biological engineering is an appropriate major and to sharpen communication and teaming skills; and to encourage civic responsibility.

Project Description

Students enrolled in this course complete a playground design, usually for a public school. The goal of this program is to ensure that every child enrolled in Baton Rouge public schools has access to a safe, accessible, fun playground. Students work in groups with 3–4, and with their community partner There are approximately 45 students enrolled in two laboratory sections. Each section has a separate playground to design.

Students learn about playground design by studying the Consumer Product Safety Commission's Handbook for Public Playground Safety and the Americans with Disabilities Act. They learn about the community's and school's history from the community partners, and learn more about playground design from the children at the school. Elementary school students create drawings and descriptions of their dream playgrounds, and the college students work with these ideas and others provided by the community partner to create initial playground designs. These designs are presented to the community partner approximately 12 weeks into the 15 week semester. Students then make changes suggested by the community partner and submit a final playground design and comprehensive report during the last week of the semester.

After the semester is finished, students with a strong interest in completing the project merge the 6–8 designs into one. The consolidated design is checked by a certified playground safety inspector, and any necessary adjustments are made. The students and the community partner work to secure donations and grants to build the playground.

Community Partners

Community partners are primarily public school communities in Baton Rouge, LA. The "average" school has approximately 300 students, pre-K through grade 5, 20 teachers, an assistant principal, and a principal. School improvement teams or parent-teacher organizations are also involved. Most schools have a corporate partner that assists in raising and/or providing funds for playground construction. Other community partners include agencies that serve children with special needs.

Student Profile

Freshman and sophomore students in biological engineering with approximately 25% of the students who are thinking about majoring in biological engineering but

Figure 9.11 Portion of the playground students drew in AutoCAD, a picture of the playground during the construction process, and after construction was complete.

are enrolled in other majors such as general studies (undecided), biology, biochemistry, or chemical engineering.

Community Needs Addressed Through the Project

Childhood development experts assert that well designed play spaces for children are critical to advancing their physical, mental, social, and educational development. The majority of the Baton Rouge public schools have no playground, or have a playground built in the 1960s or 1970s, long before appropriate safety standards were established.

Challenges and Successes

The biggest challenge with this program is securing funding to construct the playgrounds. This challenge is compounded by liability issues, which result in the selection of pre-fabricated play equipment that is expensive. Many funding agencies are willing to fund a single playground, but returning to these agencies for funds for additional playgrounds has proved a challenge, even with volunteers from the community constructing the playground, and the school board paying for all playground surfacing.

The biggest successes include the sense of pride attained by the community when the playground is built. Students at the school who helped design the playground usually help fund the playground through fundraisers, and sometimes assist in the construction; their energy, motivation, ownership, and commitment are

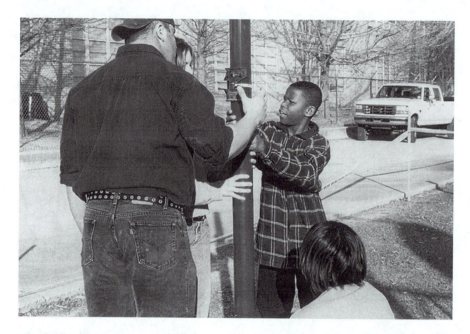

Figure 9.12 Students work together to level a pole as they set the pole in concrete.

infectious, and a great source of inspiration for the community adults and college students. The schools have responded with increased recess time and activities, and most principals have observed fewer behavioral issues during play time.

Advice for Students

In this spirit, I offer three pieces of advice:

1. **Follow through.** You will probably be in situations in which it feels like you're doing more than your share of the work. Projects take a lot more work and energy when they involve tangible, real, deliverables to actual community partners. While it is important to do your share of the work, realize that part of a service-learning project involves going that extra mile in ways that may never show up in your grade or be evident to your community partner or your peers.

2. **Get used to being outside your comfort zone.** A service-learning project is not a complete success unless students have experiences that involve creative conflict and an examination of biases. These can be uncomfortable, as can interacting with people that are very different from you and dealing with unexpected events. Be prepared to stretch yourself outside your comfort zone; while uncomfortable in the short run, these experiences will benefit you in many ways in the long run.

3. **Get into the habit of obtaining information from multiple sources and perspectives.** Designing in a community context can be challenging because of a high volume of information, a multitude of conflicting opinions

and needs, and a lack of money and time. These make the design process fun, meaningful, creative, and challenging. Take advantage of the multiple perspectives and resources available to you. You will create a design, hopefully, with everyone's buy in. You will never please everyone 100%, but people are more likely to compromise and be satisfied with the final result when everyone's voice has been heard and considered.

9.14 CONSTRUCTED WETLAND

Course Description

Engineering Projects in Community Service (EPICS) at Purdue University is a multidisciplinary and vertically integrated (freshmen through seniors) engineering service-learning program. In 2004, it had 30 teams with about 300 students per semester working with local community partners. A typical EPICS team has 12 to 20 students. EPICS programs exist on several campuses across the country http://epicsnational.ecn.purdue.edu.

Project Description

The team surveyed the site and designed the wetland cells and the piping layout and pump installations to carry water from the creek, through the cells, and back to the creek. The team designed and constructed a dam to control the water flow. A contractor was hired to excavate the site and to install the large piping and weir boxes. The students worked with a wetlands nursery to determine required plant type and quantity, and they planted 9000 plants.

To allow the wetland to serve as an experimental facility, the four cells of the wetland were arranged into two parallel trains so the students could evaluate the effect of different loading levels. The team designed and installed flow measurement and sampling equipment to collect data on the wetland's effectiveness.

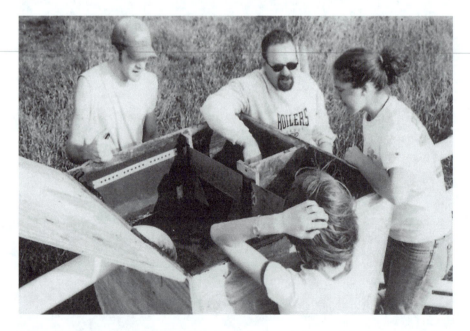

Figure 9.13 Students and their advisor examine a weir box used to measure the flow rate entering the wetland.

Figure 9.14 View of one of the four cells in the wetland from the observations platform.

When the wetland construction was completed, the students looked to expand their work's impact by turning the wetland into an environmental education center that could be a destination for school field trips and community groups. The teams designed and constructed an observation platform and signs and displays around the wetland for a self-guided tour. Information discussed the wetland issues, how the wetland removed pollutants, and the plants and animals that inhabited the wetland.

Community Partners

Department of Forestry and Natural Resources.

Student Profile

Freshman through seniors participate from 20 departments across Purdue University's campus. These projects involved students from civil engineering, mechanical engineering, agricultural engineering, electrical engineering, forestry, natural resources, biology and environmental science.

Community Needs Addressed Through Project

Purdue University operates a large agricultural facility about ten miles north of West Lafayette, Indiana. In addition to intensive farming activities, confined feeding operations exist for dairy cattle, hogs, and chickens along with an aquaculture center for raising fish. Storage lagoons collect the wastes from these operations, and the lagoon contents are applied to the farmland by spray irrigation. This common practice can have the negative effect of increasing the levels of nitrogen, phosphorus, and other chemicals in the surface runoff and the groundwater. The Constructed Wetlands EPICS team, formed in 1998, provided engineering support for the planning, design, construction, and operation of a wetland that would treat the agricultural runoff that polluted Pine Creek. This wetland would be a demonstration and research model for constructed wetland technology and an environmental education community center.

Challenges and Successes

The wetland was completed and has functioned to mitigate pollutants in the adjacent stream. The wetland's effectiveness was tested when a fertilizer line broke upstream, dumping liquefied manure directly into the stream. The water was diverted into the wetland and the pollutants were removed before the water left the wetland cells. The educational displays and observation platform has made the wetland a destination for local school field trips.

Conclusions, Recommendations, and Advice for Students

Look for possibilities to increase your impact. This project was originally designed as a demonstration of the constructed wetland technology. After it was completed, it was adapted to become an educational center for environmental education, increasing its community impact.

9.15 LIGHT MANUFACTURING ENVIRONMENT FOR ADULTS WITH DISABILITIES

Course Description

Engineering Projects in Community Service (EPICS) at Purdue University is a multidisciplinary and vertically integrated (freshmen through seniors) engineering service-learning program. In 2004, it had 30 teams with about 300 students per semester working with local community partners. A typical EPICS team has 12 to 20 students. EPICS programs exist on several campuses across the country http://epicsnational.ecn.purdue.edu.

Community Partners

Wabash Center-Greenbush Industries (WCGI) is a non-profit organization that aims to improve the lives of individuals with disabilities. The organization assists these individuals through vocational rehabilitation in an integrated environment. Greenbush Industries offers commercial subcontracting services to local businesses and industries. The industries contact Greenbush for functions such as the kitting of parts for washing machines, the packaging of medical tubing, or the rebuilding of food processing filters. These operations provide revenue to individuals who may not otherwise be employable in mainstream industry as well as subsidizing other services that the Wabash Center provides such as adult daycare services and assisted living services.

Student Profile

Freshman through seniors participate from 20 departments across Purdue University's campus. This team is comprised mainly of mechanical, electrical, and industrial engineering students.

Successes and Challenges

The WCGI EPICS team has worked with Greenbush Industries since 1998 to assist the employees perform their jobs. Many of the employees have disabilities such as cerebral palsy, brain trauma, and amputated limbs. Therefore, they may have problems performing their tasks at work. The EPICS team works with these individuals to make fixtures and machines to aid these people in their tasks. The team looks at the process to suggest more efficient manufacturing floor layouts. The team's students face the challenge of defining the project partner's problem, making observations about the working conditions and the worker's abilities, doing preliminary designs, obtaining design approval from the project partner, fabricating the designs, and field testing the design.

The team has delivered several projects. Sample projects include the following:

- A fixture that aided in the placement of a clip over airline tubing. The employee who performed this job had problems assembling the clip because

Figure 9.15 Assembled Corn Syrup Filter

his hand shook. The fixture made assembly of the clip easier by guiding the tubing into the clip.

- A device for coiling electrical cable. The previous coiler reel was flimsy and collapsed prematurely. The team's design held more weight and collapsed when a button was pushed. The team will deliver a third project, which is a mechanical device for tube winding. This motorized device winds pharmaceutical tubing automatically. Two additional projects in the design phase are a fixture to assist in the placement of rubber grommets in a heat exchanger, a clamping system, and process evaluation for rebuilding large food processing filters.
- The Individual Paper Dispenser (IPD) enables workers at WCGI to process mail and newspaper inserts for local companies with greater ease and efficiency. Employees experienced difficulty removing individual papers from a large stack. We have designed a device that allows for easy removal of one sheet every time.
- The Break Time Indicator (BTI) is a visual device that signals to the WCGI employees their respective break times. The BTI will consist of two units with different colored lights. The lights will be controlled by timers, which are hard wired into one device and communicate wirelessly with the other. The finished project resembles traffic lights, but the lights will be multidirectional.
- The Filter Assembly Device (FAD) project team has developed a device to ease the assembly of large WCGI corn syrup filters. The assembly process requires that the 40-pound filters be flipped, and the awkwardness of this manual operation means that few employees can work on the project. The

FAD project team has developed a device similar in appearance to a large sawhorse, which can secure the filter on a rotating crossbeam and lock in convenient assembly positions. This device will allow more employees to work on this project.

Community Needs Addressed Through Project

Greenbush Industries provides a work environment for adults with disabilities who may not be able to hold a similar private sector job. The student team works with the staff of Greenbush Industries to increase their work environment's safety and productivity.

9.16 HABITAT FOR HUMANITY IN LAFAYETTE

Course Description

Engineering Projects in Community Service (EPICS) at Purdue University is a multidisciplinary and vertically integrated (freshmen through seniors) engineering service-learning program. In 2004, it had 30 teams with about 300 students per semester working with local community partners. A typical EPICS team has 12 to 20 students. EPICS programs exist on several campuses across the country http://epicsnational.ecn.purdue.edu.

Project Description

The student team designed a web-based system to integrate house blueprints, elevations, and three-dimensional views of homes with information on projected utility costs for new homeowners. This system replaced a paper system with several large notebooks. The system allowed families selecting homes to use the computers at the Habitat office to examine design options, visualize the home, and estimate the home's operating cost. The web site can be accessed through the Habitat for Humanity team's web page at http://epics.ecn.purdue.edu/hfh.

The projected utility costs were found using an analysis software package called *Energy 10.* This analysis allowed the homes to be compared for energy consumption and the homes' projected utility costs. The team extended the project's analysis portion to perform parametric studies on design alternatives and their energy consumption impact.

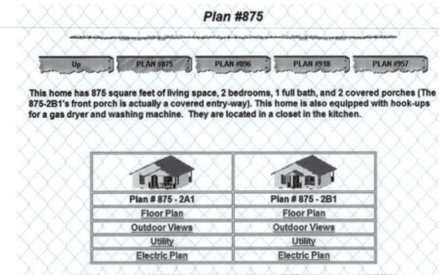

Figure 9.16 Screen Shot of the Home Selection Guide

Community Partners

Habitat for Humanity of Lafayette, Indiana. Habitat for Humanity International is a Christian organization dedicated to eliminating substandard housing in the world.

Student Profile

Freshman through seniors participate from 20 departments across Purdue University's campus. These projects involved students from electrical, computer, mechanical, and industrial engineering.

Community Needs Addressed Through Project

Habitat for Humanity partners with low income families to provide affordable, decent housing. The team worked to improve the home selection process and provide information on reducing energy consumption.

Challenges and Successes

The home selection guide replaced the paper process and has spawned other projects, including some for the national headquarters. The parametric studies on building alternatives gave the local affiliate data to make construction and design changes to their homes to reduce the homes' operating costs.

9.17 NATIONAL DATA COLLECTION SYSTEM FOR HABITAT FOR HUMANITY

Course Description

Engineering Projects in Community Service (EPICS) is a multidisciplinary and vertically integrated (freshmen through seniors) engineering service-learning program. EPICS programs at Purdue University and Notre Dame collaborated on this project. EPICS programs exist on several campuses across the country http://epicsnational.ecn.purdue.edu.

Project Description

For Habitat for Humanity International to document the impact it is having, it needs data from the families they have served. The infrastructure does not exist to collect and track such data. Students from Purdue and Notre Dame have designed a database system for Habitat for Humanity International that will allow local affiliates to enter data received from their families into a national database. The information on the families can be compiled and compared nationally or across regions. The system is designed to protect family privacy through a coding scheme. Only the local affiliates will know the families' identities.

The teams have designed several separate system components:

- A survey generator creates, manages, and edits surveys using an easy interface. The survey questions are being developed by a sociology professor at Ohio State University.
- Homeowner ID lets local affiliates request a set of homeowner identification numbers to track the families in the database. Data will be entered using the ID numbers so the families' identity is not in the database. Only the local affiliates will have the key to the family identity.
- Database stores the survey results by homeowner identification and allows longitudinal tracking through successive surveys.
- Statistical Analysis tools have been developed so the Habitat staff can view statistics on a local, regional, and national basis. Local affiliates will have access to statistics on their own families and how they compare with national statistics.

Community Partners

Habitat for Humanity International is a Christian organization dedicated to eliminating substandard housing in the world. The partners for this project are the national staff members for Habitat for Humanity International in Americus, Georgia.

Student Profile

Computer engineering and computer science students collaborated on the project implementation.

Community Needs Addressed Through Project

Habitat for Humanity partners with low income families to provide affordable, decent housing. For Habitat to assess their impact, it needs data from the families it serves. Funding opportunities, especially federal funding, are increasingly being based on their ability to document their impact. This data collection system will allow them to do that.

Challenges and Successes

The teams have produced and delivered a Beta version of the software to the staff of Habitat for Humanity International and have incorporated the feedback from the local and national users into the final production version. One challenge has been the distances between the partners at the national headquarters and the students at their respective universities. The project's impact will be much wider than the local community, but the logistics make it more difficult.

A parallel team is working with HFHI to develop training materials for volunteers. This second team involves a collaboration between the Purdue team and one from University of Wisconsin, Madison.

Advice for Students

When collaborating with students from other campuses, face-to-face meetings are beneficial. Schedule a meeting early in the semester to ensure everyone is on the same page and has the same expectations; this makes a big difference for the project. Communication can be a challenge, so identify the primary contacts at each campus.

9.18 DYNAMICS OF A PLAYGROUND

Course Description

Sophomore level, required kinematics course in mechanical engineering.

Project Description

Students were assigned in teams to assess local playgrounds for safety. They performed analyses to estimate forces on the children from the playground equipment. Their analyses included an impact analysis of the children from the rides and falls from equipment. They mapped out the playgrounds and observed how children played on the equipment to identify safety concerns. The project was 15% of the course grade, and the deliverables included a two-part report and a letter to the community on their findings.

Community Partners

Local neighborhood associations and parks boards.

Student Profile

Sophomores in mechanical engineering at the University of Massachusetts.

Community Needs Addressed Through Project

Access of safe playgrounds for local children. Many playgrounds, designed many years ago, contain equipment that can injure children and do not conform to modern safety standards.

Challenges and Successes

The results of the analyses and letters to the community have resulted in modifications to several playgrounds. Equipment has been changed and, in some cases, removed based on the students' findings.

Conclusions, Recommendations, and Advice for Students

Integrating the subject matter objectives and the service objectives should not compromise course objectives. This challenge is a creative opportunity for the instructors, the students, and the community.

9.19 PARTNERSHIPS IN REMOTE VILLAGES OF PERU

Course Description

Senior Capstone Design course in mechanical engineering.

Project Description

Professor John Duffy at—the University of Massachusetts—Lowell has established relationships with people in the mountain communities of Peru and takes teams of students twice a year to deliver the projects completed during the semester.

Projects have included the following:

- Drinking Water Purification—This project provided safe drinking water for the Peruvian village of Quian using ultraviolet radiation and solar energy for purification. The system was designed to supply a minimum of two gallons (~8 liters) per person per day of safe water based on WHO Water Guidelines.
- Portable Standalone Vaccine Refrigerator—A refrigerator was designed using solar power to refrigerate vaccines. This refrigerator is a stand-alone unit that could be carried by one person. A back-up system provided four days of refrigeration and was integrated into the design using a phase change material.

Figure 9.17 Student takes water samples from a stream in Peru

- Hydroelectric mini-turbines—The large elevation changes in mountainous terrain were used to drive a small turbine. Students designed the turbine and generator systems along with the system to channel water to the turbine inlet. The system provides power for the needs of the local village's medical clinic.

Community Partners

Villages in rural communities in Peru.

Student Profile

Seniors in mechanical engineering.

Community Needs Addressed Through Project

Like many parts of the developing world, rural Peruvian villages lack many modern technological conveniences and benefits. The student teams have dealt with safe and reliable supplies of drinking water, power to operate systems for communication, and education or refrigeration for food and medicine.

Challenges and Successes

The projects have been successful with several systems delivered and installed that are being used. For a summary of the projects completed, go to http://energy.caeds.eng.uml.edu.

Challenges of international projects include transportation and costs for students to install the projects. The trips are usually taken after the semester is over during summer and winter breaks. Students who participate in the installation leave profoundly affected by their first-hand experience with the local communities and the realization of their impact. The locations' remoteness has put additional pressure on the students to get it right the first time and has created challenges on the sites if everything does not work as planned.

Conclusions, Recommendations, and Advice for Students

The developing world has basic needs, such as safe water, education and medicine. These needs can be partially addressed with technological solutions. Students can play a key role in the implementation of these solutions as a part of their undergraduate or graduate educational experience. When implementing solutions, understanding the local culture and taking advantage of local expertise and materials are a key to success.

9.20 LOW COST COMMUNICATION SATELLITES

Taylor University

Project Description

A small, affordable satellite-based communications system was designed to provide an e-mail communication system for people in remote parts of the developing world. The satellite has been designed along with all supporting systems including solar arrays and batteries for power, as well as a monitoring, operation and management system for the satellite after launch. Multiple microcontrollers govern the operation of the satellite and the communication with ground stations. E-mail communications are sent using a central server at Taylor University, which serves as a gateway to the Internet. E-mails are sent to and collected from the satellite in batches as it passes over Taylor and the locations in the developing world.

Community Partners

The initial partners were missionary organizations in the developing world. The systems' broader impact could include communities in the developing world.

Student Profile

Physics undergraduate students at Taylor University.

Community Needs Addressed Through Project

Access to communication technology using the Internet and the many benefits it affords is largely restricted to the developed countries. In the developing world, access to the Internet and communication technology is concentrated in urban areas and reserved for the wealthy. Missionaries and aid workers in the more remote areas of the developing world are restricted in their ability to communicate with their support organizations and resource personnel while they are stationed in these areas.

Challenges and Successes

The work has demonstrated that low cost systems for e-mail communication are possible. Future work will deploy the systems and look for ways to disseminate the technology to those who can benefit most.

9.21 HIGH SCHOOL EXAMPLE

Sara Nation is a graduate from the EPICS program at Purdue and one of the co-founders of the first High School EPICS team. She writes about her experience and motivation for starting the program in high school:

> *When deciding which route I was going to take for my senior design course at Purdue University, I spoke to many students that had done the traditional courses. Many were disappointed in their experience of hours in the lab for a project that, if they were lucky, would sit on their shelves at home and collect dust. I found a group of students in Engineering Projects in Community Service (EPICS) that were able to do their project in conjunction with a community partner that would use the product. This appealed to me in that I would be doing real engineering but mostly because I had been increasingly frustrated that I hadn't fit community service into my routine. This seemed like a perfect fit.*
>
> *When choosing a team, I decided to join one that was just forming in order to see the start-up process and get the whole experience. That team was partnered with the school of education at Purdue and tasked to build a mobile computer laboratory. The experience of building a team, designing a product, and working through the issues showed me the intricacies that go into the planning of real life systems. I have built on this experience in my work experience.*
>
> *Upon graduation, I was in a position of joining a team that was just getting started. The project I joined was working on proposals for funding a full-blown project. My service-learning experiences helped me understand what needed to happen and gave me the confidence to help with the planning. Two years out of school, I was named task leader for this project.*
>
> *Recently, a fellow EPICS alumna approached me with the idea of starting a high school EPICS team. I have always felt strongly about exposing K–12 students to the world of engineering and what better way to do this than through a community-based project? We approached local teachers who agreed to collaborate in the creation of the high school program. Its hands-on approach and community context can appeal to those students who might not have considered engineering. In its third semester, the high school EPICS program has designed a product, developed a prototype, and has begun discussions for a patent.*

BEDFORD NORTH LAWRENCE HIGH SCHOOL EPICS PROJECT SUMMARY

Course Description

The intent of this program is to provide academic credit for the high school participants. Currently, it is an extracurricular activity. Discussions are in process of how the service-learning course would fit into the curriculum. As the program continues to grow and show success, more interest is being generated.

Project Description

The project is to design and develop a device to remind people with neurological disorders (who do not have the automatic swallow reflex) to remember to swallow.

Community Partners

The special education branch of North Lawrence Community Schools

Student Profile

The program is open to all high school grade levels of students attending Bedford North Lawrence High School. Students from the adjoining vocational school are also invited and have proven to be invaluable in terms of practical knowledge. The program has drawn a majority of seniors to date with a few juniors each semester. The future goal is to involve more students who are at earlier stages in their high school careers.

Community Needs Addressed Through Project

At least 20 people in the immediate community would benefit from this project. In particular, an elementary school student with cerebral palsy would have the opportunity to be more fully integrated into a normal classroom.

Challenges and Successes

Even though this engineering project involves students that have had no previous engineering experience, a working prototype was finished in the first two semesters of this project's existence. This success is due to the students from the electronics courses at the local vocational school. The students' different backgrounds have reinforced the need for teamwork and that the whole is greater than the sum of the parts. These students have been driven by the thought of helping other students and have benefited by meeting one of the potential users of this project. After meeting the student, work dramatically increased.

Conclusions, Recommendations, and Advice for Students

This and similar projects have the potential to be highly effective high school courses that would instill a larger worldview to younger students. The two main goals are to increase community awareness and to provide exposure to engineering as a career prior to the collegiate experience. Each project implementation will be different depending on the people involved, geographical location, etc.

9.22 SERVICE-LEARNING STUDENT PROFILE: STUART FEILDEN

Student Description

I am a Biological Engineering senior at Louisiana State University (LSU). My hobbies include weightlifting, rugby, and cooking. I am a student worker for Dr. Marybeth Lima and also cook at Ruffino's Italian Restaurant. I am a native of Louisiana and was born in the great city of New Orleans. During my senior year, I plan to interview with many companies in order to secure an engineering position after graduation.

Course Description

As a sophomore, I was enrolled in BE 1252 (Biological Engineering) in Spring 2002. The catalog description follows: "Effect of variability and constraints of biological systems on engineering problem solving and design; engineering units; engineering report writing; oral report presentation; laboratory demonstration of biological engineering analysis."

Community Need and Goal Accomplishment

The community need was to create a playground for a local public school that was safe and accessible, promoted physical, mental, and social growth of its children,

Figure 9.18 Stuart Feilden

and provided a comfortable environment for community members to gather. We worked on a public school playground in an effort to provide equal opportunities to access play equipment for these students as compared to those attending private schools. Most local public school playgrounds do not have equipment that meets current regulations.

We began by learning CPSC and ADA accessibility standards. The CPSC (Consumer Product Safety Commission) compiled the *Handbook for Public Playground Safety*, which became our class doctrine. Not only does it provide detailed information on dimensions and measurements, it provides insight on designing the equipment to develop the "whole child." This meant not only challenging the children physically, but encouraging their social and metal growth by providing open areas, relaxing areas, and other mental stimuli. Dr. Lima continuously encouraged our creativity as engineers and challenged us to think "outside of the box." She refers to her students as "social change agents."

Funding was provided by local grants, one of which was written by another Service-Learning class at LSU. The parts were ordered at the beginning of the summer, and construction for the new playground began in July 2002. Student volunteers (volunteers at this point in time, because the class had concluded) came to help with preparation of the land and the construction and assembly of the playground equipment. The entire job was spear-headed and supervised by a local playground construction company, Agrestics.

After the land was cleared, the concrete poured, the equipment built and the fences refinished, a special team arrived to pour the rubber pieces that formed protective safety surfacing. After a couple days of curing, the playground was completed. A ceremony was held and the playground was blessed by a rabbi, while a news crew recorded the event. The smiles of the young children enjoying their new playground capped it all off.

Successes and Challenges

One of the most demanding challenges of the project was to integrate various student designs into a single design, and to have the children and teachers of the school agree upon and approve the final proposal. This was accomplished through communication with the teachers and students, including PowerPoint presentations of the revised proposals. Also, changes under the advice and expert leadership of the local playground company ensured that the playground design met all regulations. Other minor challenges included the timely arrival of the equipment, weather conditions delaying construction (we worked through a tropical storm), final exams affecting student volunteer hours (for summer classes), and the heat of a Louisiana summer.

Advice

Service-Learning provides a platform for students to take initiative and develop their leadership ability. Under leadership, I include the leadership of others and leadership of oneself. Students may be interested in one class more than another, depending on their interests and abilities. Service-Learning allows an opportunity to more deeply understand or experience (with "hands-on" experience) an educational discipline that is talked about in the classroom environment. Therefore, Service-Learning ultimately gives the student another avenue to approach classroom education, which is reinforced with personal responsibility, leadership, pride, and reflection. My advice to you, the student, is to give yourself fully to a service-learning project and to take responsibility for the outcome. You will find that the journey may inspire your compassion, reinforce your classroom engagement/participation, and further your personal growth through reflection on the project.

Reflection

In terms of my own reflections with regard to working on service-learning projects, here are the highlights:

Doing service-learning was personally rewarding because I enjoy doing hands-on projects, especially building playgrounds. It was great to design the playground on paper and then to construct it because you wind up with something physical that you actually can see and touch.

I grew up with the idea of "every man for himself," and "every community for itself." Service-learning really changed my perspective on this concept; now I think about civic responsibility, and working together to make the world a better place. We all have a responsibility to our local and national communities, and it's really about teamwork. I believe that engineering can aid in social justice: Through your design and effort, everybody can get the same opportunity and access to goods and services, and equal treatment and respect. The main thing I've gotten from service-learning is the realization that I am a member of a community and must respect and serve that community and the communities around me.

I also believe that service-learning forces you to develop skills and behaviors that build character, and reinforce a moral value system. Service-learning did that for me by challenging me to take personal responsibility for a project. Successfully working with the community to complete playground projects built a sense of pride in me; I believe that I grew as an individual by developing respect for the environment and respect for other people.

Post-script: Stuart graduated with a B.S. in Biological Engineering from LSU in May 2004. He is now a sales engineer with Johnson Controls in Houston, TX.

REFERENCES

Bullard, Lisa G., Clayton, Patti H and Peretti, Steven W. "Service-Learning in CHE Senior Design", *Proceedings of the 2004 American Society for Engineering Education Annual Conference, Salt Lake City, Utah, June 2004.*

Coyle, E.J., Foretek, R., Gray, J.L., Jamieson, L.H., Oakes, W.C., Watia, J., & Wukasch, R. (2000). EPICS: Experiencing engineering design through community service projects. The 2000 Annual Conference of the ASEE, Charlotte, NC.

Coyle, E.J., Jamieson, L.H., & Sommers, L.S. (1997, Fall). EPICS: A model for integrating service learning into the engineering curriculum. *Michigan Journal of Community Service Learning, 4,* 81–89.

Duffy, J., Tsang, E., & Lord, S. (2000). Service-learning in engineering: What, why, and how? *Proceedings of the 2000 Annual Conference of the ASEE.*

Guedelhoefer, L., Jones, J.D., Davies, P., Coyle, E.J., & Jamieson, L.H. (2000). Engineering education, beyond the books. The 2000 Annual Conference of the ASEE, Charlotte, NC.

Holmes, W.C., Voss, H.D., et al, "TU Sat 1: An Novel Communications and Scientific Satellite", *16th AnnualAIAA/USU Conference on Small Satellites,* August 2002.

Jamieson, L.H., Coyle, E.J., Harper, M.P., Delp, E.J., & Davies, P. (1998). Integrating engineering design, signal processing, and community service in the EPICS program. *Proceedings of the 1998 IEEE International Conference on Acoustics, Speech, and Signal Processing,* 1897–1900.

Jamieson, L.H., Oakes, W.C. & Coyle, E.J. (2002). EPICS: Serving the community through engineering design projects. In Kenny, M.E., Simon, L.A.K., Brabeck, K., & Lerner, R.M. (Eds.), *Learning to serve: Promoting civil society through service-learning* (pp. 277–295). Norwell, MA: Kluwer Academic Publishers.

Lima, Marybeth, (1998) "Principles of living systems and engineering design for freshmen level students in biological engineering: design of a tiger habitat", *Proceedings of the 1998 ASEE Annual Conference.*

Linos, Panagiotis K, Stephanie Herman and Julie Lally, "A Service-Learning Program For Computer Science And Software Engineering", *Proceedings of the 8th Annual Conference on Innovation and Technology in Computer Science Education,* Thessaloniki, Greece, June 2003.

Lord, Susan M., "Service-Learning in Introduction to Engineering at the University of San Diego: First Lessons", *Proceedings of 29th ASEE/IEEE Frontiers in Education Conference,* San Juan, Puerto Rico, November 1999.

Michaud, F., Clavet, A., Lachiver, G., & Lucas, M. (2000). Designing toy robots to help autistic children—an open design project for electrical and computer engineering education. *Proceedings of the 2000 Annual Conference of the ASEE.*

Oakes, W.C., Krull, A., Coyle, E.J., Jamieson, L.J., & Kong, M. (2000, October). EPICS: Interdisciplinary service-learning using engineering design projects. 2000 Frontiers in Education Conference.

Oakes, W.C., Duffy, J., Jacobius, T., Linos, P., Lord, S., Schultz, W.W., & Smith, A. (2002, November). Service-learning in engineering. *Proceedings of the 2002 Frontiers in Education Conference.*

Simon, L.A.K., Kenny, M., Brabeck, K., & Lerner, R.M. (Eds.) (2002). *Learning to serve: Promoting civil society through service-learning.* Norwell, MA: Kluwer Academic Publishers.

Stott, N.W., Schultz, W.W., Brei, D., Winton Hoffman, D.M., & Markus, G. (2000). ProCEED: A program for civic engagement in engineering design. *Proceedings of the 2000 Annual Conference of the ASEE.*

Tsang, E. (Ed.). (2000). *Projects that matter: Concepts and models for service-learning in engineering.* Washington DC: AAHE.

Zlotkowski, E. (Ed.). (2002). *Service-learning and the first-year experience.* Columbia, SC: National Resource Center for the First-Year Experience & Students in Transition, University of South Carolina.

EXERCISES

1. Find a profile that is related to your own project. Prepare a short oral presentation on the project for your classmates.

2. Find a past or current service-learning project from another service-learning program (see the resources chapter) and create a profile for this project to share with your classmates.

3. Select two projects, one done by first year students and one by seniors. Write a one to two page essay that compares and contrasts the two projects.

4. Select one of the profiled projects and write a one page essay on how that project would have enhanced the learning objectives of the course it was done through.

5. Select one of the profiled projects and write a one page essay on what aspects of engineering that were involved in the project.

6. Select one of the profiled projects and prepare an oral presentation on how that project enhanced the learning objectives of the course it was done through.

7. Select one of the profiled projects and write an oral presentation on what aspects of engineering that were involved in the project.

8. Select one of the profiles and write a two to three page proposal to a company asking them to support the project. Outline why they would want to sponsor the project, including direct and indirect benefits for themselves, and ways they could partner on the project.

9. Select one of the profiles and write a two to three page proposal to a local foundation or organization asking them to support the project. Outline why they would want to sponsor the project, including direct and indirect benefits for themselves, and ways they could partner on the project.

10. Create a profile for your own project from what you know at the beginning of the project.

11. Assume that you have finished your project, write a profile for your completed project. Project what your deliverables will be and include a discussion about the challenges and success of your project as well as the experience you would have had.

12. After you have completed the project, create a profile and post the profile on a web page.

Chapter 10

Helpful References for Service-Learning in Engineering

'Tis well to borrow from the good and the great.   —J.G. Saxe

10.1 INTRODUCTION

In a traditional class, the instructor plans the activities and assignments for the entire semester or quarter before the class begins. He or she identifies the resources needed for the class with text or reference books plus any supplemental materials such as lecture notes. Students will solve answers to all prepared and available course problems. Students expect the instructor to answer any questions related to the course content.

Service-learning courses do not always work this way. The instructor may not have all the answers and resources needed to accomplish a community project. Service-learning projects are driven by real community needs and people. Therefore, anticipating all the information and resources your class will need to respond to these needs is difficult. A team needs to identify potential resources outside of class that can help get over the hurdles during the service portion of the experience.

Your instructor may play a different role in the service-learning experience from what you may be used to. Each instructor is not necessarily the expert and keeper of all knowledge. In a more traditional class, the instructor will have all the answers. If the instructor does not know the answer, it is not important and he or she will not put it on a test (so we do not need to know it either. Right?). Service-learning can differ because we are dealing with subject matter in one area of expertise, and we are addressing real community issues needing a wide range of experience and knowledge.

Your instructor usually does not have all the experience and knowledge you need. In a typical situation, you will need more expertise or resources from people outside of the class. In this case, your instructor will serve as an advisor or coach to guide your experience, set the project up, and help you through the process. The instructor will not, however, have every answer to every question. The instructor has elected to use service-learning to help you and your classmates learn and is a coach is by design.

This service-learning experience looks like the real world. In the public or private sector, your manager or supervisor will not have all the answers to your questions, and you will need to consult outside experts. Many companies have a chief engineer's office staffed with technical experts to help the other engineers with specific issues. They do not rely on the managers to answer all questions. As an engineer, you might have to talk to marketing, finance, or sales people for questions involving their areas of expertise. Finding outside help for your work is the norm and is expected. Resourcefulness, the ability to find the information, materials, and resources to solve a problem, will help you develop as an engineer and will serve you well as you enter the profession. Service-learning students need to be resourceful to meet the community's needs.

This chapter provides ideas of where you can look for these resources as you accomplish your tasks. These resources will vary based on school, community, and project, but they will make you think of how to proceed to answer your questions. Your instructor can provide additional ideas for whom to talk to and how to answer your questions. Many people can help and, because of the compelling work you are doing, are usually willing to do so.

10.2 CAMPUS RESOURCES

Your campus has many resources that can meet your community needs. Campus resources can be the easiest available resources and fastest to find.

Faculty

When you and/or your team needs information from a content specialist, find other faculty at your school. Almost every department will have a list of faculty by research area. If there is not an explicit list, you will find links to personal web pages which will have faculty areas of interest and expertise. In research institutions, each department will publish a research annual report listing the each faculty member's activity. Another way to identify faculty is to identify who teaches the topics that interest you. For example, if you are designing an interactive display to demonstrate an historic U.S. event and do not have anyone from history on your team; look for someone who teaches U.S. history. In engineering, faculty who teach design classes are excellent resources.

Graduate Students

If your institution has a graduate program, graduate students can be another great resource for content specialists. When contacting faculty, you could ask for graduate students working for them who are knowledgeable in your topics. You or your classmates may know graduate students that work as teaching assistants. Sometimes graduate students are easier to get in touch with and may have more time than faculty members.

Technical Staff Members

All of the technical expertise on campus is not with the faculty. The support staff and organizations on campus also have the expertise to help you. These organi-

zations will vary from school to school. Here are some of the examples of on-
campus support:

- For manufacturing-related or construction-related topics, the staff members
  who work in the machine shops on campus possess a wealth of knowledge.
  Most institutions have facilities that support the university's activities and
  have machinists and technicians in these facilities. They will have years of
  experience and can help students overcome their problems.
- For information technology, most institutions have computer or information technology support organizations. These people have knowledge and
  practical experience to help students implement these technologies in the
  community.
- For facilities management, your campus probably has a group that works
  with facilities. They manage new construction as well as maintenance and
  remodeling of existing structures. They will be familiar with building practices
  and codes as well as local suppliers.
- For purchasing, most schools have organizations that purchase items for
  the school. They will be familiar with local vendors and can provide products
  and services you might need.

Whenever dealing with staff members on campus, you and your classmates
should be sensitive that they will be helping you as a favor and possibly on their
own time. Go out of your way to be respectful and gracious. Sending them a thank
you note for their help will go a long way to keeping good relations. If you need
significant amounts of their time, talk to your instructor to see if it can be arranged
with their supervisor.

Student Organizations

Most majors have honorary societies and student chapters of professional societies. These organizations will have student leaders who are juniors, seniors, or
graduate students who may provide assistance in their area of expertise. Many of
the organizations, especially the honoraries, have service requirements. Tau Beta
Pi, the engineering-wide honorary, requires all initiates to fulfill a service obligation. Working with these organizations, provides resources for you while enabling
the organization to meet its goals.

Service-Learning/Community-Service/Volunteer Office

Many campuses have a center for service-learning or community service. Almost
all have at least a volunteer office that coordinates student volunteers. These offices may have contacts and ideas to help your team and have other contacts who
might help you locally.

Extension Offices

If you are at one of the 106 land grant institutions in the United States, your school
has a statewide network of extension offices. These offices are designed to link

the state with resources from the university. Every state has such a network and the network can be a resource whether or not you are at the land grant university. Typically, an office is in each county. When the offices began in the 1800s, they were designed to assist farmers. Their mission, however, has evolved as our society has become more urban, and they are much broader in their areas of expertise. Extension offices are a distributed network of professionals with experience in meeting needs in your state's communities. They can be a great resource for you and your classmates and can help you find additional resources.

The Library

> The library is the temple of learning, and learning has liberated more people than all the wars in history.   —Carl Rowan

Librarians can be your best friends when it comes to finding the resources that you need in your engineering endeavors. Reference librarians in particular are information experts and can provide you with multiple strategies for efficiently locating information. The following section is intended to provide basic library skills in terms of searching for technical information and resources. We strongly suggest consulting the reference librarian at your school's main library for further assistance.

There are two main ways to search for information at the library: in person and on the computer. A combination of these methods is the best way to go; although taking a trip to the library tends to be less fun and efficient than a computer search, it will probably be necessary for you to actually get your hands on the references that you need! However, your "hands-on" library trip will be much more efficient if you complete some computer work first!

The following approach should prove useful during your search for information

- Identify your topic
- Generate search terms and keywords on this topic
- Search computer databases using key words or key phrases
- Record the full citations that you need from this computer search
- Proceed to the library to get the citations (if necessary; sometimes you can obtain the full citation on the computer, though you may have to pay for it. The library is free.)

The following paragraphs contain more detailed information on this approach.

Identify your topic. It may sound trivial, but identifying and fully describing the topic of your information search is an important step to locating desired information efficiently. You can use the encyclopedia to get general, background information on your topic. If you run across terms that you don't understand, look up their meanings in the dictionary, and add this information to your topic description. You can also identify different aspects of your topic for search which will help to identify more specific information on your topic. For example, what are the ethical, technical, financial or social aspects of your information topic?

Generate search terms and key words on this topic. Sometimes finding the information you need is like finding a needle in a haystack! When you are searching for information, you need to locate the correct "scale" of information. If your search is too broad, you will get millions of citations, references, books, etc. and will never have enough time to work through everything. If your search is too narrow, you will not have any information to analyze, or very little. The trick is to identify an intermediate scale which is general enough to contain all the information you need, but is specific enough to eliminate the things you don't need. You must generate search terms, key words, and key phrases that are representative of this intermediate scale.

To do this, look at the description you prepared of your topic from step 1. What words or phrases best represent your topic? Write these key words and phrases down on a page of paper. Then use a thesaurus to generate keyword synonyms (words that mean the same thing). Take all your key words and phrases and organize them into similar areas or groupings. You will use this organized information to search computer databases.

Too broad: environmental engineering
More specific: methods for cleaning oil spills

Search computer databases using the key words and phrases you generated. Library information is organized into subject areas. The major subject areas include:

- Humanities
- Social sciences
- Sciences
- Applied sciences

Your on-line university library may have a separate subject area for engineering. If it does not, search under applied sciences. See the information in the next box for places to search for engineering information. When you have located the information that you would like to collect, *write down the full citation for this information so that you can easily locate it at the library.*

Proceed to the library with your the citations. Your computer search will most likely provide full reference information that you will collect in its entirety at the library. Much of this information will be in **the stacks**, which is the area in the library in which books and periodicals are stored in an organized format. Use information provided at your school library to locate your desired resources in the stacks. Material in library stacks can be checked out from the library for your use, usually for two to three weeks. The information that you desire may also be contained in the **reference section** of the library, which means that you have access to the information, but you cannot remove it from the library.

Sometimes the library will not possess the resources that you need; libraries have limited budgets, and may not carry certain journals or books because of these limitations. There are several things that you can do if this is the case.

"Librarians are a tribe."

—Rita Mae Brown

Places of Importance When Searching for Information on Engineering

National technical information service (http://www.ntis.gov): comprehensive source of information for the US Government in terms of engineering, technology, scientific and business knowledge generated by or for the government.

Science citation index (also known as the web of knowledge): comprehensive listing of all publications in scientific journals (includes engineering). You can use this knowledge to locate specific publications and can find related publications. The web of knowledge will be available at your university library.

US Patent and Trademark Office (http://www.uspto.gov): Patents are documents that grant an inventor(s) the sole rights to their invention. Trademarks can be a word, phrase, design, symbol, or slogan that differentiates individual products from their competitors. Patents and some trademarks are registered with the US Government. A patent search can be important in determining the most cutting edge information being used in an area of design, or can illustrate the evolution of the design of a device.

Thomas register (http://www.thomasregister.com): a complete resource for locating engineering companies and products manufactured in North America. You can find an engineering company's catalogs and can order parts and information through the register.

Compendex (also known as the Engineering Index or the Engineering Information Village 2), http://www.engineeringvillage2.org). A complete bibliographic database for engineering research and publication.

Did You Know?

- The amount of technical knowledge published worldwide is doubling every 10 to 15 years
- Approximately one-third of all technical knowledge published is communicated in a language other than English?
- The US Government funds or executes approximately 35% of all the research and development in the United States. Thus, it can be an important place to search for information!

Use interlibrary loan. This free service is available at your university library. See the reference librarian and ask for an interlibrary loan request form. On this form provide the full citation of the information that you need and your contact information. The library will locate partnership libraries that have the materials you need through the interlibrary loan system. Your library will contact you when they receive a hard copy of your reference, or will mail it to you directly. Interlibrary loan takes approximately four to eight weeks.

Use electronic means for securing your reference. Sometimes, your reference may be fully available on-line. Many times, only part of the reference is given, and you need to pay a fee to view and print out the entire document. This fee may be nominal (many journal articles are available for under $5) and within your budget. It may also be within your time frame (most of us don't want to wait).

Try another library. Your city, county, and state library/archives may have the information that you need. Nearby university libraries may also have the information you need.

10.3 OFF-CAMPUS RESOURCES

Professional Societies

Professional societies, such as the National Society of Professional Engineers, have professional members in addition to the student members we discussed on campus. They have local and state organizations and your team may want to contact the local organization to request expertise or to ask if their organization has someone who could help you. Most of the organizations have e-mail lists they can use to forward your request to their members, or they may ask you to come to one of their meetings to make your request.

Every major has a professional society in engineering. In engineering, one of the umbrella organizations is the American Association of Engineering Societies (www.aaes.org). Its web site has links for most of the professional organizations in engineering. A listing of engineering-related professional societies is at the end of this chapter for reference. For professional societies in other disciplines, look to the academic departments at your own school. Their web sites often have links to the professional societies in their field. If they do not, contact the department which can give you the information. Most professors will belong to at least one professional organization in their field.

Community Partners

Do not overlook the community partners as a resource to your questions. It can be a big mistake to assume what they know and do not know. First-year students at one university were surprised to find out that the director of their community partner, a local homeless shelter, was an electrical engineering graduate from their school. He had the experience that they needed, but they had overlooked him. Many community members will have good experiences that you can use, even if they do not have an official degree in an area.

If your community partner contacts do not have the background or expertise, they probably have a Board of Directors or an advisory board. Many times, these members come from a wide cross-section of the community and will have the skills to complete the project. An extra benefit is that they are interested and knowledgeable about your issues. Even if they do not have the expertise, they may have contacts in the community or within their own organizations who do.

Community Volunteer Bureau

Your community probably has a volunteer bureau to match volunteers with local needs. It will have access to many people in the community with the expertise you need. It will have suggestions of where to look for the resources you need.

Service Organizations

A number of organizations consist of community members who want to help others through service. These organizations have a focus on service and consist of professionals from a wide range of ages, experiences, and areas of expertise. These groups include the following:

- Rotary (http://www.rotary.org/)
- Lions (http://www.lionsclubs.org/)
- Kiwanis (http://www.kiwanis.org
- Optimists (http://www.optimists.org/)

These kind of groups are international organizations with a local chapter or club in many communities. They may have a club or chapter in your community that can help you and your classmates. If they can't help, they can provide a great network to help find the right people to talk to. The members of these organizations are usually well connected in the community and since they are dedicated to service, they will be more likely to help with service-learning.

Local Companies

Corporate partnerships are common in engineering-based service-learning. Many local companies have resources to help you and your team and have programs to engage the community. If the students approach the right people, they can get companies involved in their projects. Some companies even financially sponsor projects or their employees lend some support. The EPICS program at Purdue University, for example, (http://epics.ecn.purdue.edu/), has engineers from local companies that work with teams to provide technical guidance on a weekly basis.

PATENTS

All engineering students should learn how to do a patent search whether or not in service-learning. Patent searches should be done early in your project and can help identify benchmark products that address similar issues. Existing patents might show that a product exists to meet your need. More often, the existing products do not quite meet your community partner's needs. Commercially available projects can be prohibitively expensive for the community and the need you and your classmates serve is to make the technology affordable. Knowing what exists can save you time reinventing the wheel, provide ideas for your own application, and identify patent-protected ideas.

Several ways exist to explore patents. The most direct is through the U.S. Patent and Trademark Office at http://www.uspto.gov/. This service is free and allows you to access the patent database.

Other search engines are available for student use. Delphion, for example, operates a search engine developed by IBM. You can use the basic search engines free if you register with them. You can access additional subscriber features for a fee. The search engine is available at http://www.delphion.com/. Select *Basic Registration* for the free access to the database and search engine.

The Community of Science provides a search engine for patents at http://www.cos.com/. Free patent searches are available by selecting *services* at the top of the web page and then selecting *U.S. Patents* on the lefthand menu.

Intellectual Property

Patent searches will help you identify ideas for solving similar problems to yours. The results of these searches may reveal that you have created a novel approach to meeting a community need, an approach you could patent. If your solution provides community value, the next logical question is how others could benefit from your solution. Some ideas can be given away. However, disseminating your solution could require some sort of support structure for manufacture, distribution, and support in the field. Perhaps the solution is a company founded to meet community needs.

Some students have explored community-focused entrepreneurship, and have started their own companies. One way this is happening is the Idea-to-Product (I2P) entrepreneurial competition through the National EPICS Program. For more information on this competition and the teams that have presented, go to: http://ims.ecn.purdue.edu/entrepreneurship/

OTHER SERVICE-LEARNING PROGRAMS

Another great information resource is other students and professors who are or have worked on similar projects. Many students across the country are engaging in engineering-based service-learning. You can find national networks of organizations for engineering service-learning that are focused on local and international projects. These programs can be useful resources for students if they can find teams working on similar problems. Students who have made contacts with students from other schools working on similar problems have found the programs helpful and the teams fun to collaborate with. Examples are contained in the sections below.

Local Communities

Engineering Projects in Community Service (EPICS) is a national network of 15 universities that brings teams of undergraduates together with local community organizations. EPICS projects exist in most engineering disciplines. Contact information for each EPICS program is found on the National EPICS web site at http://epicsnational.ecn.purdue.edu/. Selecting Current Sites will give access to all of the local programs in EPICS.

One of the initiatives of the National EPICS Program is to organize projects that span multiple campuses. Their pilot national project is with Habitat for Humanity, where teams from different schools work on different aspects of the same project for the staff at the Headquarters of Habitat for Humanity in Americus, Georgia.

ProCEED is another organization that works with local community organizations. University of Michigan's ProCEED Program http://www.engin.umich.edu/soc/pts/ProCEED/ uses a student organization as the management structure for matching community projects with engineering courses.

International Projects

Organizations that have focused on international projects for their service-learning include the following:

Engineers Without Borders (EWB) USA (http://www.ewb-usa.org/) is an organization started at the University of Colorado, Boulder, to promote international development projects through service-learning. The program was modeled after the organization Doctors Without Borders. These projects are done with university students in collaboration with practicing engineers. The communities are in developing countries and students travel to these communities to deliver or install community-based projects. Several universities have EWB student chapters on their own campuses.

A similar organization started about the same time in Canada, Engineers Without Borders Canada (http://www.ewb.ca/content/en/index2.shtml). This organization is less focused on the curriculum integration of international projects and more focused on marshalling the technical community to help address the developing world's needs.

A third organization, Engineers (http://www.esustainable.world.org/), brings international projects into the service-learning classroom. Similar to Engineers Without Borders, it has student chapters at a number of campuses around the country.

While not an organization, Professor John Duffy at the University of Massachusetts in Lowell has been successfully engaged in international projects in Peru for many years. See the Profiles chapter for more deatils.

Other Resources

Massachusetts Institute of Technology (MIT) has two organizations that work with engineering service-learning: The Edgerton Educational Center (http://web.mit.edu/Edgerton/) and the Public Service Center (http://web.mit.edu/mitpsc/). Other service-learning programs are described in the text, *Projects that Matter: Concepts and Models for Service-learning in Engineering.* (Tsang, E., Ed., American Association of Higher Education, 2000). Dozens of faculty and students are working in service-learning that are not part of large centers.

OUTREACH AND EDUCATION

Many service-learning classes work in the area of outreach and/or education, and several great resources can help. If your campus has a school of education, that is the first place to look. The school will have faculty and students who can help your team meet your educational needs. Faculty or graduate students may be willing to work directly with your class. You may be able to partner with undergraduate or graduate education classes. Education students have student organizations that could make great partners. Look at the department web page or go to the department to investigate possibilities.

One thing to remember is that many institutions have their secondary education (high school) teachers in majors that they will eventually teach. For example, someone studying to be a math teacher will be in the math department, not in education. If you are looking for a physics education student, you may need to look in the physics department.

Many engineering-related outreach programs and resources exist. The American Society for Engineering Education has a web site resource for K-12 engineering outreach at http://www.engineeringk12.org/default.cfm. This web site has links to many other sources. Almost every engineering professional society in engineering has its own K-12 resources. NASA (www.nasa.gov) has many educational resources and information for outreach related activities to engage younger students.

OTHER SERVICE-LEARNING RESOURCES

You can find resources for service-learning programs that are not just focused on engineering. Though most are designed for professors and student affairs professionals leading service-learning, these resources can provide needed information for students as well. They can be resources in themselves or they can lead to others who are working on similar problems.

- The American Association for Higher Education (AAHE) published a series of volumes on service-learning within different disciplines. The 25 volumes provide excellent examples of service-learning in different disciplines. The engineering volume was edited by Edmund Tsang and titled *Projects that Matter: Concepts and Models for Service-learning in Engineering* (2000).
- Campus Compact is a national organization that promotes service-learning within higher education. It has many resources and examples on its web site (www.compact.org). State compacts can be found at the national web page. These state compacts can be great local resources for students and faculty with projects, training, and funding. Some have grant programs for projects. Others sponsor student conferences that bring students together to share their community work.
- The National Service-Learning Clearinghouse (National Information Clearinghouse; www.servicelearning.org) is provided through the Corporation for National and Community Services and has a vast array of resources for service-learning including some on environmental and educational projects.
- The *Michigan Journal of Community Service-learning* (http://www.umich.edu/~mjcsl/) is an academic journal that is totally focused on service-learning.

Fundraising

Part of being resourceful may require your student team to find financial resources to meet the community need. Suggestions and resources for fundraising are detailed in sections 6.13 and 7.3.2.

10.4 CONCLUSION

Many people and organizations can help you and your classmates meet your service-learning project objectives. These people and resources are needed when addressing real problems. Your instructor can help you find these outside resources but you and your classmates must take responsibility to make contacts, too. The skills you develop in this experience will benefit you long after graduation. You may want to stay connected with organizations and people you have met.

At the successful conclusion of any project, recognize all of those who helped you succeed. If you have delivered a tangible community project, put the organizations' names that supported you on the project as a way of thanks. Sending thank you's to the organizations or hosting a luncheon for them partially repay their help. Taking care of those who were helpful will help students who participate after you leave the class and will serve you and your classmates later in life.

REFERENCES

ABET. *Criteria for accrediting engineering programs.* Baltimore: The Engineering Accreditation Commission of the Accreditation Board for Engineering and Technology, 2000. (www.abet.org/eac/eac.htm)

ABET. *Engineering criteria, 2002–2003.* Baltimore: Accreditation Board for Engineering and Technology, 2002. (Available at www.abet.org/criteria.html.)

Boyer, EL. *Scholarship reconsidered: Priorities of the professoriate.* Princeton, NJ: Carnegie Foundation for the Advancement of Teaching, 1990.

Bransford, JD, Brown, AL & Cocking, RR, Eds. *How people learn.* Washington, DC: National Academy Press, 2000.

Coyle, EJ, Foretek, R, Gray, JL, Jamieson, LH, Oakes, WC, Watia, J & Wukasch, R. EPICS: Experiencing engineering design through community service projects. Charlotte, NC: *The 2000 Annual Conference of the ASEE*, 2000.

Duffy, J, Tsang, E & Lord, S. Service-learning in engineering: What, why, and how? Charlotte, NC: *Proceedings of the 2000 Annual Conference of the ASEE*, 2000.

Eyler, J & Giles, DE. *Where's the Learning in Service-learning?* San Francisco: Jossey-Bass, 1999.

Jamieson, LH, Coyle, EJ, Harper, MP, Delp, EJ & Davies, P. Integrating engineering design, signal processing, and community service in the EPICS program. *Proceedings of the 1998 IEEE International Conference on Acoustics, Speech, and Signal Processing*, 1897–1900.

Jamieson, LH, Oakes, WC & Coyle, EJ. EPICS: Serving the community through engineering design projects. In Kenny, ME, Simon, LAK, Brabeck, K & Lerner, RM, Eds. *Learning to Serve: Promoting Civil Society Through Service-learning.* Norwell, MA: Kluwer Academic Publishers, 2002.

Michaud, F, Clavet, A, Lachiver, G & Lucas, M. Designing toy robots to help autistic children—an open design project for electrical and computer engineering education. Charlotte, NC: *Proceedings of the 2000 Annual Conference of the ASEE,* 2000.

Oakes, WC & Rud, AG Jr. The EPICS model in engineering education: Perspective on problem-solving abilities needed for success beyond school. In Doerr, H & Lesh, R, Eds. *Beyond Constructivism: A Models & Modeling Perspective.* Hillsdale, NJ: Lawrence Erlbaum Associates, 2001.

Oakes, WC, Duffy, J, Jacobius, T, Linos, P, Lord, S, Schultz, WW & Smith, A. Service-learning in engineering. *Proceedings of the 2002 Frontiers in Education Conference,* Boston, MA, November 2002.

Simon, LAK, Kenny, M, Brabeck, K & Lerner, RM Eds. *Learning to Serve: Promoting Civil Society Through Service-learning.* Norwell, MA: Kluwer Academic Publishers, 2002.

Stott, NW, Schultz, WW, Brei, D, Winton Hoffman, DM & Markus, G. ProCEED: A program for civic engagement in engineering design. Charlotte, NC: *Proceedings of the 2000 Annual Conference of the ASEE,* 2000.

Tsang, E Ed. *Projects That Matter: Concepts and Models for Service-learning in Engineering.* Washington DC: AAHE, 2000.

Zlotkowski, E. Ed. *Successful Service-learning Programs: New Models of Excellence in Higher Education.* Bolton, MA: Anker Publishing, 1998.

Zlotkowski, E. Ed. *Service-learning and the First-year Experience.* Columbia, SC: National Resource Center for the First-Year Experience & Students in Transition, University of South Carolina, 2002.

APPENDIX: ENGINEERING AND TECHNICAL ORGANIZATIONS

The following list of engineering technical societies represents but is not necessarily a comprehensive listing of the societies available for engineers. These societies are a tremendous source of information and many have student branches that allow engineering students to meet other engineering students as well as practicing engineers in the same field.

American Association of Engineering Societies
111 19th Street
Suite 403
Washington, DC 20036
(202) 296-2237

http://www.aaes.org/membership/index.asp

American Association for the Advancement of Science
1200 New York Avenue, NW

Washington, DC 20005
(202) 326-6400
www.aaas.org

Association for the Advancement
  of Cost Engineering
  International
209 Prairie Avenue
Suite 100
Morgantown, WV 26505
(304) 296-8444
www.aacei.org

American Ceramic Society
735 Ceramic Place
Westerville, OH 43081-8720
(614) 890-4700
www.acers.org

American Chemical Society
1155 16th Street NW
Room 1209
Washington, DC 20036-1807
(202) 872-4600
www.acs.org

American Concrete Institute
38800 Country Club Drive
Farmington Hills, MI 48331
(248) 848-3700
www.aci-int.org

American Congress on Surveying
  and Mapping
5410 Grosvenor Lane
Suite 100
Bethesda, MD 20814-2122
(301) 493-0200

American Consulting Engineers
  Council
1015 15th St., NW #802
Washington, DC 20005
(202) 347-7474
www.acec.org

American Gas Association
1515 Wilson Blvd.
Arlington, VA 22209
(703) 841-8400
www.aga.com

American Indian Science and
  Engineering Society
5661 Airport Blvd.
Boulder, CO 80301-2339
(303) 939-0023
www.colorado.edu/AISES

American Institute of Aeronautics
  and Astronautics
1801 Alexander Bell Drive, #500
Reston, VA 20191-4344
(800) NEW-AIAA or (703) 264-7500
www.aiaa.org

American Institute of Chemical
  Engineers
345 East 47th Street
New York, NY 10017-2395
(212) 705-7000 or (800) 242 4363
www.aiche.org

American Institute of Mining,
  Metallurgical and
  Petroleum Engineers
345 East 47th Street
New York, NY 10017
(212) 705-7695

American Oil Chemists' Society
1608 Broadmoor Drive
Champaign, IL 61821-5930
(217) 359-2344
www.aocs.org

American Railway Engineering
  Association
8201 Corporate Drive
Landover, MD
(301) 459-3200

Society for Engineering in
  Agricultural, Food and
  Biological Systems
  (American Society of Agricultural
  Engineers)
2950 Niles Road
St. Joseph, MI 49085-9659
(616) 429-0300
www.asae.org

American Society of Civil
  Engineers
1801 Alexander Bell Drive
Reston, VA 20191-4400
(800) 548-2723 or (703) 295-6000
www.asce.org

American Society of Naval
  Engineers
1452 Duke Street
Alexandria, VA 22314
(703) 836-6727
www.jhuapl.edu/ASNE

American Nuclear Society
555 North Kensington Avenue
La Grange Park, IL 60526
(708) 352-6611
www.ans.org

American Society for
  Engineering Education
1818 N St. NW #600
Washington, DC 20036-2479
(202) 331-3500
www.asee.org

American Society for Heating,
  Refrigeration and Air
  Conditioning Engineers
1791 Tulie Circle NE
Atlanta, GA 30329
(404) 636-8400
www.ashrae.org

American Society of
  Mechanical Engineers
345 East 47th Street
New York, NY 10017-2392
(212) 705-7722
www.asme.org

American Society of Plumbing
  Engineers
3617 Thousand Oaks Blvd.
Suite 210
Westlake Village, CA 91362-3649
(805) 495-7120
www.aspe.org

American Society of
  Nondestructive Testing
1711 Arlingate Lane
P.O. Box 28518
Columbus, OH 43228-0518
(614) 274-6003
www.asnt.org

American Society for Quality
611 East Wisconsin Avenue
Milwaukee, WI 53202
(414) 272-8575
www.asq.org

American Water Works Association
6666 West Quincy Avenue
Denver, CO 80235
(303) 443-9353
www.aws.org

Board of Certified Safety
  Professionals
208 Burwash Avenue
Savoy, IL 61874-9571
(217) 359-9263
www.bcsp.com

Construction Specifications
  Institute
601 Madison Street

Alexandria, VA 22314-1791
(703) 684-0300
www.csinet.org

Information Technology
    Association of American
1616 N. Fort Meyer Drive, #1300
Arlington, VA 22209
(703) 522-5055
www.itaa.org

Institute of Electrical and
    Electronics Engineers
1828 L Street NW, Suite 1202
Washington, DC 20036
(202) 785-0017
www.ieee.org

Institute of Industrial Engineers
25 Technology Park
Norcross, GA 30092
(770) 449-0461
www.iienet.org

Iron and Steel Society
410 Commonwealth Drive
Warrendale, PA 15086-7512
(412) 776-1535
www.issource.org

Laser Institute of America
12424 Research Parkway, Suite 125
Orlando, FL 32826
(407) 380-1553
www.laserinstitute.org

Mathematical Association of
    America
1529 18th Street, NW
Washington, DC 20036
(202) 387-5200
www.maa.org

NACE International
1440 South Creek Drive

Houston, TX 77084-4906
(281) 492-0535
www.nace.org

National Academy of Engineering
2101 Constitution Avenue, NW
Washington, DC 20418
(202) 334-3200

National Action Council for
    Minorities in Engineering, Inc.
The Empire State Building
350 Fifth Avenue, #2212
New York, NY 10118-2299
(212) 279-2626
www.naof cme.org

The National Association of
    Minority Engineering Program
    Administrators, Inc.
1133 West Morse Blvd., Suite 201
Winter Park, FL 32789
(407) 647-8839
(407) 629-2502 Fax

National Association of Power
    Engineers
1 Springfield Street
Chicopee, MA 01013
(413) 592-6273
www.powerengineers.com

National Institute of Standards
    and Technology
Publications and Programs Inquiries
Public and Business Affairs
Gaithersburg, MD 20899
(301) 975-3058
www.nist.gov

National Science Foundation
4201 Wilson Blvd.
Arlington, VA 22230
(703) 306-1234
www.nsf.gov

National Society of Black
 Engineers
1454 Duke Street
Alexandria, VA 22314
(703) 549-2207
www.nsbe.org

National Society of Professional
 Engineers
1420 King Street
Alexandria, VA 22314
(888) 285-6773
www.nspe.org

Society of Allied Weight Engineers
5530 Aztec Drive
La Mesa, CA 91942
(619) 465-1367

Society of American Military
 Engineers
607 Prince Street
Alexandria, VA 22314
(703) 549-3800 or (800) 336-3097
www.same.org

Society of Automotive Engineers
400 Commonwealth Drive
Warrendale, PA 15096
(412) 776-4841
www.sae.org

Society of Fire Protection
 Engineers
7315 Wisconsin Avenue
Suite 1225W
Bethesda, MD 20814
(301) 718-2910

Society of Hispanic Professional
 Engineers
5400 East Olympic Blvd.
Suite 210
Los Angeles, CA 90022
(213) 725-3970

www.engr.umd.edu/organizations/
 shpe

Society of Manufacturing Engineers
One SME Drive
P.O. Box 930
Dearborn, MI 48121-0930
(313) 271-1500
www.sme.org

Society for Mining, Metallurgy
 Exploration, Inc.
8307 Shaffer Parkway
Littleton, CO 80127
(303) 973-9550
www.smenet.org

Society of Naval Architects and
 Marine Engineers
601 Pavonia Avenue
Jersey City, NJ 07306
(800) 798-2188
www.sname.org

Society of Petroleum Engineers
P.O. Box 833836
Richardson, TX 75083-3836

Society of Plastics Engineers
14 Fairfield Drive
Brookfield, CT 06804-0403
(203) 775-0471
www.4spe.org

Society of Women Engineers
120 Wall Street
11th Floor
New York, NY 10005
(212) 509-9577
www.swe.org

SPIE-International Society for
 Optical Engineering
P.O. Box 10
Bellingham, WA 98227-0010

(360) 676-3290
www.spie.org

Tau Beta Pi
508 Dougherty Engineering Hall
P.O. Box 2697
Knoxville, TN 37901-2697
(423) 546-4578
www.tbp.org

The Mineral, Metals and Materials
    Society
420 Commonwealth Drive

Warrendale, PA 15086
(412) 776-9000
www.tms.org

Women in Engineering Initiative
University of Washington
101 Wilson Annex
Box 352135
Seattle, WA 98195-2135
(206) 543-4810
www.engr.washington.edu/
    ~wieweb

EXERCISES

1. Generate a list of at least ten people on your own campus who could provide technical assistance during your project. Include contact information and their area of expertise.

2. Identify three off-campus resources or organization that could help you with your project. Summarize each person or organization including contact information and areas of expertise.

3. Select one service organization that has a chapter in your community or close by that would be a resource for you and your classmates. Who are typical members of this organization and how could they provide assistance? Summarize your findings in a memo to your instructor.

4. Find three patents on products that address similar issue to the ones you are addressing. Prepare a memo summarizing the attributes of these products.

5. Find a service-learning project at another institution that addresses similar issues or that developed similar products. Summarize your findings in a one page essay.

6. Find a service-learning project at another institution that addresses similar issues or that developed similar products. Summarize your findings through a short oral presentation.

7. Find at least one additional resource that is not identified in this chapter that could be useful to you and your classmates. Summarize the resource in a memo to your classmates.

8. Prepare a memo to your classmates on how your library and its staff can be used as a resource for your project.

9. Select one of the service-learning web resources (e.g., Campus Compact, Service-Learning Clearinghouse) Prepare an oral presentation on ways this resource could be helpful to your classmates.

10. Prepare an oral presentation on the resources that could be useful for your project that can continue to be a resource as you enter practice as an engineer.

Chapter 11

Reflection and Self-Discovery

I may not have gone where I intended to go, but I think I have ended up where I intended to be.

—Douglas Adams

11.1 INTRODUCTION

In Chapter 1, we introduced service-learning with the definition

> *We view service-learning as a credit-bearing educational experience in which students participate in an organized service activity that meets identified community needs and we* **reflect** *on the service activity in such a way as to gain further understanding of the course content, a broader appreciation of the discipline, and an enhanced sense of civic responsibility.*

Reflecting on the service activity is a critical component of a service-learning experience, but is different from what you might expect in a traditional classroom. Many engineers respond to the idea of reflection with the reaction that they do not reflect. Reflection sounds like a warm and fuzzy thing that would happen in a liberal arts class but not in an engineering class. Not that there is anything wrong with a liberal arts class, but you are in an engineering class. Engineering is rigorous, right?

The reflection referred to in the definition of service-learning is not a fuzzy activity designed to make you feel better. It is a vital and rigorous component of the learning process. The engineering processes, problem solving, design, and skill sets presented in this text follow systematic procedures to produce optimal results. Reflection follows the same principles to maximize learning.

While many engineers do not see themselves reflecting, they regularly analyze. That is what engineers do. Reflection can be recast in terms of analysis. Reflection is a process whereby you, your instructor, and your classmates analyze the processes, experiences, and results of your service-learning course.

In educational practice, the process of reflecting on the course topics is called metacognition. Metacognition has been shown to improve learning in all classes, traditional and service-learning. Good educators use research-based techniques like metacognition to improve their classroom learning environments.

Reflection, analysis, and metacognition are the same things with different names. Whatever we call these activities, they are an important part of the educational process and are critical in service-learning. The learning that takes place within service-learning can be complex and sometimes hard to understand without reflection, analysis, and metacognition.

It may be difficult to relate the service component to the other parts of the course and vice versa. Since they have been put into the same course, there is a connection; otherwise, your instructor wouldn't have placed them together. Reflection provides a way to see the connections and develop a deeper understanding of both.

Some of the learning that can take place in service-learning occurs outside of the classroom and is beyond what one would normally expect in a traditional course. These learning experiences can be complex, messy, and can vary depending on personal experiences and backgrounds. Service-learning can put us in places we are not used to or in contact with people we would not associate with. These experiences can stretch us personally and professionally. Reflection can help you process these experiences so that you can better understand what happens and the context for the experience as well as learn something about how your background and views affect the experience. Having an opportunity to reflect and process these experiences can help you grow as a person and a professional.

The purpose of this chapter is to provide background on why reflection is important and what you might expect. Later material in the chapter will give examples of areas you might explore in reflection activities and why they are important for engineering students. The questions we raise will help you think about your experiences as you develop as a person, a professional, and a citizen.

11.2 METACOGNITION AND LEARNING CYCLES

From a learning standpoint, reflection provides benefits to the classroom experience. Cognitive scientists who study how people learn have found that reflective, also called metacognitive, activities, enhance learning. (Bransford, 2000,) Revisiting what has been presented is a part of the learning process that transcends traditional and service-learning classrooms. Metacognitive activities can take many forms including discussions, writing assignments, or oral presentations.

One of the most influential models for learning is Kolb's (1984) learning cycle, which shows the integration of metacognitive (reflective) activities into the learning process. As Kolb puts it, "learning is the process whereby knowledge is created through the transformation of experience." Learners gain new knowledge by testing and adapting their existing knowledge through a process that involves abstract conceptualization (e.g., posing a theory or planning a project), active experimentation, concrete experience (observing and tracking results), and reflection (thinking about how to improve on the original abstract conceptualization). The metacognitive activities (reflection) become links between the experience gained through the service and the conceptualization of covered topics.

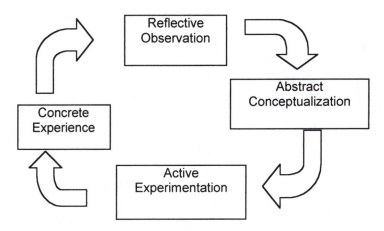

Figure 11.1   Kolb's Learning Cycle

The same principle applies to other experiences, such as a course's laboratory component. Theory might be presented in the course's lecture, and the lab gives you an opportunity to explore with hands-on activities. If nothing ties them together, they may feel like separate components and not integrated into the whole course. Tying them together requires intentional activities, which we would call reflection, analysis, or metacognition.

The same reflection process is followed in service-learning, but it may be even more important than a laboratory component. The service component is often harder to connect to the traditional course content than a more familiar experience, such as a lab or in class project. The service component can push your understanding of engineering beyond traditional boundaries and conceptions. This is why part of the reflection or metacognitive activities will address the academic material covered and how the course material relates to the service.

Another reason that reflection is so important is that so many things can be learned from the service, thus, an opportunity to digest and process them is important. As Kolb's model shows, to understand experiences you may need reflection; otherwise, things may go by without you seeing or taking time to understand these experiences. For these reasons, part of the reflection will address your personal experiences, the implications of the social context and issues associated with the need being met, and the role of engineering in the context of large social issues.

Each person will observe different things in a service experience based on the views and insights s/he brings to the experience. You must become aware of what these are as you develop as a professional. Understanding the views you bring to a situation will help you think beyond your preconceptions to develop better engineering solutions.

Reflection activities can take several forms and can include open-ended questions, written or oral guided discussion topics, periodic written summaries of the work and its implications, and assigned readings. Many of the forms are not typical for engineering courses and students must keep an open mind and understand that the activities support sound learning principles.

Personal Discipline

Taking time to reflect on your activities and experiences is a practice that can serve you well as a person. Some of the most successful strategies for personal success include the personal reflection model. For example, Stephen Covey, in his highly acclaimed book *The Seven Habits of Highly Effective People,* writes about the importance of taking time to do personal reflection. Taking time to reflect and looking at how you are doing is a strategy which separates effective, successful people from those who are not.

For example, Covey and many others talk about setting goals and organizing daily tasks to accomplish these goals. He ranks tasks with two criteria: urgency and importance (shown in Figure 11.2).

Covey points out that most people spend their time in quadrants I and III. To achieve your long-term goals, quadrant II is the most important. By looking at activities in II, you can take more control over your activities. The urgency is something imposed by others whereas importance is something you assign.

Covey points out that most people spend their time in quadrants I and III because they do not take time to analyze and reflect on what is important for achieving their goals. Those who develop the discipline to reflect on their personal tasks and goals have a higher probability success.

Reflection activities may seem to fall into these same categories. Taking time to process how things are going during service-learning is important but not urgent. These activities may seem to take away from urgent activities, like getting the project done. Again, researchers who have studied successful people have found that those who are successful take time to prioritize and reflect on the implications of their actions.

An example of a leader who uses personal reflection in a different way is Bill Hybels, senior pastor of one of the nation's largest churches, Willow Creek Community Church near Chicago. He has been invited to address management organizations, such as Harvard's MBA program, about his successful organization and leadership characteristics. He talks about personal disciplines including reflection. For him, taking time to write his thoughts using a daily journal has been

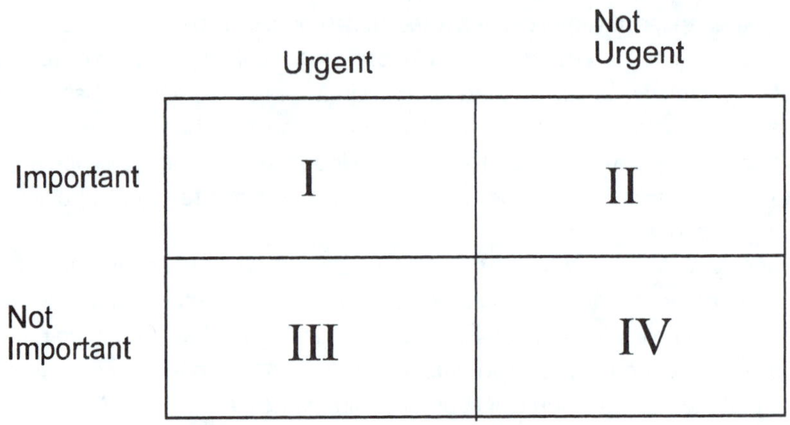

	Urgent	Not Urgent
Important	I	II
Not Important	III	IV

Figure 11.2   Covey's quadrants for daily tasks.

valuable. He is a prolific writer and credits journaling as one way that he organizes his ideas and stays focused on the most important tasks for success for his organization and himself.

Life-Long Learning

Personal reflection can help you stay disciplined, stay focused on your own goals, and continue to grow as a person. Another term for continued growth is *life-long learning*. Engineers have to continue to develop as new technologies and challenges arise. Life-long learning is one of the program outcomes recognized by the Accreditation Board of Engineering and Technology (ABET). Every American engineering program has life-long learning as one of its goals for its students.

An important part of life-long learning is continuing to learn the latest technical information and techniques as our society rapidly advances. Another aspect of life-long learning is understanding yourself and how you can continue to develop as a person. Engineers typically take on more responsibility and challenges as they progress through their careers. Some of you will become managers, while others will become technical leaders. You may need to develop new skills to handle these challenges.

Personal reflection can be a powerful tool to identify the kinds of experiences, education, or training you might need to continue to develop as a person and professional. Ask yourself this classic question: "What are my strengths and what are my weaknesses?" In your service-learning reflection opportunities, you may be led through activities to fully examine your experiences, perceptions, motivations, and misconceptions. Look at these experiences as a way to build on the discipline of life-long learning.

> *How far you go in life depends on your being tender with the young, compassionate with the aged, sympathetic with the striving, and tolerant of the weak and strong. Because someday in your life you will have been all of these.*
>
> —George Washington Carver

Analysis and Engineering Discipline

Reflection can become a barrier for engineers and sometimes generates negative connotations of a touchy-feely activity with no intellectual purpose. Earlier we discussed how the education community calls these activities metacognition. In engineering, we call the process analysis. All three are the same process and follow the same principles.

Good engineers analyze everything they do, including their designs, processes, and results. Engineers use disciplined and systematic approaches to design and manage projects and solve complex problems. In each of these processes, part of the process is analyzing the process itself and revisiting the process when needed. All of these processes are cyclic, with smaller cycles inside larger cycles. Analysis (reflection) is what we use to determine when to go back to an earlier process and when to advance.

Bill Hybels states that journaling is a reflection method. Okay, he is a pastor and that might work for him. He writes books, so that makes sense for him. Do engineers journal? Many of you are probably thinking, "this sounds too much like an English assignment."

Many engineers talk about recording their ideas in a disciplined way. They record their work, ideas, and reactions to these ideas. They do not write in what they call a journal; they write in what they call a design notebook.

The practice of keeping a design notebook has a long history in the engineering and scientific community. Thomas Edison, one of the nation's most prolific inventors, filled over 2,500 design notebooks. Edison still holds the record for the number of patents awarded to any single person: 1,093. He recorded his ideas so that he could come back to them later. He recorded his ideas, gathered data, developed specifications, and analyzed the ideas.

Keeping a daily record of your work and ideas is one form of documentation recognized by the US Patent Office for patent protection. If you come up with a new idea, you need to produce documentation that proves that you were the originator and the date you developed the idea. The practice of keeping a daily notebook to record your work, ideas, and potential applications can help you protect ideas for future patents.

Though Edison did not write essays per se in his design notebooks on the social and global impacts of his ideas, he, like other great engineers, did consider these issues as part of the invention process. To help you develop this same discipline, your instructor may ask you to write on aspects of your service-learning experience. Reflection assignments are intended to help you learn and practice the discipline of analysis. Activities may take the form of keeping a daily log or journal, responding to questions, or writing an essay about an aspect of your service-learning project.

These activities will teach you this important aspect of good engineering practice. Analyzing activities, experiences, findings, and processes is sound engineering practice and can help you develop as a professional and a person.

11.3 CRITICAL THINKING

Reflection, metacognition, or analysis (whatever we choose to call the process) is good educational practice, and a sound method for problem solving, self-improvement, and engineering methodology. We should be clear, however, that we want to move beyond this. Engineering is so dominated by systematic problem solving, that it is easy to get caught up in the methodologies and look at everything as a problem needing a solution or goal. We have presented problem-solving methods that give a systematic approach for analyzing and solving problems. However, many of life's issues are more complex and have no single solution; some cannot be solved. I (Oakes) once assigned a project to design a program using MATLAB® to predict students' financial future and life plans, including a potential spouse. I jokingly suggested that the class use the program when dating to evaluate the financial impact of a potential spouse or life partner ("Sorry, MATLAB says we wouldn't be compatible. . . ."). The class laughed at the suggestion. Clearly, whom you marry, or if you marry, is a complex question and not one that can be solved by some stepwise methodology or computational algorithm. Life is more complex than that.

Issues and challenges you face in your service-learning experience have a similar complexity and require a critical perspective. Effectively addressing engineering issues with human, environmental, or ethical impacts requires a critical perspective.

For example, many programs have sought to address poverty, and many programs and "solutions" involved engineering. Poverty, however, has remained a pressing social issue in this country and abroad. Solutions to these larger social issues are complex and do not have a single or simple solution.

Many of the issues a service-learning student will be exposed to are problems that cannot be easily or quickly solved. It is easy to get caught up in the processes and methodologies and move to solutions and implementation plans. Sometimes this is appropriate, but other times we need to evaluate our actions and examine the larger issues of our actions. Being able to evaluate why and how you are doing something by taking a step back to gain perspective is an important skill. At each step, one of the divergent questions you can ask is "why?"

There are times when you need to evaluate your actions, to discover deeper meanings and larger issues. One example involves the design of toys for children with physical challenges in a program where students work on engineering solutions to community issues, EPICS (Engineering Projects in Community Service http://epics.ecn.purdue.edu). As the students worked with the children, families and therapists, they gained an appreciation for the many complex issues facing these children. When engineering students design toys, they must design them so they can be used within the physical abilities of the children. This is fairly straightforward.

What the students have learned is that they can address many other issues, such as socialization issues, also critical in the design process. Some of the toys are designed so that children with physical challenges can interact with their peers by using these toys. The students have also learned to design these toys such that children with disabilities can control the play. Normally, the children who are not physically challenged control the games and allow the other children to participate. The engineering students have learned about the socialization of children with and without disabilities and its impact on self-esteem. Armed with this knowledge, the engineering students can design toys that meet a wider spectrum of needs.

When working with issues such as children or adults with disabilities, there is often no simple or straightforward answer. These are not simple problems to be solved but are complex issues that need to be addressed and pondered. By working through these issues and their multiple dimensions, students have become aware of the social and emotional issues of their work. They have become better designers, and have become better educated about relevant issues. When they work with people with disabilities to design inclusive environments, the students are able to effectively engage in these conversations and design appropriate solutions.

As engineers, we have significant responsibilities because our work has great potential for good and for harm. While having the highest of ethical standards is important, having a critical eye on the context and direction of your work is equally vital. Creating opportunities to gain perspective and evaluating your actions, experiences, and perceptions is as important as the problem-solving methodology presented in this text. At the beginning of the creative problem-solving process as well as the design process, we discussed how important it was to get the question right. Similarly, when evaluating an issue, framing the right question will enable you to generate an appropriate solution.

We use our personal background and experience to evaluate problems, and this perspective can limit our thinking. When evaluating a solution, getting an outside opinion has value. You must become aware of the perspective you bring to issues based on your background so it does not limit you. Thomas Edison wanted people around him who would not limit their thinking by jumping to conclusions. He would take every prospective engineer to lunch to his favorite restaurant, which was known for their soup and which he would recommend. Of course, the candidate would order soup. Edison wanted to see if he or she would salt the soup before tasting it. Salting without tasting, he reasoned, was an indication of someone who jumps to conclusions. He wanted people who were open to questioning. Periodically, ask yourself if there are things that you are salting without tasting. Are there issues to which you jump to conclusions based on your background, personality, or thinking style?

Critical thinkers ask the why question about themselves as well as about the things around them. Periodically take a step back and ask why or what about yourself. Why are you studying to become an engineer? What will you do as an engineer to find personal fulfillment? Becoming a critical thinker will make you a better problem solver and engineer and one who is more engaged in society and more fulfilled.

> *"I learned about the importance of perspective in engineering. I had to think like a child to design the best playground. I had to think like a parent to design a safe playground. I had to think as a member of the community to design a playground that reflected the unique aspects of the community. I had to think like a politician to sell the playground to potential funders."*
>
> —Service Learning Student

11.4 REFLECTION COMPONENTS

The analysis (reflection or metacognition) of service-learning has several components that can take different forms. In a traditional engineering class, reflection is centered around reinforcement of class concepts. Reflection activities might include the following:

- Writing a report to summarize your work on a lab or a project.
- Giving an oral presentation that summarizes work on a project.
- Participating in a review session to bring together the topics of the last few weeks.
- Keeping a design notebook to record your ideas during a design.
- Writing a short report on a practical application of the course concepts.

Rarely will engineering professors use the word *reflection* to describe what they are doing in class, but they will use a cyclical model to learn and revisit concepts, connect them with real applications, and pull different concepts and components of the course together as the course progresses. The activities tend to be focused on the class content or on the technical aspects of a project.

Service-learning uses these same components and some of the same techniques, but there is more. Since service-learning can put you into new situations or in contact with different people, other dimensions to your learning can and should be processed in a systematic manner.

We can think of service-learning as an economical way to learn. Traditionally, we would take different classes to learn different things. We take engineering courses to learn about technical issues. We take humanities courses to learn about society. Service-learning experiences, like life after graduation, often have many aspects that cut across academic areas. In reflection, we systematically explore these aspects to take full advantage of the learning opportunities.

One model for exploring the different dimensions of the service-learning experience has been presented by Edward Zlowkowski (shown in Figure 11.3). This model shows three concentric circles to represent the three dimensions that can occur during the service experience and will be explored during reflection activities. The center of the circles is the technical or academic material related to the course. This is placed in the center as it is service-learning's primary reason: to develop a deeper understanding of the academic content of the course. The next level is related to you as a participant: your experiences, values and perceptions. The third and broadest level is the social systems and implications of the project at a societal level.

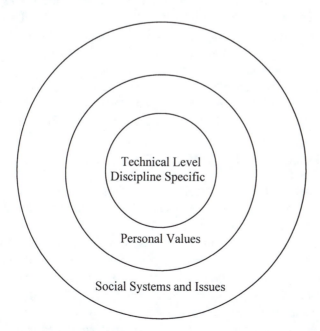

Figure 11.3   Levels of Reflection (Developed by Edward Zlotkowski, used with permission)

Your instructor may focus on one, two, or all three of these dimensions and can use various methods to achieve this focus. We should keep in mind that service-learning, like real-life applications, introduces variability that makes predicting the precise outcome difficult. When we deal with real people and issues, the student's experience will vary. Some projects lend themselves to different experiences or levels of involvement. Reflection activities can help you and your classmates to process these diverse experiences and identify the knowledge learned at each level.

Reflection activities that address personal and social dimensions can look similar to the activities reinforcing course concepts, but with an expanded view or a new twist. Your reports, for example, may have additional sections that address specific questions provided by your instructor. You might be asked to make an oral presentation on your experiences or the needs that were addressed by your service-learning project. In your design notebook, you might be asked to respond to guided questions and record your answers in the notebook.

Other activities may include small group discussions within your class. Writing assignments may be dedicated to the service components of the experience. Additional readings may be assigned for discussions or writing assignments to add to your learning as a future professional, person, and citizen in your community. In the sections below, we will expand on the three levels of reflection in Zlotkowski's model.

Technical Level

Level 1. At the core of any service-learning experience is the academic course content. As we stated in the introductory chapter, service is not added to the course just because it is a good thing; it was added because it will enhance learning the academic material. A student should expect to spend time revisiting the course topics or learning objectives to make the connections. Your instructor may spend some time connecting the service experiences and the theoretical course components. These reflection activities should help your understanding of the course content and are based on sound educational theories and research.

Personal Values

Level 2. The second component to this core level of reflection is your engineering discipline and personal values. Many students engaged in service-learning find that their view of their engineering discipline is expanded by the service experience. Most engineering students do not associate their discipline with the social issues that service-learning requires. Computer engineering students, for example, might not have thought their discipline could address the needs of children with disabilities, but many programs employ students to do just that.

Taking time to look at your discipline and how it can or does connect with the broader issues addressed in the service-learning experience has value. It can open your eyes to more career options and ways to apply your knowledge to markets and products. It can open ideas for future community work. Communities need people with the special skills you have. Looking for ways you can use these skills can open doors within your community.

Social Systems and Issues

Level 3. Beyond your specific discipline, there are implications for the engineering profession and social and community issues. In the first chapter, we discussed how other professions, law for example, have imbedded the expectation of pro bono work into professional responsibilities. Lawyers embrace this ethic as they understand that access to basic legal counsel is critical for our free society, and all citizens do not have the means to pay for these services. Could it be argued that with all the advantages that technology has brought about, access to basic technology is equally important?

Dr. William Wulf, President of the National Academy of Engineering, in testimony to Congress, talked about the impact that engineers have had on our world:

> ". . . what engineers do has had profound impacts on our quality of life. If one reflects on the day-to-day existence of someone in 1899 and 1999, virtually all of the differences are due to technology—to what engineers have created. If one wants to have a positive impact on people's lives, engineering is a great career."

If we have improved the quality of our citizens' lives so much, is it our responsibility as a profession to see that these benefits are provided to as many people as possible? In chapter two, we quoted ABET's definition of engineering:

> Engineering is the profession in which a knowledge of the mathematical and natural sciences gained by study, experience, and practice is applied with judgment to develop ways to utilize, economically, the materials and forces of nature for the benefit of humankind.

The definition does not end with "benefit of those citizens who can afford it." It states that we "benefit humankind," which includes all people.

So what is the engineering profession's role in bringing these benefits to everyone? Clearly, the engineering profession by itself cannot bring modern advances to every citizen. Technological solutions are not always the best solutions nor are they always appropriate. However, many basic technologies can improve and save lives. For example, billions of people in the world do not have safe and reliable drinking water or sanitation systems. These conditions directly contribute to premature deaths and disease.

In our own country, thousands of children do not have access to playgrounds that meet current safety codes and standards. Social services devote people and resources to managing information that could be automated, freeing people to provide more assistance. Barriers remain for people with and without disabilities to have full access to educational and employment opportunities.

Oakes: Personally, it was not until I began teaching with service-learning that I saw the connections between my discipline, mechanical engineering, and the professions related to the social issues. This is ironic since I had grown up in a household with socially active parents, one a physician and the other a social worker. They were personally and professionally engaged in the community's social issues. I figured these issues didn't apply to me since I was an engineer. Oh, I did understand I could volunteer to work in the community but could not volunteer professionally. Through teaching service-learning, I have seen how we are connected. My mother, the social worker, and I now joke about how obvious our connections are but how long it took to see them.

Those in the technical community and in social services often do not see connections between their disciplines and the issues they can and do address. This is why we reflect on the discipline, to see potential connections. The other side of the equation is to help those in the social services see the connections to one's expertise. You are taking time to examine ways to make connections, and the service providers may need a similar process. You may need to discuss with community service providers how to apply your skills and abilities to their problems. You have started the process by working with your community partner in this service experience. In a new community or with new partners, you might have to start with a tangible project to get to know each other. The process may take some time and you need to be patient. The potential benefits are enormous. Once the connections are made, we can make a tremendous impact working together.

As a profession, we cannot solve every problem. We can and should be a major player in working with community to improve the quality of people's lives. That is, after all, what engineers do.

SELF: PERSONAL VALUES

If we do not take time to examine the impact on ourselves in the service-learning experience, we have lost a tremendous opportunity to learn. Service-learning is designed to meet the community's needs and we must look at how we approach these needs. How do we think about the problems we are addressing? How do we feel about the people we are working with? What do we think about the solutions we are developing?

One of the program objectives for all engineering programs is a recognition of the need for and an ability to engage in life-long learning. We talked about this earlier in the context of developing a self-discipline of personal reflection and analysis. A key aspect of being a life-long learner is to develop ways to identify areas in which you need to develop as a person and professional. If we do not under-

> **Lima:** The engineering profession became much more fascinating to me after I figured out how to use my engineering skills to directly address community issues through service-learning. Math, science, and engineering have always been interesting to me, but I believe that intrinsically, these subjects have no soul. The act of bringing these subjects to life through community action is the most rewarding part of my career in engineering, and in my mind, is what gives engineering its soul.
>
> In your engineering classes, you will learn about transducers, devices that change one type of energy to another and can multiply their effects. For example, you can't lift a car by yourself, but if you press down on a lever arm attached to the car, you can lift the car by yourself because the lever arm acts as a transducer, and multiplies the effect of your "single person" force. I think of service-learning as a human energy transducer. It is impossible to complete a service-learning project yourself, but if you can work together with people and concentrate your team's efforts and talents, that collective action is a lever arm in itself. Your service-learning team can accomplish amazing things with this approach. I believe that harnessing and directing this kind of human energy is also part of engineering.

stand ourselves, we cannot progress. Failure to examine ourselves is akin to not defining the problem in a design process. We will miss key information.

The reflection that your instructor designs can help identify how you view the work you do as well as the people and situations you encounter. Looking at what you do and how you feel can help you understand what views and perspectives you bring to the experience. Your perspective is a result of how you were raised and the experiences you have had. There is strength in that perspective and in the diversity of the perspectives we bring to a problem. Dr. William Wulf, President of the National Academy, stated:

> *The quality of the work produced by the workforce depends on the variety of perspectives and life experiences brought to the job by its members. Without diversity, we limit the set of life experiences that are applied, and as result, we pay an opportunity cost—a cost in products not built, in designs not considered, in constraints not understood, and in processes not invented.* (Wulf, 1999)

Though we bring dimensions from our personalities, experiences and perspectives can strengthen a solution, we bring dimensions that may make it harder to come together to achieve solutions. An important part of self-reflection is to be aware of the dimensions that strengthen a solution and to identify those areas that make it more difficult.

One of impediments that we have in coming together is the filter through which we see people, events, and experiences. When we come in contact with a situation or person, we look for analogies to previous experiences and people and make initial decisions based on these analogies. Work in artificial intelligence seeks to replicate this process. Computers may learn from previous experiences, but we can and do.

We may prejudge situations and people based on previous experience and knowledge. We do not like to use the word prejudice in today's society because being prejudiced is bad. We do not want to admit we are prejudiced, but we do make initial judgments. Service-learning can be a terrific way to explore what these pre-judgments are and how they influence us.

Service-learning can be a great way to look at your own thoughts, views, and values. What is important to you? How do you view the people and circumstances in which you have been working? Service-learning is not teaching you there is a right way to think about the issues, but it provides an opportunity to take a look at yourself and how you look at society and the issues we face. Self-reflection can be a powerful tool to show you how you see the world and how you can engage others to make the world better. That is why, after all, we are engineers.

SOCIETY

I was working with some guys to build planter benches. It took a long time to drive in all those nails, but at the end of the day, when I looked at all the planter benches I'd put together, I realized that those tiny nails held together a structure much bigger than the nails. It made me think about how something small can hold up something large, and this analogy can be extended to service-learning. Your small contribution to community can hold up something much larger: our democracy.
—Julianne Forman, NSF Graduate Fellow, Louisiana State University

A certain parable tells the story of a man who was sitting by a swiftly flowing river. He saw a young child caught in the flow and immediately dove in. He frantically swam to reach the child. Fighting against the strong current, he rescued the child and struggled back to shore. People gathered to see if the child was all right. As the people dried the child off and covered him with blankets to keep him warm, someone saw another child in the river. The man quickly jumped back in rescued the second child. Then they saw another, and he rescued that one. Then more. Finally, as the exhausted man was coming out of the river with the last child, he turned to the crowd gathered along the bank and said someone needed to go upstream to see how the children were getting into the river.

In service-learning, you are typically engaged in meeting an immediate need, pulling the children out of the river. We will lose an important opportunity to learn if we do not take time to look at the larger societal issues that created the issues. Why were the children in the river in the first place? What were the societal circumstances or institutions that have contributed to these problems or are preventing the problems from being addressed?

Like the other steps in the reflection process, looking at the larger issues is good engineering practice. Good engineers seek root causes of problems, not just symptoms to treat. I (Oakes) learned this early in my engineering career as we worked with an engine component that developed cracks in the field. The part was designed to reduce the stresses but failures continued. Sophisticated finite element analyses were conducted and the part was designed again. The part still developed cracks in service. When an engineer looked for the root causes, he found that the manufacturing process was introducing micro-cracks as the part was being created. The real problem was not the stresses but the cracks from the machining. All of the work had been dealing with the children in the river, but the problem was upstream, as the parts were being made.

The same is true for social issues. We talked at length in the problem-solving and design chapters about identifying the real problems to solve. There are times when the need you are addressing is the result of a larger issue that could be addressed. This is not to say that the immediate need is trivial. The analogy of the children in the river is a good one. Saving the children is a good thing, but finding the reason they are in the river could stop the problem. If you are working with Habitat for Humanity, you are providing access to housing for families in the community. The families who become homeowners for the first time are grateful, and your work is important. We have to look though at the larger issue of why our society has poverty and a lack of access to housing for a significant percentage of its citizens. Reflection can help us examine the upstream or root causes and potential solutions to these larger issues.

CIVIC ENGAGEMENT

Though not a separate "level" of the reflection process, an increased sense of civic engagement is an explicit goal for service-learning, not just in engineering. Our hope is that by engaging in service early in your life, you will begin to see that community needs must be addressed and you can play a personal and professional role in meeting those needs. Civic engagement can include volunteering, voting, serving on non-profit or governmental boards, or even running for office.

With so many issues involving technology, the technical community must become engaged. People who understand technology and its implications must become involved in public policy. The National Academy of Science and The National Academy of Engineering serve as consultants for the Congress and the President and have advocated for an increased engagement from our professions. The National Society of Professional Engineers has seen this need for engagement and states:

> *NSPE recognizes its responsibility to participate in the democratic process and to offer significant contributions to the development of technical public policy. NSPE, in its dedication to the advancement of*

the engineering profession, recognizes the need to contribute to and
influence legislative and regulatory activities at all levels of govern-
ment. Furthermore, as society becomes more technical and complex
it is vital that more technically trained individuals become active.

Of the 435 members of the 2003–04 US Congress, two were licensed professional engineers, five had an engineering degree and eight had a science degree.
A total of 15 out of 435 have any formal education in technology-related fields. We
talked earlier about how important technology is and the impact it has had on
modern society. If we, as a profession or technical community, should be more engaged in helping to guide public policy, then how can we do so? Ask yourself how
you can become engaged in guiding public policy with your expertise in technology and experience in the application of technology to social issues.

Beyond Partisanship

Contrary to what some may think, service-learning is not nor should it be politi-
cally partisan. In the United States Congress, both Republicans and Democrats
have supported service-learning and civic engagement. Indeed we can approach
service-learning from the current "liberal" position or "conservative" position.

Liberals can view service-learning positively as it gives participants first hand
experience to the needs of the community. It puts faces and names with these
needs which can build the governmental programs that support these needs.

Conservatives can view service-learning positively as it actively engages individuals in addressing local needs and builds an engaged citizenry to meet these
needs without large governmental programs.

Notice that with each definition, both groups assumed there were real needs
and wanted to address them. In all political parties, there are groups of people
who want to address real issues and those who want power. This should be the
biggest political difference, rather than which party you belong to.

In today's political climate, people label each other with unflattering terms. This
only serves to shut down useful dialogue. Public discourse about relevant social
issues is critical to finding those upstream solutions. In your reflection sessions,
do not jump too quickly to traditional positions. Look for ways to engage in con-
structive dialogue or debate. You may find more in common with other people than
you think.

I (Oakes) found this to be true early in life with one of my cousins. We used to
take walks along the beach during family gatherings and we loved to discuss politics and the issues. We were on opposite ends of the political spectrum, but we
found so much to agree on. We understood society's needs had to be met. What
we disagreed on were the methods to solve the problems. We were not emotion-
ally tied to our own methodology and could debate and discuss and refine our
ideas and put them into action.

When solving problems, engineers brainstorm to collect ideas. They will develop criteria to select the best ideas. When they do this, they show respect for
the team's ideas and contributions. When the idea is implemented, they will col-

lect data to see if the data were effective. We can follow the same principles and processes looking at solutions to today's problems. Reflection sessions can model this.

11.5 ENGINEERING AS A CAREER

A concerned and confused student came to me (Oakes) in his first year in engineering. He had come to the university to study electrical engineering but felt he needed to change his major. He had attended a missions retreat and felt that he was going to be called into the mission field, specifically in Africa. He had considered this calling for a long time and genuinely felt that was where he was headed after graduation. He felt that a college degree and its training would benefit him in his calling, but he had a problem. He didn't think he was in the right major and had come to my office to help figure out where he should go. We talked about his interests. He loved working with circuits and tinkered with electronics in his spare time. He had done well in his first semester of engineering courses. I thought he had chosen the right major and was confused as to why he wanted to change his major. The answer was simple. He didn't see a connection with the international service he felt called into and electrical engineering.

We talked about communications technology and how critical it was for missionaries spread out in remote areas. We talked about the resources that could be provided through communication technologies that could stream text and videos into remote areas to support the mission work and its missionaries. Someone had to provide and manage these services. Initially, this student did not see any connection with technology and specifically his discipline and where he saw his own career leading him. It was only after we reflected upon these connections that he saw how well equipped he would be to make strong contributions. In fact, the kind of skills he would have were those the mission organization needed.

Service-learning puts students into situations that many do not associate with engineering. Some students enjoy the service experiences and look at potential career and major changes as a result. For some students, this is a good move. For many, however, the answer lies in how to apply their engineering skills to their problems and interests. Like that young man who came into my office, engineering may be the best path to do what interests you. Engineering is full of possibilities and can open many doors to future careers and opportunities. We hope that your service-learning experience has opened your eyes to more exciting possibilities, whether they are integrated into your career plans or become part of your volunteer efforts.

11.6 CONCLUSIONS

Although social change does not come overnight, we must always work as though it were a possibility in the morning.

—Martin Luther King, Jr.

Many engineering students report that their service experience is nothing like they envisioned doing in an engineering class, and some miss any connection to the academic components of engineering. Many find their service experience placed them into new situations that stretched them personally or professionally. Others miss many of the experience's aspects and the larger issues that they could have seen.

Reflection is integral to the whole learning experience and helps all participants process their experiences and complete the learning cycle. Taking time to reflect and analyze your experiences allows all engineers to understand more about themselves, the communities they serve, and the issues they address. These activities can take many forms from writings, discussions, or additional readings.

Author Reflections

The discipline of reflection and analysis is important to engineers. It is part of every process we are involved in and helps guide progress in complex projects

---

Oakes: A danger of looking at these larger problems in detail is to get discouraged or afraid of the future. When that happens to me, I think back to my great-uncle Archie and the discussions we had when I was a high school and college student. He was in his 80s and philosophical. We would sit on his porch overlooking the lake and talk about the issues, and the conversation always seemed to turn to discussions about the future. Half the time, he said he was glad he was old and would not be around to see the future. The problems seemed too daunting and he feared what would happen. This discouraged me no end. However, during the other half of our visits, he talked with envy of being young today and the incredible opportunities the future held.

I realized that both could be true. The issues we face are daunting, but the possibilities are equally exciting. We have problems that people have never faced or have never faced on this magnitude. But we have capabilities to address problems that have been with us from the beginning of history. The future will be determined by how well we use our resources and energy to address the real issues that face us as a global community. People who see the possibilities and opportunities and act on them will determine the future.

The technical community will play an important role in our future's success. To be an engineer who will play an important role in these solutions is exciting. I hope that you have begun to see the connection with your future as an engineering professional. You have the potential to have a tremendous impact on our world and to improve the quality of people's lives.

and designs. As individuals, we must grow and develop as people and professionals. We are all works in progress. The discipline you practice in reflection will develop you into a life-long learner.

Service-learning's explicit goal is to expose you to some of today's broader issues. The ABET lists awareness of contemporary issues and a global awareness as critical for engineers. As citizens, we must join to address the larger issues and the upstream causes.

REFERENCES

ABET. (2002). *Engineering criteria, 2002–2003.* Baltimore: Accreditation Board for Engineering and Technology. (Available at www.abet.org/criteria.html.)

Lima: Technology is often offered as a solution to the world's ills. Technology by itself will not address global issues, and in fact, is projected to increase the gap between rich and poor people, communities, and nations (Dieter, 2000). The engineering profession requires you to understand and execute technological solutions to societal problems. I encourage you to strive to learn how to direct those solutions in responsible directions. Translated to service-learning, this means working with a community partner to effect a positive change, but also working on the societal structures and policies that helped to create the problem in the first place.

To this end, it is critical to learn about how societies embrace and adopt technology. This requires you to know something about people and the ways in which they relate to technology, and to public policy, which drives the widespread use and adoption of technology in society. Remember that appropriate technology already exists for many of our problems, but often there are barriers to implementing these technologies. I encourage you to study and understand these barriers, and through this process, you will be able to use societal forces to effect positive change.

I offer the following list of books that offer insight in this regard. Good luck in your studies and in your engineering travels!

- *Building America: The Democratic Promise Of Public Work,* by Harry C. Boyte and Nancy N. Kari
- *The Tipping Point,* by Malcolm Gladwell
- *Soul of a Citizen: Living With Conviction In A Cynical Time,* by Paul Rogat Loeb
- *My Ishmael, The Story of B,* or *Ishmael,* by Daniel Quinn
- *Democracy Matters: Winning The Fight Against Imperialism,* by Cornel West

Boyer, E.L. (1990). *Scholarship reconsidered: Priorities of the professoriate.* Princeton, NJ: Carnegie Foundation for the Advancement of Teaching.

Bransford, J.D., Brown, A.L., & Cocking, R.R. (Eds.). (2000). *How people learn.* Washington, DC: National Academy Press.

Duffy, J., Tsang, E., & Lord, S. (2000). Service-learning in engineering: What, why, and how? *Proceedings of the 2000 Annual Conference of the ASEE.*

Eyler, J., & Giles, D.E. (1999). *Where's the learning in service-learning?* San Francisco: Jossey-Bass.

Hatcher, J.A., & Bringle, R.G. (1997). Reflection: Bridging the gap between service and learning. *College Teaching, 45* (4), 153–158.

Howard, J. (Ed.). (1993). *Praxis I: A Faculty Casebook on Community Service-Learning.* Ann Arbor, MI: Office of Community Service Learning Press, University of Michigan.

Jacoby, B., "Service-Learning in Today's Higher Education", in Service-Learning in Higher Education: Concepts and Practices, ed. B. Jacoby and Associates, Jossey-Bass Publishers, San Francisco, CA, 1996.

Kolb, D. (1984). *Experiential learning: Experience as the source of learning and development.* Upper Saddle River, NJ: Prentice Hall.

McAuliffe, Kathleen (1995) "The Undiscovered World of Thomas Edison", *The Atlantic Monthly;* December 1995 Volume 276, No. 6; pages 80–93.

National Society of Professional Engineers, *Issue Brief:* Professional Engineers in Congress, *June 6, 2003, Publication #4048*

Slivovsky, L. A., Oakes, W. C., Zoltowski, C. B., DeRego, F., and Jamieson, L. H., "An Analysis of the Reflection Component in the EPICS Model of Service Learning", *Proceedings of the 2004 ASEE Annual Conference* , Salt Lake City, Utah, June 2004

Stanton, T.K., Giles, D.E., & Nadinne, I.C. (1999). *Service-learning: A movement's pioneers reflect on its origins, practice, and future.* San Francisco: Jossey-Bass.

Simon, L.A.K., Kenny, M., Brabeck, K., & Lerner, R.M. (Eds.) (2002). *Learning to serve: Promoting civil society through service-learning.* Norwell, MA: Kluwer Academic Publishers.

U.S. Department of Commerce. 1997. The Image of the Information Technology Professions: a Report of the Image and Information Technology Professions Task Force. Washington, D.C.: U.S. Department of Commerce.

Tsang, E. (Ed.). (2000). *Projects that matter: Concepts and models for service-learning in engineering.* Washington DC: AAHE.

Tsang, E., (2000) "Service Learning: A Positive Approach to Teaching Engineering Ethics and Social Impact of Technology", *Proceedings of the 2000 ASEE Annual Conference & Exposition,* St. Louis, MO, June 18–21, 2000

Tsang, E., (2002) "Use Assessment to Develop Service-Learning Reflection Course Materials", *Proceedings of the 32nd ASEE/IEEE Frontiers in Education Conference,* Boston, MA, Nov. 6–9, 2002

Wulf, W. A, (President, National Academy of Engineering), *Testimony to the Commission on the Advancement of Women and Minorities in Science, Engineering, and Technology Development. Committee on the Diversity of the Engineering Workforce,* July 20, 1999

Zlotkowski, E. (Ed.). (1998). *Successful service-learning programs: New models of excellence in higher education.* Bolton, MA: Anker Publishing.

Zlotkowski, E. (Ed.). (2002). *Service-learning and the first-year experience.* Columbia, SC: National Resource Center for the First-Year Experience & Students in Transition, University of South Carolina.

EXERCISES

1. Write a brief essay on how metacognitive activities are used in your other classes. How do professors get students to think about their learning and make connections between different parts of the class?

2. Write a one-page paper to your classmates on why reflection or analysis is important as part of service-learning.

3. Create a short presentation to your classmates on why reflection is an important part of service-learning.

4. Write a one-page paper on ways to develop a personal ethic of reflection and analysis to continue to grow personally and professionally.

5. We used the analogy of being "upstream on a river" for larger social structures and issues that have contributed to or created the social issues and needs you are addressing. Write a three page essay identifying the immediate need you have worked to address and what the "upstream" larger social issues or structures are.

6. Prepare an oral presentation on the issues you have helped to address. Include the river analogy in your presentation. Have you been pulling the children out of the river or working on the causes for the children being in the river? If you have not been working on the "upstream" issues, what are they?

7. Prepare an oral presentation on why the needs you are addressing exist? What or who has either contributed to these problems or have allowed the problems to develop?

8. Write an essay about the expertise in the community that can help you and your classmates accomplish your project's goals.

9. Write an essay about the expertise in the community that can help you and your classmates learn the course material.

10. Write a three-page essay describing your reactions to the service experience. Include how you felt about the work, the people, the issues you addressed, and the results you achieved.

11. Write an essay on how the service-learning experience has reinforced or changed your career goals.

12. Prepare a short oral presentation on how this experience has reinforced or changed your career goals.

13. Write an essay on how this experience has reinforced or changed your personal goals.

14. Prepare a short oral presentation on how this experience has reinforced or changed your personal goals.

15. Write an essay on how this experience has reinforced or changed your career goals

16. Write a one-page essay on how your service-learning experience was connected to the learning objectives for your class.

17. Write a one-to two-page essay on the aspects of engineering you used and/or learned about during this service-learning experience.

18. Lawyers and other professionals, as part of their ethical responsibility, perform pro bono work for the community. Write a short opinion paper arguing FOR engineering having the same professional expectation.

19. Lawyers and other professionals, as part of their ethical responsibility, perform pro bono work for the community. Write a short opinion paper arguing AGAINST engineering having the same professional expectation.

20. Investigate how many of your state's federal and state legislators have an engineering or science background. Summarize your findings in a one-page memo.

21. Prepare an oral presentation on the reasons why engineers should be civically active.

22. Prepare an oral presentation on the impact that engineers could have on state or federal policy if a critical mass of legislatures had engineering backgrounds.

23. Write an opinion paper discussing the position that congressional policy would be BETTER if a majority of legislators were engineers or had an engineering background.

24. Write an opinion paper discussing the position that congressional policy would NOT be better if a majority of legislators were engineers or had an engineering background.

25. Our own experiences and backgrounds can give us preconceptions about circumstances and people we encounter. Write a two page essay on what you have learned about your own views, perceptions and preconceptions from your service-learning experience.

26. We can bring tremendous benefits from technology to the issues in our local communities. There are limitations to these benefits and sometimes even negative ramifications. Write an essay on what some of the limitations or negative ramifications could be.

27. We can bring tremendous benefits from technology to pressing issues in the developing world. There are limitations to these benefits and sometimes even negative ramifications. Write an essay on what some of the limitations or negative ramifications could be.

28. Write a three-page essay on what you have learned during your service-learning experience.

29. Prepare a memo to a future class on what you would do differently knowing what you know now after your project has been completed.

30. Write a two-page essay on the expertise that you found in the community. Include how this expertise helped the project and what you learned.

31. Write a one-to two-page essay on what you learned from the people in the community you were serving.

32. Prepare an oral presentation on the expertise and experience that were in the community you served. How have they addressed issues similar to your project in the past and how will they continue to address these issues after you have left?

33. Prepare a one-page essay to evaluate how effective you and your class-mates were in forming a reciprocal partnership with those who were being served. Estimate the balance between the community and your class in re-gards to what was learned and who benefited, and show this result on two spectrum illustrations:

Community	Student
Benefit	Benefit

←——————————————————————————————→

Community	Student
Learning	Learning

←——————————————————————————————→

34. Write a letter that could be sent to your institution's governing board (e.g., board of trustees) that makes the case, why service-learning helps your in-stitution to fulfill its mission.

35. Write a letter to your a respected elder (such as a grandparent) explaining your project, what you learned, and what you accomplished in the commu-nity you served.

36. Write a two-page essay on what impact the service-learning experience has had on you as a person and future professional.

37. Create a one-page flyer for entering first-year students on why they should enroll in a service-learning class.

38. Ethics is an important part of engineering. Write a two page essay on the eth-ical issues of your project. Identify specific ethical decisions your team had to make as well as other potential ethical issues surrounding the project.

39. Chapter 2 presents the NSPE Code of Ethics, including the Fundamental Cannons. Use the Fundamental Cannons as an outline and write a para-graph for each cannon describing how well you and your classmates abided by the cannons.

40. Prepare an oral presentation on the ethical issues surrounding or associ-ated with the community need you and your class addressed.